THE INSANITY FILE

THE CASE OF

Mary Todd Lincoln

Mark E. Neely, Jr.

R. Gerald McMurtry

Southern Illinois University Press
Carbondale and Edwardsville

Copyright © 1986 by the Board of Trustees,
Southern Illinois University
All rights reserved
Printed in the United States of America
Edited by Teresa White
Designed by David Ford
Production supervised by Natalia Nadraga
Paperback edition, 1993
98 97 96 95   5   4   3   2

Library of Congress Cataloging-in-Publication Data

Neely, Mark E.
    The insanity file : the case of Mary Todd Lincoln / Mark E. Neely,
Jr., R. Gerald McMurtry.
        p. cm.
    Includes bibliographical references and index.
    1. Lincoln, Mary Todd, 1818–1882—Mental health. 2. Presidents—
United States—Wives—Biography. 3. Lincoln, Abraham, 1809–1865—
Family. I. McMurtry, R. Gerald (Robert Gerald), 1906–
II. Title.
    [E457.25.L55N44   1993]
    973.7'092—dc20
    [B]   92-33847
    ISBN 0-8093-1895-4 (pbk.)   CIP

The paper used in this publication meets the minimum requirements
of American National Standard for Information Sciences— Permanence
of Paper for Printed Library Materials, ANSI 239.48-1984. ∞

CONTENTS

ILLUSTRATIONS

FOREWORD

Stored away in my grandfather Robert Todd Lincoln's Manchester, Vermont, home, Hildene, was a bundle of letters, papers, and documents marked by him "MTL Insanity File." Tied with a ribbon, the file had lain in his file room just off his study, undisturbed since his death on July 26, 1926. At my sister Mary Lincoln Beckwith's death in 1975, Hildene's use as a family residence came to an end.

Many items and this file therefore came to me. What to do with this file and the information it could contribute on this very controversial subject was not easily decided. I have decided to have the contents published by two competent Lincoln scholars R. Gerald McMurtry and Mark E. Neely, Jr.

My reasons are several. First, it is likely that this is the only definitive record of this tragic story. Second, as the last member of my family I must either take this course or destroy the file. Third, it would seem to me that although my grandfather destroyed much of his incoming correspondence and many personal family letters, this file he retained. I believe that he did so knowing that in the future its contents should be made known.

Fourth, and most important, I believe that because of this file history will treat my great-grandmother Mary Todd Lincoln more kindly in regard to this very disturbing period of her life and most of all recognize that my grandfather acted in the best possible way towards his mother.

Robert Todd Lincoln Beckwith

May 1981

PREFACE

On Christmas Eve, 1985, the last member of the Lincoln family died. Robert Todd Lincoln Beckwith was the grandson of Robert Todd Lincoln, the firstborn son of Abraham and Mary Todd Lincoln. Beckwith was eighty-one years old and had long been in ill health. Despite a reputation for reclusiveness and extreme reticence about his famous ancestor, Abraham Lincoln, Beckwith decided toward the end of his life to reveal what he knew of the remaining secrets about his famous family.

These secrets, if such they can be called, did not involve Abraham Lincoln but his wife and son, and they were more or less unknown, except through hazy family tradition, to Beckwith himself until late in his life. Only the bare, official court documents stemming from the insanity trial of Mary Todd Lincoln were available to historians until the 1980s. When Beckwith learned that his grandfather's personal file on the case had been discovered in a closet in one of the family's estates, he decided to make these documents available as well.

When we first saw the documents, we were having cocktails before a dinner at a farmhouse in central Illinois. The scotch seemed to lose all its effect in the startling and sobering light of these documents. The two of us had worked in the Lincoln field, between us, some sixty years, and we had never seen anything like this cache of documents in private hands.

As we returned to our hotel after dinner, driving a rented car over a dirt road through flat Illinois farmland in a pitch-dark night, we were seized with the idea of being able to write a book based on these documents. Like most writers on Lincoln, we were accustomed to reading and interpreting documents that had, most of them, been known for a hundred years and read by hundreds of historians before us. The idea of writing a book on manuscripts unseen by any other historian led us to pursue the project with vigor.

Eventually, we were allowed to use the Insanity File, the Lincoln family's retained file of documents on the case of Mary Todd Lincoln. Once again, certain sobering realities caused us to see that this would be a different sort of book for us. For one thing, it would not be a Lincoln book in the traditional sense, for the event it would chronicle occurred a decade after Abraham Lincoln's death. It would be a book about Mary Todd Lincoln and Robert Todd Lincoln and, as it turned out, some other rather surprising characters from the Abraham Lincoln story, but they would now appear out of the shadow of the great man's reputation. For better or worse, these people would figure in their own right as forceful protagonists for whom Abraham Lincoln was only a memory.

As it turned out, the book would depart the Lincoln tradition in other important respects as well, for we found that familiarity with such standard subjects as the historiography of the causes of the Civil War and the major issues of Lincoln's presidency was not really adequate preparation for understanding the Insanity File. We needed to learn about medical jurisprudence, for example, and we were ourselves surprised in the end to see how much of the book was based on research outside the Insanity File itself. These documents provided only the makings of a narrative, but an understanding of the events would have to come, if at all, from other sources.

Finally, it would be a departure for us as writers because of the peculiarly controversial nature of the materials. We sensed immediately in conversations about our work in progress an intensity of visceral feeling about the issues that was different from the attitudes toward more familiar historiographical debates over the causes of the Civil War or the presidential policies of the Lincoln administration. People seemed to expect us to defend or justify one protagonist and to denounce another. There was little consensus about heroes and villains, but people definitely had their heroes and villains.

Strangely enough, we did not seem to live in this highly charged atmosphere ourselves. When we attempted to transport ourselves back to Chicago and Springfield in 1875, we experienced fascination but not moral engagement. We could not at first understand how the trial and its aftermath worked and we wanted to figure it out very badly, but we did not much care how the story turned out—as long as it seemed true to the documentary record. The whole event held for us the fascination of a puzzle but not the passionate engagement of a moral melodrama, and we sensed a certain surprise among our early readers in finding that the manuscript was less a brief than an analysis, that it did not exactly crackle with moral electricity relevant to modern political and social concerns, and, in fact, that so much of the manuscript dealt with legal history. It surprised us, too, but then we had often before been surprised at the conclusions historical evidence drives us toward. Historical research certainly does begin with a theory, but the interesting thing about it is that it often does not end with the same theory. We changed our minds about many things, and we hope this book will change some readers' minds as well.

One thing about which we did not change our minds was the controversial nature of the Lincoln family, as a family. From Abraham Lincoln's first engagement to Mary Todd in 1840, the couple seemed destined for controversy and perhaps for tragedy. Even their engagement was troubled, once broken off on the "fatal first of January" 1841, and salvaged only in defiance of certain family wishes. Historians have argued endlessly about the marriage union that ensued after November 4, 1842, and have been able to agree only on the ultimate tragic dimensions of the Lincoln family, caused by the early deaths of three of their four children: Edward Baker, William Wallace, and Thomas "Tad" Lincoln. Robert Todd Lincoln, alone of the four boys born to Abraham and Mary, survived to live a full life and have an adult career.

Yet deep tragedy would mar that life as well as the later life of Abraham Lincoln's widow, for this pathetic remnant of Abraham Lincoln's family would fall apart in 1875. Robert in that year caused his mother's commitment to an insane asylum. This book is an attempt to explain that tragic coda to the history of the Lincoln family.

The manuscript received many helpful readings. Those by John Y. Simon and Gerald N. Grob led us to revamp the manuscript in important ways, stylistic, organizational, and substantive. James T. Hickey has been of great help at all stages in the preparation of this book. Roger Bridges and the late Jack Nortrup kindly gave us the benefit of their astute readings as well. Ralph G. Newman called a crucial letter to our attention. And many of our other friends in the Lincoln field have given patient encouragement and advice on technical points, among them, Paul Beaver, Gary Planck, George Painter, Frank J. Williams, Georgia Wralstad-Ulmschneider, and John R. Chapin. Sylvia Neely assisted with the Index.

Grateful acknowledgment is made to the following for permission to reproduce the photographs used in this book: The Illinois State Historical Library, Old State Capitol, Springfield, Illinois; The Louis A. Warren Lincoln Library and Museum, Fort Wayne, Indiana.

THE INSANITY FILE

THE TRIAL

Because Mary Todd married Abraham Lincoln somewhat in defiance of her family's hopes, she put her all into proving that she had made the right choice. She idolized him and she idealized family life. Lincoln was "lover—husband—father & *all*[,] *all* to me," she said after his death. "A nice home—loving husband & precious child are the happiest stages in life," Mrs. Lincoln recalled, and she thought any woman had "grown worldly" who regarded "housekeeping & babies" as "an uncomfortable state of existence for a young married lady." Over twenty-five years after the event, she could recall vividly "my darling husband, . . . bending over me, with such love and tenderness—when . . . [Robert] was born."[1]

Nevertheless, Mrs. Lincoln always had a free spirit inside her. She appreciated freedom to travel where she wanted and to say what she felt and to buy what struck her fancy. As an aging widow, Mrs. Lincoln advised her young daughter-in-law to hire a servant to tend her baby so that she could "go out *every* day" and "be as gay as a lark." It was perhaps "all the better . . . for young men to settle down early," but, Mary once told a friend, "if I had a daughter—I think I would not give her up so easily."

"Trouble comes soon enough," Mrs. Lincoln warned her daughter-in-law, and she spoke from bitterest experience. The death of four-year-old Eddie, her secondborn, in 1850 brought a grief only partly consoled by deepening religious conviction and the birth later the same year of another son, Willie. Tad's birth in 1853 ended Mrs. Lincoln's childbearing, so that Willie's death in the White House in 1862 caused more inconsolable grief and desperate religious experimentation.

The American nation, sharing Mrs. Lincoln's idealization of the family, sympathized with the Lincolns when Willie died. Even the rigid lines of nineteenth-century political partisanship could be crossed in the name of family sentiment. Ex-president Franklin Pierce, a Democrat sourly opposed to almost all the policies of the administration, had lost a young son in a railroad accident just before assuming the presidency in 1853, and he now wrote President Lincoln a touching letter of condolence. "I realize fully," Pierce admitted, "how vain it would be, to suggest sources of consolation."[2]

Mary Todd Lincoln was never really able to tap those sources, but this fact was for some time obscured from the American people by what might now be called the "cult of the First Family." The phenomenon was growing rapidly in the fertile soil of Victorian sentimentalism. Its roots reached back to the presidency of George Washington. By Lincoln's time the tendency of the American people to idealize the family led them virtually to demand that the president have a home. Without it, he would be an entirely public man, all calculation, ambition, and business without any "sympathy[,] honor[, or] virtue." He would have no refuge from the cares of office. The Victorian era invested the idea of the family with a peculiar sense of solemnity. It was supposed to be a haven from the anxieties of business and public life and a shelter for moral and spiritual values—altruism, religion, and culture—at odds with commercial hustling and political hurly-burly. Mrs. Lincoln shared her era's values in this regard and thus reproached herself and her husband, after Willie's death, for having "become so wrapped up in the world, so devoted to our own political advancement" that God afflicted them with a grim reminder of the sin of "worldliness."[3]

In truth, President Lincoln, and likely most other presidents as well, found little refuge from the cares of office. Only in 1864 did he have a door cut to lead directly from his office in the White House to the family apartments. Before that he had walked down a corridor crowded with office seekers and other troubled supplicants, stopping to talk with them on his way to meals or rest. He seemed to his family always to arrive late and exhausted. "I consider myself fortunate," said his lonely wife in 1864, "if at eleven o'clock I once more find myself, in my pleasant room & very especially, if my tired & weary Husband, is *there*, resting in the lounge to receive me—to chat over the occurrences of the day."[4]

If work was pulling Abraham away, grief and escapism pulled Mary in the opposite direction. She maintained a darkly rigorous mourning for almost three years after Willie's death on February 20, 1862, leading Lincoln at one point to warn her that excessive sorrowing might force him to send her to "that large white building on the hill yonder," the government hospital for the insane, built on high ground between the Potomac and Anacostia rivers. Mary sought to escape unpleasant associations by travel and was absent from Washington a good deal. She later confessed that on their last carriage ride together, on the afternoon of the day Lincoln was shot, he had insisted that they "must *both*, be more cheerful in the future—between the war & the loss of our darling Willie—we have both, been very miserable."[5]

The Lincoln family, or what was left of it after 1862, was rarely together. Robert, as a Harvard undergraduate and afterward a member of Gen. Ulysses S. Grant's staff, was absent most of the time the Lincolns were in the White House. As a result, he knew little of his mother's increasingly unhappy condition.

The cult of the family—the cult of the First Family in particular— hid from view the evidence of decreasing closeness in the Lincoln family in the 1860s, buried it, in fact, under an avalanche of sentimental lithographs picturing all of the members of the Lincoln family in an imaginary parlor. Most modern historians have slighted the evidence too. Eager to set the record straight after Lincoln's old law partner, William H. Herndon, depicted Mary's role in the Lincoln marriage in a most unflattering light, they have generally sentimentalized the relationship and ignored its changing nature over time by saying the marriage as a whole was solid. It no doubt was, but the fact remains: the Lincolns' home life deteriorated steadily through his presidential term.[6]

Then, in the spring of 1865, it ended. Mrs. Lincoln lost her husband to the assassin's bullet and her home to the inexorable processes of the law of presidential succession. The ideal of womanhood in nineteenth-century America allowed no opportunity for happiness outside the home, and Mary believed in that ideal. Through the rest of her unhappy life, she longed for a home she could never re-create. She traveled restlessly over America and Europe, living in boardinghouse and hotel rooms mostly, lamenting bitterly that the nation showered houses on Grant, a man her husband had made, while ignoring the martyr's widow. She recalled the dislocations of her childhood, when a stepmother and new half brothers and half sisters had made her true home a boarding school. Indeed, one of the bonds that had forged the Lincoln marriage so tightly into a happy home in the early years was Mary and Abraham's memories of rather unhappy childhoods. These memories had made them indulgent parents who wanted their children to be happier than they had been. Longing, impossibly, throughout her sad widowhood for a return to that happy home of early marriage, Mrs. Lincoln purchased trunkloads of drapes to hang over nonexistent windows. She blamed her unhappiness on others—a fickle and forgetful American public, cold Chicago, ungrateful politicians, but she seemed to guarantee it herself by refusing to settle down.[7]

One cause of Mrs. Lincoln's unhappiness which had perhaps even deeper roots was her anxiety about money. President Lincoln had been too busy to notice his wife's increasingly erratic course in matters financial. Even before Willie's death, Mrs. Lincoln had given dramatic evidence of this aberration by wildly overspending the appropriation for redecorating the White House. Lincoln exploded in anger at the spectacle of extravagance displayed by his wife while soldiers shivered without blankets, but Congress covered the possible scandal up by burying a supplemental appropriation amidst other legislation.

The president was too preoccupied to think much about his personal family finances and estate, as his intestate condition and uncashed salary warrants found in his desk after his death attest. Here, too, Mary moved in the opposite direction. She became obsessively preoccupied with getting and spending. The Lincolns had more money than ever, an income almost twenty times higher than before and the nearly limitless credit of the president of the United States, and Mrs. Lincoln was unable to restrain her lavish extravagance. At Abraham's death in 1865, Mary found herself suddenly saddled with enormous debts which she had managed to keep secret from her husband in his lifetime.

The executor of Lincoln's estate, David Davis, learned about Mary's debts as a matter of course. She seemed positively insane to Davis. Why else would she buy eighty-four pairs of kid gloves from merchant Jos. J. May in less than a month? What other explanation could there be for $3,200 worth of jewelry purchased from Galt & Brothers in the three months immediately preceding Lincoln's assassination? Mary tried to hide her $6,000 indebtedness from Davis and from her oldest son. Robert told Davis that he had not been "aware that there were any claims" like those against his father's estate. It seemed "mysterious" to him, and he began to suspect that his mother was insane on the subject of money. Indeed, she spent money the same erratic way the rest of her life, but without the president's $25,000 annual salary, it made her more anxious than ever to do so.[8]

Without her husband or Republicans in Congress to cover for her, Mrs. Lincoln was, after 1865, almost certain to cause some spectacle of financial mismanagement. The "Old Clothes Scandal" of 1867 convinced Robert that his mother was "on one subject not mentally responsible." Driven by irrational fears of destitution, the president's widow attempted to sell her old finery through dealers in New York City. The clothes did not sell well, in part because people knew that Mrs. Lincoln was not really destitute. Urged on by the unscrupulous dealers, she wrote letters pleading for sales, generally chastising Republican politicians "for whom my noble husband did so much" for having "unhesitatingly deprived me of all means of support and left me in a pitiless condition." When the press got wind of Mrs. Lincoln's scheme, it ridiculed the vulgarity of the martyred president's widow.

The scandal was a major factor in driving Mrs. Lincoln to flee to Europe in 1868, attending Robert's wedding to Mary Harlan less than a week before sailing. She wandered to Frankfort, Nice, various watering spots, and London, all the while keeping an eye out for news that Congress would grant her a pension. She sent a barrage of letters to politicians in a campaign as single-mindedly conducted as that of any lowly soldier's widow seeking her pension. Finally, Congress granted her $3,000 a year for life. Like the $22,000 it had earlier granted her as the remainder of President Lincoln's salary for 1865, the pension soothed her for only a short while.[9]

Mary returned to the United States in 1871 for the sake of Tad's education, but he proved to be mortally ill and died the same year. Her restless misery was sharply renewed. She spent the summer of the next year in Waukesha, Wisconsin, taking the waters, apparently visiting spiritualists, and, if the recollections of two aged Waukesha ladies can be believed, talking to Tad. Mrs. Lincoln spent several months in Canada in 1873 on a trip so obscure that it is not even known what province she visited. Throughout the period she complained of poor health.[10]

In November 1874 Mary decided to go to Florida. Newspapers reported that she had been confined to her Chicago residence for the previous nine months because of "nervous exhaustion." She was seeing a physician regularly, and it was not thought safe for her to travel without a nurse. On her first tour of the Reconstruction South, the Great Emancipator's shattered widow, accompanied by her nurse-servant, stopped in Chattanooga and Savannah. She changed hotels in Savannah, seeking more privacy. The local newspaper reported her "in feeble health." Near the end of the month she reached Jacksonville, where she stayed in Mrs. J. T. Stockton's boardinghouse and continued to avoid publicity. Her passion for privacy caused her to pull the shades, keep her room dark, and use only candles to light it (gas was the invention of the devil, she told her nurse). She spent the winter quietly among the limes and oranges.[11]

Neither the warm climate nor the seclusion did Mary much good. As spring approached, she was seized with the conviction that her sole surviving son was dying. On the evening of March 12, 1875, appearing "nervous & somewhat excited," she entered the Western Union Telegraph Office in Jacksonville and sent Robert's law partner, Edward Swift Isham, this message: "My Belief is my son is ill[.] telegraph me at once without a moments delay—on Receipt of this I start for Chicago when your message is received[.]" Her agitation revealed in two redundancies in the space of one short telegram, Mrs. Lincoln admonished the telegrapher to "Deliver tonight without fail."

Mrs. Lincoln's delusion pictured Robert prostrate, too ill to receive a telegram through ordinary channels, so she sent Isham another message, this one meant for Robert. "My dearly beloved Son Robert T. Lincoln rouse yourself—and live for my sake[.] All I have is yours from this hour. I am praying every moment for your life to be spared to your mother[.]" Her old nemeses, money and death, had become ideas confusedly intertwined in Mary's mind: she seemed to think almost that she could bribe Robert into living by giving him his inheritance now.[12]

Mrs. Lincoln's son was robustly healthy—"flourishing," he would have said—and when Isham brought the telegrams, Robert suspected what the trouble was. He requested a discreet inquiry. A Western Union official in Chicago told the Jacksonville manager: "Please make inquiry and let it be strictly confidential if Mrs. Abraham Lincoln now at Jacksonville is in any trouble mentally or otherwise and advise me at once[.] do not allow her under any circumstances to know of this and please give me prompt reply." Mrs. Lincoln's quest for privacy proved all too successful. The local superintendent in Florida "tried every hotel and all the principal boardinghouses" but could not find her.[13]

The telegrapher knew, however, from the message she had sent that Mrs. Lincoln would return to his office the next morning. With ideas of death and money still churning in her head, Mrs. Lincoln telegraphed her son: "Start for Chicago this evening[.] hope you are better today[.] you will have money on my arrival." The superintendent of the Jacksonville telegraph office tried to convince her that Robert was fine, but in the end he had to send this message to Chicago: "Mrs. Lincoln and nurse left this evening for Chicago[.] She will not be convinced that her son is not dangerously ill[.] Nurse thinks Mrs. L. should be at home as soon as possible." By March 16 Mary reached Indianapolis, where the watchful telegraphers informed Robert of her departure for Chicago via Kankakee just after noon.[14]

Robert met his mother at the station where, after getting over her amazement at his healthy condition, she told him that someone had tried to poison her on the train. She said that a wandering Jew had stolen her pocketbook but would probably return it. She appeared otherwise healthy and spoke normally of her stay in Florida and everyday matters.

Robert took a room next to his mother's at the Grand Pacific Hotel. He observed her restless wanderings in her nightdress and eventually had to let her sleep in his room to calm her nocturnal fears. Mrs. Lincoln appeared to need a guardian, so Robert hired Pinkerton detectives to watch her thereafter.

On April 1 Mrs. Lincoln, half-clad, left her room to go to the Grand Pacific lobby. When Robert attempted to stop her at the elevator, she screamed, "You are going to murder me." Sometime in the following six weeks, Robert Todd Lincoln decided to take the necessary legal steps to have his mother committed to a mental hospital.[15]

About the time of his inquiry via the telegraph office about his mother's "trouble mentally or otherwise," Robert naturally sought medical advice in Chicago as well. Since his law partner's nephew Ralph N. Isham was a physician, Robert's in fact, he first consulted him. Dr. Isham was not an expert on mental medicine, so he apparently consulted Dr. Robert T. Patterson, proprietor of Bellevue Place (a private sanitarium for women near Chicago), former superintendent of the state hospitals for the insane in Indiana and Iowa, and one of the area's more experienced specialists in diseases of the mind. Robert paid Dr. Patterson ten dollars for the consultation on April 10, 1875.[16]

Robert also engaged legal counsel, hiring the Chicago firm of Ayer & Kales to handle his problem. They in turn brought Leonard Swett into the case. He was one of the greatest trial lawyers in Illinois and an old friend of Robert's father to boot. With Swett on his side, Robert was well on his way to mustering perhaps the greatest team of experts on the medical jurisprudence of insanity brought together for a trial before the famous trial of Garfield's assassin, Guiteau.[17]

Swett immediately began to assemble medical talent. Drs. Charles Gilman Smith and Hosmer Allen Johnson had helped treat Tad Lincoln, in what proved to be his last illness, after Mrs. Lincoln returned from Europe in 1871. Mary herself had described them as "two excellent physicians." Johnson, fifty-three years old in 1875, had risen rapidly in his profession after graduation from Chicago's Rush Medical College in 1852. He and Ralph Isham had been instrumental in founding what became the Chicago Medical College. Although not a specialist in mental medicine, he had taught medical jurisprudence at Rush Medical College.[18]

Naturally, Swett consulted Dr. Willis Danforth. He had been treating Mrs. Lincoln since 1873 and was the physician most familiar with the clinical details of Mrs. Lincoln's recent medical history. As a result, he would testify at length at her trial.[19]

Swett called in two more doctors on the case, both obviously chosen for their professional eminence and for their familiarity with mental disease. Nathan Smith Davis, a New Yorker born in 1817, had graduated from medical school in Fairfield, New York, in 1837. He quickly gained considerable fame for publishing papers on the nervous system. After practicing first in Binghamton, he moved to Chicago in 1849 to assume the chair in physiology and pathology at the Rush Medical College. Dr. Davis became the editor of Chicago's *Medical Examiner* in 1860 and helped establish a national medical association, of which he was president from 1864 to 1865. Eventually he would become the editor of the *Journal of the American Medical Association*. Mental medicine was not his specialty, but he had won a prize from the New York State Medical Society in 1840 for an essay on the physiology of the nervous system. He had once taught medical jurisprudence in New York as well. A Methodist teetotaler and an ardent temperance advocate, Dr. Davis was considered an expert on the relationship between alcoholism and insanity. As an expert on lungs as well, he had helped treat Tad Lincoln, who apparently died of pleurisy.[20]

When Swett engaged the services of James Stewart Jewell, he added one of the Midwest's foremost experts on mental medicine to the prosecution team. Jewell was the founder and editor of the *Chicago Journal of Nervous and Mental Diseases* (which survives as the *Journal of Nervous and Mental Diseases*). Born near Galena, Illinois, in 1837, he graduated from the Chicago Medical College in 1860. During the Civil War he served as a contract surgeon with Gen. William T. Sherman's command. From 1864 to 1869 he was professor of anatomy in the Chicago Medical College. By the time Swett consulted him, Jewell had been a professor of mental diseases at the same college for three years, a position he would hold until his death in 1887. He had founded his psychiatric journal a year before his involvement in Mrs. Lincoln's case and became the first president of the American Neurological Association the year of the trial.[21]

Leonard Swett himself had impressive credentials in the medical jurisprudence of insanity. Most often regarded today as a political wire-puller and flashy criminal lawyer, Swett was known in his own time as an expert on the insanity defense. Dr. Andrew McFarland, one of the state's leading experts on mental disease, proudly noted in 1880 that Illinois had the "lasting honor" of seeing "some of the most advanced maxims of law" on the insanity defense "born in her courts." And he attributed much of this pioneer case law to the work of Leonard Swett.[22]

Chance had first brought Swett's attention to the insanity defense in a case which also involved Abraham Lincoln. In June 1855 Isaac Wyant was embroiled in a street brawl over a land boundary dispute. A man named Anson Rusk shot Wyant in the arm. After the limb was amputated at the elbow, Wyant murdered Rusk in the county clerk's office in Clinton, Illinois, on October 12, 1855. In 1857 the case of the *People v. Wyant* was tried in Bloomington on a change of venue. Swett defended Wyant and Lincoln aided the prosecution. David Davis was the judge. Wyant was acquitted on grounds of insanity. Several doctors, including Andrew McFarland, testified for the defense that Wyant's sanity had been questionable long before the murder. The court sent Wyant to the State Hospital for the Insane at Jacksonville, where he remained an inmate for several years until he was released on condition that he return to his native Indiana to stay.

Responding to testimony during the Wyant trial that the defendant's insanity was evident from his habit of picking painful sores on his head, Lincoln said, "Now, I sometimes pick my head, and those joking fellows at Springfield tell me that there may be a living, moving cause for it, and that the trouble isn't at all on the inside. It's only a case for fine-tooth combs." Swett soon became adept at blunting such folksy attacks on the insanity defense. By way of preparation for the Wyant trial, he went to Boston to consult Dr. Luther V. Bell, superintendent of the McLean Asylum for the Insane. Thus began those studies which, Dr. McFarland said, "eventually made him [Swett] master of all medical evidence ever likely to appear in court in the department of mental disease." He grew legendary as the defense counsel who could whip out a copy of Gray's *Anatomy* and correct an arrogant doctor on the nature of the brain.[23]

Within a few months of the Wyant trial, Robert Sloo, of Shawneetown, Illinois, killed a man named Hall who had written a newspaper article critical of Sloo's father. The elder Sloo, a friend of Lincoln's, had been running for a minor office. He wrote Lincoln for help with his son's defense. Lincoln could not oblige, but impressed with the opposing attorney's performance in the Wyant case, he recommended Swett. The Sloo trial occurred in the summer of 1857, and Swett again proved victorious. Sloo was found not guilty by reason of insanity. Later, he enlisted to fight in the Civil War and was found dead, either from exposure or suicide. By this time, McFarland recalled, Leonard Swett was "master of all the mental moods of men that are suggested in relation to human action. Science could not instruct him, but he needed its representatives in court as a part of the formality of justice."[24]

By the middle of May 1875, Robert's lawyers had assembled about the best representatives of science available for a Chicago court. On May 16 they met in the Ayer & Kales law offices and heard Mrs. Lincoln's symptoms described by Robert. They all agreed that she was insane and should be committed to an asylum for treatment.[25]

Mrs. Lincoln's mental health had been in precipitous decline since 1873. She had been under a doctor's fairly constant care for a year and a half before Robert's move to commit her. Dr. Danforth treated her as early as November 1873 "for nervous derangement and fever in her head." He noticed "peculiar symptoms" which may have been "indications of derangement." Mrs. Lincoln told him that someone was removing wires from her eyes, especially the left one, and bones from her cheeks. This was no mere metaphorical description of the sort of pain she had endured in her frequent bouts of headache, for she attributed the fiendish work inside her head to an Indian spirit. Occasionally, she claimed, he lifted her scalp and replaced it. Dr. Danforth attributed the hallucinations to physical ailments. They improved gradually and he ceased visiting her.

In March 1874 he resumed treatment, seeing Mrs. Lincoln almost daily until September. Her complaints were much the same as before, but she now added that her husband had informed her she would die on the coming sixth of September. Danforth described this condition as "debility of the nervous system" and concluded now that her symptoms were "not dependent on the condition of her body, or arising from physical disease." She apparently remained confined to her room until mid-November. She doubtless went to Florida because of this condition, and it is no wonder a nurse went along.

Mrs. Lincoln's hallucinatory impression that Robert was desperately ill constituted her next symptom, one solidly documented by surviving telegrams and not only by the secondhand reports of witnesses. Danforth visited his patient again on May 8, 1875. Mrs.

Lincoln did not complain of any particular physical symptoms this time. Instead, the doctor remembered,

> He called upon her . . . at the Grand Pacific Hotel, when she spoke of her stay in Florida, of the pleasant time she had there, of the scenery, and the manners and customs of the Southern people. She appeared at the time to be in excellent health, and her former hallucinations appeared to have passed away. She said that her reason for returning from Florida was that she was not well. She startled him somewhat by saying that an attempt had been made to poison her on her journey back. She had been very thirsty, and at a wayside station not far from Jacksonville she took a cup of coffee in which she discovered poison. She said she drank it, and took a second cup, that the overdose of poison might cause her to vomit. He did not see any traces of her having taken any poison, and was of the opinion that she was insane. On general topics, her conversation was rational.

Danforth's description of Mrs. Lincoln's case, as it was reported by Chicago newspapers when he testified at her trial, is the only clinical evidence based on lengthy personal examination of the patient available in the case of Mary Todd Lincoln.[26]

Otherwise, mostly conclusions of medical authorities drawn from secondhand descriptions of her behavior, are available. All of the doctors consulted by Robert's lawyers agreed that his mother was insane and required institutionalization. Each wrote a letter to that effect, basing his conclusion on what Robert told them in the lawyers' office. This was part of the solid preparation of the case, but doubts remained. "Robert," Swett recalled later, "was so careful to keep within the truth that the physicians doubted whether we would be able to make out a case sufficiently strong to satisfy the general public, and perhaps not strong enough to secure a verdict." Swett himself "never had any doubt because of my conviction in regard to her real condition, and because I did not doubt when the case was put together it would appear stronger than when described in the manner it was" in the conference with the doctors. Robert, the doctors, and the lawyers knew that Mrs. Lincoln was insane, and Leonard Swett knew that he had the requisite skills to convince the jury.

Still, the case had to be "put together." After the meeting, the doctors wrote their formal letters, and Robert and Swett awaited other advice and evidence. There seemed to be plenty of time. Mrs.

Lincoln "had been buying expensive lace curtains, perfumery and watches," but "she paid for very little, . . . arrangements having been made with the traders to return the goods" at a future date. There was little "danger of serious loss," therefore, and a Pinkerton agent was watching her movements.[27]

Two days after Danforth's discouraging examination of Mrs. Lincoln in the Grand Pacific Hotel, Robert sent a telegram to John Todd Stuart, a cousin of Mrs. Lincoln's and an old law partner of Abraham Lincoln's. Robert wanted to meet with Stuart to discuss his mother's condition, but Stuart's wife was ill and he was too busy with business in Springfield to leave. Robert had earlier sent Stuart two letters describing her condition. At last, after the prompting of the telegram, Stuart responded with a letter which endorsed the notion that Mrs. Lincoln needed a conservator. But he was "not so sure about the necessity of *personal restraint*," that is, of institutional confinement. Stuart thought it probable, if a conservator were appointed, "that she would consent to remain at some private hospital." "I have no doubt but that she is insane," Stuart added.[28]

After the meeting of May 16 with the battery of medical experts in the Chicago law office, Swett contacted David Davis in Indianapolis. Davis had discussed the subject with Robert and Stuart earlier. "I believe her to be a fit subject for personal restraint," Davis said, "and fear the consequences, unless action is taken soon." Swett reported that Mrs. Lincoln was talking of traveling again, to California or Europe this time, and a "departure from Chicago at all, in her present condition would be very embarrassing," Davis thought. The doctors only confirmed what Davis already thought, and if Swett and Ayer were convinced "as lawyers" that there was "evidence enough to warrant you in expecting a favorable verdict from a jury, then proceedings should be commenced at once."

Davis was fully "aware that an unfavorable verdict would be disastrous in the extreme, but this must be risked." He could "not see how Robert can get along at all, unless he has the authority to subject his mother to treatment." Appointing a conservator, "without the confinement, will not answer the purpose."

It might do with persons of different temperment from Mrs. Lincoln, but with her it would not do at all—Like you I have been satisfied for years, that her unsoundness of mind, affords the proper explanation for all the

vagaries she has developed. . . . I do not see the propriety of waiting until
the commission of some act which w[oul]d arrest public attention—It
may be that medical attention, in a Retreat for Insane persons, would
operate favorably upon her. This chance should not be lost.

Davis' letter convinced Swett, if indeed he needed more convincing,
that Robert must not lose the chance to get his mother into a
sanitarium before she left Chicago.[29]

On May 18 the detective reported suspicious visitors to Mrs.
Lincoln's hotel room. Robert learned that she had about $1,000 in
cash on her "which must have come through sale of some of her
bonds." Mrs. Lincoln had grown so grasping and paranoid that she
now carried the bulk of her capital on her person, some $56,000 in
government securities sewn into pockets in her petticoats. Swett's
news that she was "contemplating leaving town for parts unknown"
was unsettling to Robert as well. When Swett urged Robert to move
quickly "in consideration of the danger of injury to herself, the loss
of her bonds through sharpers, the certainty in my mind of her
condition," Robert assented. Swett jumped into a cab and visited all
the witnesses to be called at the trial. These visits convinced him
that "the case [was] very much stronger than represented [at the
doctors' conference], and . . . admitted of no doubt."[30]

Although the trial that ensued has been the subject of two book-
length treatments, both suffer from a serious oversight. By faulting
the legal system of the day, blame for the verdict falls in these
accounts on the statute, and what happened in the courtroom becomes irrelevant and farcical. Thus previous accounts ignore the
essence of legal history under the American system: the possibility
that any trial may have more than one outcome. David Davis, the
doctors, and maybe even Robert himself feared an adverse verdict.
Only Swett seemed confident of victory, and that confidence
stemmed from the one factor which all previous accounts of the trial
have ignored: his skill as a lawyer. Swett pushed for the trial and
Swett won the verdict. Some other lawyer might well have lost the
case, and that is why Robert hired Swett.[31]

Judge Marion R. M. Wallace assembled a jury hastily because
Swett and Robert decided to press the case at the last moment. Even
so, it was studded with the names of prominent Chicagoans: Charles
Benjamin Farwell, a member of the United States House of Repre-

sentatives and a successful wholesale dry goods merchant; Lyman
Judson Gage, cashier of the Merchants Loan & Trust Company, who
would become secretary of the treasury under President William
McKinley; S. C. Bale, physician; jeweler Thomas Cogswell of the
Cogswell-Weber Company; William Stewart of Stewart and Aldrich
Company; J. McGregor Adams of the railway supply firm Crerar
and Adams Company; realtor Silas Moore; prominent foundryman
James A. Mason; grocer Henry C. Durand; S. B. Parkhurst; C. B.
Cameron; and Charles M. Henderson.[32]

Both Mrs. Lincoln's insanity and her need for a conservator had to
be proved in court. Robert's "APPLICATION TO TRY THE QUES-
TION OF INSANITY" was a form printed by the State of Illinois. A
clerk filled in the blanks with the particulars of Robert's "petition"
that *"his mother, Mary Lincoln widow of Abraham Lincoln, deceased,* a resident of Cook county is insane, and that it would be for
her benefit and for the safety of the community that *she* should be
confined in the Cook County Hospital or the Illinois State Hospital
for the insane." The petition listed the witnesses who could prove
Robert's allegations and then continued: "and that the said *Mary
Lincoln* has property and effects consisting of *negotiable securities
and other personal property* the value of which does not exceed the
sum of *Seventy-five thousand* Dollars, and that the said *Mary Lincoln* is absolutely non compos mentis and incapable of managing his
estate, wherefore your petitioner prays that a Warrant be issued for
a jury of *twelve* good and lawful men, to determine the truth of the
allegations in the foregoing petition contained; and also, that a
subpoena be issued for the witnesses named, . . . and that said *Mary
Lincoln* be declared an insane person after due hearing and proof,
and that a Conservator be appointed to manage and control *her*
estate."[33]

Proving Mrs. Lincoln incapable of managing her estate was the
work of witnesses like Mrs. Harrington, the Grand Pacific's house-
keeper, who saw Mrs. Lincoln's closet "piled full of packages, which
were [un]opened, just as they came from the stores." Mary Gavin, a
hotel servant who stayed with Mrs. Lincoln when she was afraid to
remain alone in her room, also testified that Mary "was out shopping at least once a day and sometimes twice" and that "there was a
large number of packages in the closet." A jewelry salesman had
witnessed "expensive and reckless purchases," a curtain salesman

had sold her $300 worth of lace curtains, and another clerk had sold her $300 worth of watches and spectacles. Robert himself devoted a substantial part of his testimony to the subject of his mother's reckless spending, $600 for lace curtains, $450 for three watches, $700 worth of jewelry, $200 worth of soaps and perfumes, and "a whole piece of silk." Yet she had no home in which to hang curtains, she had trunks full of dresses she never wore, and she had not worn jewelry since her husband's assassination.[34]

Swett's witnesses played their parts as expected, even without his masterly direction. After putting the case together and himself breaking the news to Mrs. Lincoln and bringing her to court, he left the courtroom work to Ayer. Dr. Danforth was the first witness called, and he detailed Mrs. Lincoln's two-year history of mental illness. The manager of the Grand Pacific Hotel, S. M. Turner, was next. He testified that on April 1, Mrs. Lincoln, "carelessly dressed" and with a shawl over her head, told him that all the south side of Chicago was in flames. She then asked him to accompany her to her room. She complained of a man communicating with her through the wall of her room. She claimed to have a note to visit a Mr. Shoemaker in room 137. There was no such room in the hotel. After going to rooms 127, 107, and 27, they returned, but she asked to be allowed to stay in some other lady's room, as she feared the hotel was going to burn down. Mr. Turner left a servant with Mrs. Lincoln. She appeared better the next day.

Mrs. Harrington confirmed testimony about Mrs. Lincoln's "nervous and excitable" manner. She had noticed that Mary mixed medicines from several bottles Dr. Isham had left with her and took the mixture all at once. Mary Gavin had seen her have conversations with an imaginary person. The servant added that Mrs. Lincoln frequently thought she heard voices through the walls and floor of her room. The unhappy widow reportedly said at various times that Chicago was on fire, that her pocketbook had been stolen and would be returned by a man at three o'clock in the afternoon, and that someone was trying to kill her.

A waiter in the hotel, John Bessinger, had been called to Mrs. Lincoln's room. She asked to see the tallest man in the dining room. On the way down in the elevator, she exclaimed, "I'm afraid!" The cashier varified that Mrs. Lincoln wanted to see the tallest man in the dining room.

Edward Isham recounted the strange events surrounding Mrs. Lincoln's return from Florida to Chicago. Robert added further details and described her expression of fear that he was trying to murder her in the Grand Pacific. Drs. Johnson, Smith, and Davis testified that they knew Mrs. Lincoln and were satisfied from the evidence that she was insane.

After three agonizing hours in the hot courtroom, the case was rested. Swett gave a brief summation to the jury. Isaac Arnold an old friend and biographer of Abraham Lincoln, acted as Mary's counsel at Swett's urging. Upon entering the courtroom, Arnold had second thoughts about defending her, for he was as convinced as Swett that she was insane. When he expressed his doubts to the exhausted Swett just as the trial began, Robert's lawyer snapped, "That means you will put into her head, that she can get some mischievous lawyer to make us trouble; go and defend her, and do your duty." Arnold apparently did it quietly, for newspaper accounts of the trial do not mention his defense.[35]

After the proceedings, the jury stepped aside briefly and returned its verdict. Following the form standard for such cases, they judged Mary Todd Lincoln insane and a fit person to be committed to an asylum. The verdict also stated that she was neither suicidal nor homicidal.

The verdict may have been entirely correct at the moment the jury announced it, but the trial made Mary desperate. Within hours she would attempt suicide. In a few months she would contemplate murder.

The trial of Mary Todd Lincoln has been termed a "kangaroo court," a "brazen injustice," and a "high-handed denial of her civil rights." Authors have denounced the 'snake pit' laws which summarily 'put her away,' " laws which were "in large areas of the country . . . still in force" as late as the 1950s. Mary, it is said, "deserved her day in court, and never had it." Nearly every aspect of the trial has been criticized: lack of pretrial notice, judge, jury, testimony, and defense counsel.[36]

Most of the criticisms are unfair, and all of them miss an important point. By denouncing the laws rather than studying them, previous accounts of the trial have led to a complete misunderstanding of its significance. By asking whether Mary Todd Lincoln got a fair trial, historians have failed to ask a far more crucial question: why did she have a trial at all?

At most other times in American history, before and after, she would not have had a jury trial. And in most other places except Illinois even then, she would not have had one. When the trial of Mary Todd Lincoln is studied, not as an isolated piece of Lincolniana, but as a phenomenon of American history, it takes on an entirely new significance.

In colonial America there were no statutes prescribing the manner in which the mentally ill could be committed. The common law alone governed the problem, allowing anyone to arrest "dangerous" or "furiously insane" persons for commitment until the dangerous condition disappeared. Unsystematic legal custom, also inherited from England, allowed judges to appoint conservators for the estates of insane persons likely to squander them. As late as 1850 Isaac Ray, the United States' leading expert on the medical jurisprudence of insanity, could complain that "the confinement of the insane is regulated in most, if not all the States, by no statute law whatever." Civil cases involving insane persons who were not "furiously" mad or "dangerous" to the community, by far the most numerous, were handled by family and friends outside the law, with the hoary writ of habeas corpus as the only route of release for most who felt themselves wrongly confined.

By mid-century, statutes in most New England states empowered a magistrate to commit "persons furiously mad and dangerous to be at large." Two justices of the peace could do it in New York. Procedures for the rest of the insane population remained hazardously unregulated even with the advent of state hospitals for the insane in the great reform movement of the 1830s and 1840s.[37]

The above description of early American commitment laws is adequate as far as it goes, but it does not extend to westerners or to persons of property. Isaac Ray, whose work on this subject formed the basis for later histories, was an easterner, unfamiliar with the laws of the west. And because legal history was until very recent times a neglected subject, American historians are only now coming to understand that justice was a strictly two-tiered system in the nineteenth century.

The law governed those who owned property in ways far different from those without property. The latter could be summarily committed to poorhouses, prisons, or hospitals by relatives, associates, or magistrates, and were thereafter the wards of the overseers of the poor. Propertied people on the other hand, mattered to the law. And nowhere moreso than in the west. Illinois' 1823 "Act regulating the estates of Idiots, Lunatics, and persons distracted" gave the person accused of insantity the ultimate legal safeguard, a jury trial. Section 1 of the statute provided

> That whenever any idiot, lunatic, or distracted person has any estate, real or personal, the judge of the circuit court of the county in which such idiot, lunatic, or distracted person lives, shall, on the application of any creditor or relation, then any person living in such county, order a jury to be summoned, to ascertain whether such person be a lunatic, insane, or distracted; and if the said jury return, in their verdict, that such person is a lunatic, insane, or distracted, it shall be the duty of the judge aforesaid to appoint some fit person to be the conservator of such idiot, lunatic, or distracted person.

Until the construction of the State Hospital for the Insane in Illinois in 1851, the overseers of the poor apparently had responsibility for confining and supporting even insane persons with estates.[38]

After the establishment of the state hospital in Jacksonville, the result of a carefully orchestrated tour of the state by the crusader for the mentally ill in America Dorothea Lynde Dix, Illinoisans relaxed their concerns about wrongful commitment somewhat. Property still mattered too much for the western lawyers to disturb the provision for jury trial for propertied *men* accused of insanity, but the state legislature eased the process of commitment for wives and children in 1851, exempting them from the safeguards of the earlier law: "Married women and infants who, in the judgement of the medical superintendent are evidently insane or distracted, may be entered or detained in the hospital at the request of the husband, of the women, or parent, or guardian of the infants, without the evidence of insanity or distraction required in other cases."[39]

Thus at times the sex of the person accused of insanity mattered too. The sex of one person committed to the State Hospital for the Insane in 1860 mattered a great deal. Elizabeth Parsons Ware, who became a Jacksonville inmate in 1860, had been born in Massachusetts in 1816. She married the Reverend Theophilus Packard, a Congregationalist minister fifteen years her senior, in 1839. The

Packards had six children and settled eventually in Manteno, Illinois, in 1857.

Over the years Mrs. Packard came to regard her husband as a stodgy Calvinist. She flirted with Universalism and phrenology and, after the move to Illinois, grew increasingly interested in spiritualism and Swedenborgianism. Reverend Packard regarded his wife's theological vagaries as insane. For her part, Mrs. Packard thought her husband's objections stemmed from a selfish preference to see her at home cooking and cleaning instead of performing religious labors on her own. Her platonic love letters to a Swedenborgian widened the domestic rift. When she sought to leave her husband's faith and become a Methodist in 1860, the Reverend Packard was convinced of Elizabeth's madness. He brought the sheriff and two doctors, members of his congregation, to his home. The doctors took her pulse and declared Mrs. Packard insane. She was committed to the Jacksonville asylum.

State Hospital Superintendent Andrew McFarland, formerly superintendent of the New Hampshire Insane Asylum, had a difficult patient on his hands in Mrs. Packard. She insisted from the start that she was sane and a victim of persecution for her spiritualist religious ideas (like several other women in the seventh ward at Jacksonville, she said). Dr. McFarland disagreed, and the conflict between them grew into a titanic struggle. He, after all, was president of the Association of Medical Superintendents of American Institutions for the Insane, roughly the equivalent of the American Psychiatric Association today. She was clever and articulate.

After a protracted and somewhat sordid battle (at one point Mrs. Packard either fell in love with Dr. McFarland or pretended to in order to gain her freedom), she was released to the care of her husband in June 1863. A legal dispute with the reverend naturally ensued, and an Illinois court pronounced her sane early in 1864. Because of President Lincoln's Emancipation Proclamation, freedom was in the air, and soon after her trial Mrs. Packard published *The Exposure on Board the Atlantic and Pacific Car of the Emancipation for the Slaves of Old Columbia . . . or, Christianity and Calvinism Compared with an Appeal to the Government to Emancipate the Slaves of the Marriage Union.* She sold about 6,000 copies of her book, the first of several she wrote, in Illinois and took her campaign against loose commitment laws to other states as well.

The Illinois legislature had repealed the 1851 statute which had made it easy for the Reverend Packard and Dr. McFarland to commit Mrs. Packard. In 1867 she testified before the Illinois legislature, and in March a bill was passed which required a jury trial for any person committed to an insane asylum or threatened with commitment in the future. Dr. McFarland lobbied against the bill but it became law by unanimous vote. Before leaving Illinois to take her crusade to Iowa (where she brought about a similar reform in 1872), New England, and New York, Elizabeth Packard worked for passage of an 1869 law which afforded some protection to the earnings of married women. Hers was in part a feminist crusade, aimed at giving women equal protection of the laws either as persons accused of insanity or as property owners, but she always steered clear of the movement for women's suffrage. In her 1869 campaign she enlisted the support of two ardent Chicago feminists, Myra Bradwell and her husband Judge James B. Bradwell. Mrs. Packard doubtless heightened their sensitivity to issues affecting the insane—a development which would have profound effects on Mrs. Lincoln's case six years later.

Elizabeth Packard's achievement was considerable, especially since she was a woman in a man's century and since she worked alone most of the time. But it was not as great as either her detractors or her admirers have maintained. What she did was to return Illinois to the tough commitment standards of the past by restoring the rights of women and children to trial by jury and to extend these safeguards to all persons, whatever their economic station in life. It is worth noting, however, that Mary Todd Lincoln, even under the provisions of the laws in 1851, would apparently have had a jury trial because her accuser was not her husband or father, but her son.[40]

By virtue of being a citizen of Illinois, Mary Todd Lincoln did have her day in court. Thanks to a long tradition of scrupulous safeguards in such matters and to Mrs. Packard's more recent efforts, Robert was forced to comply with the country's—perhaps the world's—strictest legal standards for commitment of the insane. Mrs. Lincoln's sex proved to be no barrier to justice under Illinois law. Her wealth, no longer necessary to qualify her for such legal protection, did afford her the privilege of exemption from confinement at Jacksonville. The law allowed relatives of persons who could afford it to choose a private asylum.

By the standards of Mrs. Lincoln's day, Illinois offered greater legal protection to the accused than any other state. In a survey of commitment procedures conducted in 1864, Isaac Ray noted that only a few states had any "positive enactments" to curtail the "right of disposal" of insane persons by relatives or friends. He singled out Illinois for special comment because it left that right only to the husbands, parents, or guardians of women and children, requiring in all other cases application to the county court and subsequent disposition by a jury. Ray found jury trials necessary for "the guardianship of the insane" only in Illinois, Indiana, and Kentucky.[41]

Even by more modern standards, Mrs. Lincoln's legal protections were impressive. Illinois repealed its peculiarly tough commitment law in 1893, and jury trials were no longer necessary there. As late as 1947 only two states in the United States required jury trials for involuntary commitment of the insane. Less than half the states offered a jury trial to the accused at any stage of the commitment process, including appeal.[42]

The use of jury trials in such cases has long been regarded with jealous suspicion by the medical profession. Nineteenth-century psychiatrists, or "alienists" as they were called then, detested juries. As was typical of groups keen on establishing or maintaining their professional status, they thought such determinations should be left to experts—themselves, in other words. Alienists were then, as some psychiatrists are today, particularly critical of jury trials because the prospect of public humiliation in open court was certain to prevent or delay many a family from committing relatives in serious need of professional help.

An article which typified the alienists' outlook appeared in the *American Journal of Insanity* in 1878. It singled out Illinois' law for special criticism, terming its provision for jury trial cruel and inhuman and sure to prevent or delay treatment. "The law of Illinois," said the author, "requires a husband or father to drag a sick and insane wife or daughter, for many miles perhaps, and in any weather, before a judge and jury, that her insanity may be judicially determined or decided, before she can be properly treated or restrained of her liberty." Isaac Ray, who worked for years to reform commitment laws, championed the model statute proposed by the Association of Medical Superintendents of American Institutions for the Insane which pointedly recognized "the sacred right of the family, under the great law of humanity, to place one of its members in a hospital for the insane, restricted by no other condition than that of the medical certificate." The Illinois statute, in other words, went too far for him.[43]

Such articles, of course, never discussed the threat to civil liberties posed by the doctors' ideals, but they did at least describe the effect of laws requiring jury trials accurately. The very existence of Illinois' peculiar law must have been a deterrent to Robert's taking the legal steps necessary to commit his mother. Only the direst of circumstances would have compelled this publicity-shy man to offer the Chicago newspapers, which both he and his mother detested, such scandalous fare in open court.

Surely then, it is wrongheaded to regard Mrs. Lincoln as a victim of the system. On the contrary, she had the greatest protection the law allowed anywhere in the country, a trial by jury. The law's only deference to the prestige of medical science was its provision, by a statute passed in 1853 just after the building of Illinois' first state hospital for the insane, that one member of the jury must be a physician. That original statute required only a six-man jury, but a change in the Illinois constitution before Mary's trial permitted the use of six-man juries only in civil cases tried before a justice of the peace. Her jury, therefore, consisted of twelve men.[44]

Only when the fact that Mrs. Lincoln had a trial is properly appreciated, is it appropriate to examine what kind of trial she had: whether she was given proper notice, whether the judge and jury were fair, and whether she had adequate defense counsel. It is certainly true that Mrs. Lincoln did not have enough time to prepare her defense. After the alarming discovery of May 18, Swett pressed for immediate action and got it. Robert's application to the court in his mother's case was dated May 19, 1875, and the judge's warrant for her appearance bore the same date. These documents were filled out in the morning, and the time for the trial set at two o'clock. Swett came to Mary's room with the warrant perhaps an hour before that time.

Failure to give proper notice in such cases was a serious offense, and the Illinois Supreme Court had made a ringing pronouncement on the question in 1854. Justice John D. Caton had ruled in *Eddy v. The People* that, though the "statute is silent upon the subject of notice," the "consequences resulting from the determination are of the most momentous character to the lunatic, both personally and pecuniarily, and so long as it is possible that a sane person might, upon an *ex parte* examination, be found to be insane, every principle of justice and right requires that he should have notice and be allowed to make manifest his sanity, and to refute or explain the evidence tending to prove the reverse."

> The idea is too monstrous to be tolerated for a moment [Justice Caton continued], that the legislature ever intended to establish a rule by which secret proceedings might be instituted against any member of the community, by any party who might be interested, to shut him up in a madhouse, by which he might be divested of his property and his liberty, without an opportunity of a struggle on his part. Should such a principle be sustained, the most sane man in the State is liable to be surprised at any moment, by finding himself bereft of his property, and on his way to a lunatic asylum. Such justice as this would be worthy of that dread tribunal of the *holy vehme*, whose first notice to its victim was the execution of its sentence; but it cannot be tolerated where just and equal laws prevail and can be enforced.

The sort of legal notice described by Justice Caton and demanded by Illinois law was, once again, greater than that demanded by most states. In Isaac Ray's 1864 survey of commitment laws he found that notification of "the accused party and, if notified, his appearance in court" were "points . . . on which there is a variety of practice." Those few states requiring jury trials likewise expected the appearance of the accused at the trial, but most New England states required neither notice nor appearance, and Massachusetts positively discouraged having the accused present.

The mere fact of the presence of the accused or his counsel at the inquisition did not constitute proof of legal notice, Judge Caton had argued in 1854. "If notice was given the record should show it affirmatively." The Illinois Supreme Court was otherwise silent in regard to what constituted proof of notice in the record of the trial. Presumably, the writ commanding the sheriff of Cook County to produce Mrs. Lincoln at the court at 2:00 P.M., docketed by the court's clerk and signed by the sheriff's deputy, constituted adequate proof of legal notice. Justice Caton's decision had said nothing of time to prepare a defense and engage counsel: the accused must only "have notice and be allowed to make manifest his sanity, and to refute or explain the evidence tending to prove the reverse." Caton's concern was for the possibility of secret proceedings, and Mrs. Lincoln's trial was embarrassingly public. The record of her case was dryly correct, and no lawyer working in Mrs. Lincoln's behalf later ever questioned it.[45]

Questions about judge and jury seem quite insubstantial. Judge Marion R. M. Wallace and the jurymen were never mentioned in the correspondence about preparations for the trial nor in recollections of it. The court itself was mentioned only in fear and respect: Davis and the doctors worried only about the ability to get a favorable verdict, given the limits of the evidence Robert would allow to be used against his mother.

Nor is there reason to see in the jury one chosen to convict. Rather, one can see a worried judge who was not about to preside over the trial of the Great Emancipator's widow without having an impeccably prestigious group of jurors to render judgment. One can glimpse in the prominence of the jurymen America's two-tiered justice system at work: presidents' widows did not run the risk of unfavorable verdicts at the hands of the *hoi polloi.* Mrs. Lincoln truly had a jury of her economic peers.

There is no record whatever of Judge Marion R. M. Wallace's role in the trial. He allowed testimony that has provoked distaste among critics of the trial—evidence from servants and tradespeople about Mrs. Lincoln's irrational purchases, which had about it an air of sordid and envious gossip. This was, however, the very sort of evidence necessary to prove Mrs. Lincoln's financial incapacity, and that was half of what had to be proven in court.

In fact, the economy of Leonard Swett's case against Mary Todd Lincoln seems to be one of the most remarkable aspects of the trial. All of the evidence concerned her behavior since her decision to return from Florida, except for Dr. Danforth's description of her medical history, which reached back two years to describe the development of a hallucinatory condition. Most of the descriptions of her fears and foibles—from thinking Chicago was on fire to taking unprescribed mixtures of medicines—revealed behavior which endangered Mary's safety. The evidence given by an American Express Company agent named Seaton, for example, which showed that Mrs. Lincoln had asked him to take eleven trunks of her possessions to Milwaukee revealed not only the extent of her stored possessions but also her extreme fear of fire in Chicago. The evidence concerning her fear of fire was important, for the doctors had told Robert that persons who feared fire sometimes leapt from buildings to avoid imaginary flames.

The range of testimony was clearly controlled. Nothing was said, for example, about Mary's interest in spiritualism, a subject which savvy attorneys probably avoided after Mrs. Packard's campaign. And little was said about Mary's behavior before 1873.

Champions of the kangaroo court thesis have been quick to point out that Mary's lawyer, Isaac N. Arnold, offered little or no defense and had been handpicked by the prosecution. This is quite true. Mary's defense was probably purely *pro forma*, but Swett no doubt did his duty as a lawyer. Newspaper accounts mention cross-examination, and he was certainly a sympathetic friend and a knowledgeable lawyer. Years before, when William Herndon first aired the Ann Rutledge story, so injurious to Mrs. Lincoln's feelings and reputation, Arnold had cautioned him against the use of such gossip. Himself a Lincoln biographer, Arnold was always circumspect about hearsay accounts of the Lincolns' personal lives. Moreover, he was a lawyer of long experience and had some knowledge of the medical jurisprudence of insanity. Well before Leonard Swett's successful employment of the insanity defense in *The People v. Wyant*, which has erroneously been called the first use of that defense in Illinois courts, Arnold had been associate counsel in a murder trial in McHenry County in which the insanity defense resulted in a hung jury. Arnold had called in an expert medical witness from out of state in that trial.[46] Mrs. Lincoln's fate would probably have been worse in the twentieth century. Modern commitment procedures have generally made no provision for advocacy on the defendant's side. Hugh Ross, the premier modern legal student of commitment procedures, sneers at provisions requiring that the accused by given notice before an insanity hearing begins. The history of the treatment of insanity in American law provides no real evidence that Mary Todd Lincoln's fate would have been different in modern times.

COMMITMENT

Dazzled by headlines about organ transplants and genetic engineering and the outright disappearance of diseases which used to ravage Western society, the modern reader shudders to recall the state of medicine in Mrs. Lincoln's era. The horrors of medical science before germ theory are memorably symbolized by the staggering death rate in the Civil War, more the result of disease than of bullets, shells, and bayonets. Yet, even where it is most tempting, it is still dangerous to assume that the course of history presents a tale of unalloyed progress. It is always perilous to regard previous eras as backward or primitive or even quaint. It may be expecially tempting to do so in medical history, but the history of mental medicine since the eighteenth century defies any simple linear characterization.

To be sure, the assumptions of Mrs. Lincoln's era were markedly different from our own. Few Victorians in England or America, as one scholar has pointed out, "doubted that there was an essential distinction between the sane or the insane, or that most of the latter properly belonged in an asylum. This was one of the verities of the age." We have lost their easy confidence in the ability to determine who is sane or insane, but we have also lost their optimism about the curability of insanity. "There are but few diseases from which so large a percentage of the persons attacked are restored," boasted Dr.

Pliny Earle, medical head of New York's Bloomingdale Asylum in 1844. Years of sobering experience would later cause Dr. Earle to change his mind, but in his early career he voiced the era's general confidence in curing the insane. In part, that attitude led to the establishment of numerous state hospitals for the insane in the reformist 1830s and 1840s. Because of that confidence also, even liberty-loving Americans put few barriers in the way of commitment.[1]

As David J. Rothman, a modern critic of the nineteenth-century asylum movement, points out, "the promise of effective treatment seemed to obviate the need for procedural protections."[2] Illinois, as we have seen already, had stringent procedural protections anyway, but recapturing a sense of an earlier era's confidence in the ability to cure insanity helps put Mary Todd Lincoln's case in fresh perspective. "Putting her away" may not be a fair description of what Robert was doing in 1875.

What precisely these early mental institutions did to bring about their success remains to this day something of a mystery. Gerald N. Grob, the premier historian of mental institutions in nineteenth-century America, admits that "specific descriptions of care and treatment within mental hospitals are almost nonexistent for this period." Narcotics, laxatives, beer, digitalis, whiskey, and other medications supplemented the doctors' principal therapy, if it may be called that, "moral treatment." Even modern champions of old-fashioned moral treatment, like J. Sanbourne Bockhoven, have difficulty describing it vividly. Dr. Bockhoven says only that it "meant that the patient was made comfortable, his interest aroused, his friendship invited, and discussion of his troubles encouraged. His time was managed and filled with purposeful activity." All sources agree, however, that moral treatment was dependent on a low doctor-patient ratio and that it could not be effectively administered in sprawling institutions filled mostly with pauper incurables.[3]

Asylum superintendents were only gradually coming to realize this in Mrs. Lincoln's day. In the end, the form their realization took robbed moral treatment of its just reputation and plummeted asylum superintendents, the medical profession, and most other concerned observers into despair of ever curing any appreciable numbers of insane persons. Because moral treatment was always so hard to describe in any convincing way, the mainstay of its champions was to advertise its results with statistics—statistics so impressive that they still intrigue psychiatrists today. In the heyday of the "cult of curability," asylum superintendents reported steadily escalating rates of cure, often as many as 90 percent of recent cases (that is, cases of less than a year's duration before institutionalization). Unsophisticated in the use of statistics and—it must be said— naturally drawn to self-serving evidence, they based their rates of cure on the number of patients discharged.

Rates of cure, which in the early days of the mental institutions compared favorably with mid twentieth-century rates, began to fall noticeably in the 1850s. Asylums, especially public ones, took fewer and fewer curable patients and had less and less time to spend curing them as they were increasingly occupied with the merely custodial care of those who were beyond help. Rapid population increase, immigration, and poverty undermined success by so filling asylums that they had to be expanded into unwieldy factorylike units. The same demographic changes also brought patients whose ethnic diversity broke down any true bonds of sympathy between doctor and patient.[4]

The year of Mary Todd Lincoln's trial, Dr. Pliny Earle, a dedicated practitioner of moral treatment and a frugal Quaker, became so disgusted at the trend toward building extravagantly large mental hospitals that he set out to prove they could not cure as they promised. His own hospital in Northampton, Massachusetts, full of pauper incurables transferred from other hospitals to make room for new patients, could not report high rates of cure. He saw that the suspiciously high rates reported by other hospitals sustained the legislature's willingness to build larger asylums which, because of their unwieldy size, were sure to neglect their patients.[5]

Dr. Earle uncovered a fallacy in the statistics. By counting patients discharged without comparing them with numbers of patients admitted, asylum superintendents had exaggerated rates of cure by counting the same person, readmitted after previous discharge, as more than one cure. Yet the repeated commitment and discharge of the same person was hardly cause for optimism about the curability of insanity. He found one woman reported as cured forty-six times before her death.[6]

Dr. Earle was so excited at this discovery that he failed to notice

that the statistical fallacy affected so few persons in the 11,000 cases
he studied as to make almost no difference in overall rates of cure.
Less than 6 percent of the persons had been more than twice re-
committed. No one else at the time noticed it either, and Dr. Earle's
studies, first published in the annual report of the Northampton
State Hospital, soon appeared in the prestigious *American Journal
of Insanity*, the professional organ of the country's experts on mental disease. He added further studies in subsequent years and finally published a book, *The Curability of Insanity*, in 1887.

Pliny Earle's book dealt the cult of curability a death blow.
Though not themselves inspired by Darwinian intellectual currents, his studies would mesh nicely with the coming vogue of
emphasis on heredity and would lead in turn to what might be called
the cult of incurability. Overcrowded and understaffed hospitals
made Earle seem prophetic. By the 1920s asylum superintendents
thought only 4 or 5 percent of their patients were curable.[7]

Mrs. Lincoln's trial, then, occurred in a year that was a sort of
watershed in attitudes toward treatment of the insane. The cult of
curability was on the wane. Elizabeth Packard's crusade, sensational revelations of the worsening conditions in crowded state
mental institutions, popular books about nefarious conspiracies to
commit sane persons in order to gain control of their property, more
conservative estimates of the curability of insanity, and conflicting
testimony from medical experts at trials of persons using the insanity defense—all these things were altering the way educated Americans regarded mental disease. Certainty and optimism were shad-
ing into doubt and pessimism as insane asylums became more
custodial institutions than hospitals.[8]

Yet attitudes were only changing. They had not turned around
entirely yet. The views of the early post–Civil War era were mixed.
Doctors and persons forced to commit relatives to asylums naturally
clung to the hopeful views of the past. Desperate hope as much as
bitter resignation characterized the mood of the people in Robert's
camp. David Davis, for example, had thought it possible "that
medical attention, in a Retreat for Insane persons, could operate
favorably upon her. This chance should not be lost." The letter that
Robert's lawyers sent the doctors present at the fateful meeting of
May 15, 1875, skirted the tone of finality in the language of the
statute and emphasized therapy by asking, "Is it your opinion in

view of the facts and information [disclosed at our conference on the 15th instant] . . . , that her case is a proper one for treatment in an Asylum for the Insane, or, in the language of the statute, that she is a fit person to be sent to a State Hospital for the Insane?" Dr. Nathan Smith Davis' reply likewise emphasized therapeutic hope:

> *First*—From the facts and circumstances detailed to us on the 15th inst., I am decidedly of the opinion that Mrs. Lincoln *is insane*. The character of her insanity is such that she may, at times, appear perfectly sane in ordinary conversation; and yet she is constantly subject to such mental hallucinations as to render her entirely unsafe if left to herself. *Second*, I think her case is one eminently proper for treatment in an Asylum for the Insane. In such an institution she would not only be safe from harm either in person or property, but her chances of recovery would be greatly increased.[9]

By abandoning the easy assumption that medical history is a story of steady progress and by avoiding the early twentieth-century notion of commitment as putting a person away for merely custodial care, one can see Mrs. Lincoln's commitment in a different light. However, the findings of modern historical research on mental medicine suggest two more questions about the fairness of Mrs. Lincoln's treatment. The first question arises from the nineteenth-century medical profession's notorious reputation for misogyny and the second from the picture drawn here of the declining quality of treatment for the insane. Can the word of the experts, all men, who testified to this famous woman's insanity be trusted? Did she, once committed to a sanitarium, receive the sort of treatment which might have helped her? In short, if she was not exactly a victim of the legal system, was she nevertheless a victim of the medical system?

Womankind had no worse enemy in the nineteenth century than the medical doctor. This is among the principal findings of the modern literature on woman's history. Medical "science" in Mrs. Lincoln's era merely endorsed and reinforced the dominant view of woman's frailty, low intellect, and restricted social destiny. Medical school lectures and gynecological manuals provide impressive evidence of woman's degraded condition in that era.

In general, nineteenth-century medicine saw woman as biologically radically different from man, smaller and weaker, but it laid

special emphasis on her nervous system. It was at once more dominant and more prone to dysfunction. In social terms, woman seemed
more emotional and less rational. Male doctors focused obsessively
on female sexuality, seeing the woman's reproductive system in
control of her physical (and social) destiny. It was, as one doctor put
it in 1870, "as if the Almighty, in creating the female sex, had taken
the uterus and built up a woman around it." Thus sexuality was the
underlying key to woman's health, and her nervous system was at
best in delicate balance—with these basic biological assumptions
it is little wonder that the judgments on Mary Todd Lincoln by
nineteenth-century men of medicine might not inspire confidence in
modern readers.[10]

Moreover, as we know, several of the doctors, including the one
most expert in mental medicine (Jewell) concluded that Mrs. Lincoln was insane without examining her personally. They learned of
her symptoms only as Robert, his lawyers, and less expert doctors
described them.

If the testimony of the doctors were all the modern reader had to
go on, the well-documented prejudices of the medical profession
would be cause enough for profound skepticism at the judgment of
insanity in Mary Todd Lincoln's case. But there is other proof, proof
which does not come down to us via suspect sources. The fact of the
matter is that Mrs. Lincoln essentially admitted her insanity.

It is possible to say with reasonable confidence that Mary Todd
Lincoln was insane *in the spring of 1875.* Those last five words
constitute a crucial qualification of the statement, for nothing in the
available historical records allows us to say with any confidence
that she was insane before or after that. But mental medicine, then
as now, did not regard insanity as a permanent condition. Durations
of mental disease ranging from temporary to chronic have long been
recognized, so that no statement that a person was insane makes
much sense without saying at what time the condition existed.

At the time of her trial, Mary Todd Lincoln was insane—by her
own later admission. In November of 1875, about six months after
Mrs. Lincoln's trial and in circumstances which will be explained in
a later chapter, Mary's sister, Elizabeth Todd Edwards, wrote
Robert a letter which stated flatly: "I have no hesitation, in pronouncing her sane, and far more reasonable, and gentle, than in
former years." Mrs. Edwards had recently spent quite a lot of time

with her sister and could tell Robert his mother's side of the story. "Surely," she wrote, "the evidences of derangement exhibited last spring, must have arisen from physical disorder—she informs me that her health was poor before going to Florida, and during her stay there, and on her return, was often conscious of the presence of fever—moreover, had used Chloral very freely, for the purpose of inducing sleep—those causes, had doubtless much to do, with producing the sad result."[11]

Dangerous opiates were readily available in the nineteenth century in patent medicines and elsewhere, but chloral will not explain Mrs. Lincoln's hallucinatory state. Readers of detective fiction will recognize it immediately as "knock-out drops." Chloral (or chloral hydrate) is a crystalline compound introduced as a soporific for medical use around 1870. It gained such immediate popularity that it was quite expensive at first and difficult to obtain, but of course a woman like Mrs. Lincoln could afford it. One of its principal uses was as a sedative for mental patients. In more recent times it has been used to sedate alcoholics in hospital emergency rooms. It was useful precisely because it has no side effects—on mental patients or in combination with alcohol. Chloral hydrate is distinguished by its lack of side effects. It has no power to induce hallucinations. At worst, large quantities of chloral might cause a burning sensation in the stomach or a little nausea.[12]

Mary's use of that harmless drug does not explain her hallucinatory state in the spring of 1875. But her explanation is nonetheless highly significant, for it shows that Mrs. Lincoln herself felt that her behavior needed explanation. She knew her behavior in that terrible spring of 1875 had been abnormal. She more or less conceded the existence of the symptoms described at her trial, but of course she had a different explanation for them. Her explanation, physical illness (discredited by Dr. Danforth) and chloral (discredited by scientific knowledge of the drug's properties), will not suffice, and that of Robert, the doctors, and the Cook County Court must stand.

Mary Todd Lincoln was, from all outward appearances in the courtroom, "stolid and unmoved" by the verdict of the jury. But her son realized immediately that gaining physical possession of the bonds that she carried on her person at all times was going to be unpleasant. Robert told Swett that he must get them. Swett asked for them, pointing out to Mary that she could save herself the humiliation of having the sheriff take them by force. Mrs. Lincoln refused, saying that Robert could never have anything that belonged to her. How about Mr. Arnold, Swett asked; would she surrender them to him? No, Mrs. Lincoln replied, they were in her underclothing and surely they would not force her to be indelicate in the presence of all the people in the courtroom.

Mary was hot and wanted to go to her room. Swett said that he would gladly take her if she would promise to give Arnold the bonds when they arrived. She agreed at first but reneged when they arrived at her hotel. Swett wrote out a receipt and argued and cajoled. Mrs. Lincoln wept and finally stepped to the side of the room to pull up her outer skirt. She was by then too exhausted to remove the bonds, and Arnold had to tear them out of the pocket.

Mary was to spend the night in her room under guard. A strong Irish woman in the room and two Pinkerton detectives in the hall outside proved to be unequal to Mrs. Lincoln's resourcefulness. She convinced the servant that she needed to step into the hall. Once outside the room, Mary had no trouble walking down the stairs past her guards, who probably thought the servant had given her permission and who apparently were under orders not to lay a hand on Mrs. Lincoln anyway. She went directly to the hotel drugstore, Squair & Co., and requested two ounces each of laudanum and camphor. Mrs. Lincoln answered the clerk's suspicious gaze by saying that she suffered from neuralgia in her shoulder and frequently bathed it in a mixture of laudanum and camphor.

Unlike Mary's inept and overawed guards, the clerk did his duty by consulting the proprietor. Mr. Squair, suspecting the real intention of the drug order, stalled for time, telling Mrs. Lincoln it would require thirty minutes to prepare the drugs. She left the store immediately, took one of the carriages which were always waiting outside the busy hotel, and drove to the Rogers and Smith drugstore at the corner of Clark and Adams, about a block away. The clever Mr. Squair and a hapless Pinkerton agent followed. The two alarmed men somehow prevented the willing clerk at Rogers & Smith from filling the order, but Mrs. Lincoln returned to her carriage and rode two blocks down Clark Street to William Dole's store. She failed there too.

By this time it occurred to Mrs. Lincoln that Squair & Co., must have finished filling her order. She took the carriage back to the hotel. Squair filled a four-ounce vial with burnt sugar and water. Mary drank the harmless compound on the way to her room and then awaited death with composure. After fifteen or twenty minutes, she knew something must be wrong. Once again, she gave her incompetent guards the slip and returned to the lobby and the knowing druggist. She needed another ounce of laudanum for relief, she told Squair; the potion had proved too weak.

To make sure he filled the order properly, Mrs. Lincoln stepped behind the counter to watch. Squair was at his wits' end. He had sent for Robert Lincoln after Mrs. Lincoln's departure with the first drug order, but he had not yet arrived. The druggist told his troubled customer that he kept the laudanum in the cellar and went downstairs, where he poured an ounce of burnt sugar and water into a vial and labeled it "Laudanum—poison." Mary drank it right after leaving the store and went to her room to die.[13]

Robert soon arrived, and his mother had to give up her attempts at suicide. He and Swett remained with her through the night. Serene resignation reminiscent of her courtroom appearance characterized her preparations to travel to Batavia the next afternoon. While Robert waited for his mother to pack, he noticed that the numerous carpet-covered footstools, "such as are made in furniture stores to use up remnants of carpets," which his mother kept in her hotel room, were missing. She was taking "a number of carpet bags with her," and Robert "had the curiosity, when her back was turned, to look into some of them." He "found that each of the bags . . . contained nothing but one of these foot-stools." He said nothing and let them go with the rest of her baggage.[14]

Robert and Swett took her to the train. Mrs. Lincoln was civil— even warm—toward Swett, clasping his hand at the station and urging him to visit her at the asylum. When he replied that he would do so in ten days at the latest, she insisted that he come the very next week. The press reported that she took five trunks with her and that nearly a dozen more were to be sent to her later.[15]

Although the law required Mrs. Lincoln's commitment and the verdict specified the State Hospital for the Insane, the 1874 statute made other provisions for nonpaupers. If the insane person were not a pauper, the law allowed "application . . . to such one of the state hospitals for the insane as the relatives or friends of the patient shall desire." In practice, the legal system allowed even greater latitude for persons whose care would not be paid for by the state. Robert apparently considered keeping her at his home, but this was out of the question. He had tried it after Tad's death in 1871 and, as Robert later told his aunt in an unusually revealing letter, "had to break up housekeeping to end the trouble."

To "break up housekeeping" in the Victorian lexicon of euphemisms was to resort to what would be called a "separation" in modern times. In other words, Mary Todd Lincoln all but destroyed Robert's marriage. The record does not show how long Mary Harlan Lincoln was separated from Robert, but it may have been a year or more. She had returned to Chicago by 1873, and Mary Todd Lincoln then became so "violently angry" with Robert's wife "for some trifle" that the two Mrs. Lincolns were to meet again only shortly before Mary Todd Lincoln's death.

Robert was intensely miserable, but he tried to do his duty to both of the important women in his life. His mother remained fond of the grandchild named after her (and nicknamed "Mamie"). Robert and Mary Harlan Lincoln had arranged for his mother to visit the child regularly despite the awkward circumstances. On some of those occasions, Robert recalled with sadness but not with anger, Mary Todd Lincoln had "driven my servants out of the room by her insulting remarks concerning their mistress & this in the presence of my little girl."

Of all this, not a word had been said at Mrs. Lincoln's trial. Victorian juries must surely have been sympathetic to the sanctity of the family and the inviolability of the home and the marriage contract that made it. The law, for example, did not allow divorce by reason of the insanity of one of the marriage partners. Presentation of the sort of evidence Robert revealed to his aunt might well have carried weight with a jury, but Robert Todd Lincoln was not about to allow any such thing. In a rare unguarded moment, however, he told his aunt of yet another factor which, if revealed to a jury, would probably have sealed Mary Todd Lincoln's fate in a moment. In 1874, as Robert told his aunt, his mother "suggested to a lady (who told me of it in some alarm) the idea of running away with the child."

"Such a freak," Robert said long after the trial, "would be no more astonishing than a good many I could tell you that you have never heard of." The trial, Robert told his aunt, had revealed "only a part of the facts, which forced me to act. I would be ashamed to put on paper an account of many of her insane acts—and I allowed to be introduced in evidence only so much as was necessary to establish the case."[16]

Robert's home could provide his mother no sanctuary, and he did not feel that he could call upon his mother's other near relatives for help. Mary Todd Lincoln, for reasons never understood by Robert, her other relatives, or historians since, had chosen long ago to cut off relations with most of her sisters and cousins. Cousin John Todd Stuart was an exception, but he in fact never proved very helpful in this crisis. When Robert asked him to confer with him about Mrs. Lincoln's mental health in the spring of 1875, Stuart sent a letter acknowledging his belief that Mary was insane but begging off the conference because of his wife's poor health. When Robert asked him to be present at the trial, Stuart again refused, mentioning his wife's poor health again as one reason and, as another, "that the State House and Penetentiary Boards were holding on that day a joint meeting in relation to some stone cut for the New State House which was alledged to be improper to be used." Stuart felt his "reputation was too much involved in the question . . . to leave," he wrote Robert more than a week after the trial was over.[17]

Left to his own devices, Robert chose Bellevue Place in Batavia, Illinois, a private sanitarium established by Dr. Richard J. Patterson. Isaac Arnold, Dr. Patterson, and Robert took Mary there by train on the afternoon of May 20, the day after the trial. Even on this sad journey, Mrs. Lincoln traveled in style. They rode in the railroad directors' "elegant special car," complete "in all its appointments."[18]

Little is known about Mary's treatment once she became a Bellevue patient, and the Insanity File itself does not contain much to expand history's knowledge of that dark period. Part of the reason for the silence of the record lies in the geography of the place. Batavia was about forty miles from Chicago, and Robert took a ninety-minute train ride to visit his mother there weekly. His regular visits enabled him to learn what he needed to know about her condition from conversations with her and with Dr. Patterson. Therefore, there was no need for correspondence which might have revealed Mrs. Lincoln's clinical progress to history. Notations in the asylum logbook, still in private hands, are skimpy. Moreover, all nineteenth-century records of mental institutions are notoriously silent on the specifics of treatment.

Placing Bellevue Place in the context of the history of mental medicine in America and examining its typical therapies and cure rates, however, do offer some fresh insights into the nature of Mrs. Lincoln's treatment. Contemporary assessments, of course, varied wildly. Mary and her partisans regarded Bellevue Place as a gloomy prison more likely to cause insanity than to cure it. Robert thought of it as a pleasant country retreat. Neither view was entirely accurate.

Bellevue Place was a small sanitarium which could accommodate twenty-five or thirty female patients. About twenty were there during Mrs. Lincoln's convalescence. The asylum catered to women from the upper crust of Chicago society. Dr. Patterson advertised Bellevue place in the *Chicago Journal of Nervous and Mental Diseases* as a "Hospital for the Insane of the Private Class" and maintained office hours one day a week in the metropolis. He admitted "only a select class of lady patients of quiet unexceptionable habits." In other words, they were probably rich and were supposed to be only moderately troubled. Avoiding the furiously insane made it easier for him to practice "the modern management of mental disease by rest, diet, baths, fresh air, occupation, diversion, change of scene, no more medicine than . . . absolutely necessary, and the least restraint possible." Patterson's wife was the matron, his physician son was medical assistant, and a dozen attendants and nurses complemented the professional staff.[19]

Unhappy with the other alternatives, Robert "considered it a blessing" that he could "place her under Dr. Patterson's care." Batavia was in the Fox River Valley, "the most beautiful country west of New York" in Robert's estimation. His mother occupied two rooms at Bellevue Place located "in the Private residence part of the house, entirely separated from the larger Ell" in which the other patients lived. She need not see or hear the others. Mrs. Lincoln would dine at "her own private table" and would "keep the key of her own room as she would at a hotel." She could go for carriage rides whenever she liked.[20]

When Dr. Patterson referred to "the modern management of

mental disease," it may have been more than mere advertising. He was probably referring, however hazily, to the idea of moral treatment. That therapy, itself only hazily defined to this day, stressed freedom from personal restraint, comfort, the courtesies of civilized society, diversion of the mind from morbid thoughts, and programs to occupy the patients' minds. Above all, as Gerald Grob has described it, moral treatment "assumed that hospitals—like families—would remain small, and that superintendents—like firm but loving fathers—would have the ability and flexibility to manipulate an environment in order to promote the mental health of their patients." Robert himself noted that his mother was "in the private part of the house of Dr. Patterson, and her associates are the members of his family only. With them she walks and drives whenever she likes and takes her meals with them or in her room as she chooses."[21]

In other words, Mary Todd Lincoln received special care. The ordinary care at Bellevue Place seems gentle enough. Many patients were given sedatives, often chloral hydrate, at bedtime. Those who were underweight, not one of Mrs. Lincoln's problems, were given the sovereign Bellevue remedy: eggnog with two teaspoonfuls of whiskey in it. Those who refused to eat were force-fed, a remedy that appears warranted by weight as low as seventy-four pounds (as was the case with one patient). At various times in the period around Mrs. Lincoln's commitment to Bellevue Place, other patients received quinine, morphia, marijuana, cod-liver oil, beer, or ale. Besides the patients' eating habits and weight gains or losses, the medical staff also noted menstrual flow—in keeping with the regnant medical opinion of the day which saw women as dominated by their reproductive system. Otherwise, the staff seems only to have kept order while allowing the patients to play croquet, go for walks around the grounds, take carriage rides, or play the piano.

Such treatment, as this chapter noted earlier, still has its champions among writers on the history of the treatment of the insane, and they might point to Bellevue Place's record with some pride. In fifty-three cases mentioned in thirty-three months of records available today, over 10 percent recovered or left the sanitarium expected to recover. Another 10 percent left improved or greatly improved in the estimation of the staff. Two of these patients (besides Mrs. Lincoln) left in less than six months. Only two of the patients mentioned in the available records were described as "chronic." It seems certain that commitment to Bellevue Place was not necessarily a permanent arrangement. From all available evidence, the sanitarium attempted to, and sometimes did in fact, cure its patients.

On the other hand, an asylum seems always to be a harrowing place, and Bellevue Place was certainly no exception. In the same available records can be found an instance in which one woman slipped into the water closet unnoticed by the servant girls and stabbed herself just below the navel with a large carving knife stolen from the kitchen. She recovered only to snatch a pair of scissors from another patient and stab herself in the abdomen again. Women often awoke screaming in the night. One woman's hair was cut in order to keep her from pulling it out, and another sat around picking sores on her head. Mrs. Lincoln could hardly have been spared exposure to some of this depressing behavior.[22]

But she was not destined to be long exposed to it. Commitment concentrated her mind wonderfully, to paraphrase Samuel Johnson, and Mrs. Lincoln would rapidly plan her release from Bellevue Place.

Robert Todd Lincoln, February 1872. Illinois State Historical Library.

Mary Harlan Lincoln. Illinois State Historical Library.

Abraham "Jack" Lincoln and Mary Lincoln, Robert's children.

Mary Todd Lincoln, about 1872, probably in mourning for Tad and in the period of her "great bloat." The ghostly hands of Abraham Lincoln are fakes, as they are smaller than Mary's. Louis A. Warren Lincoln Library and Museum.

Edward Swift Isham. Illinois State Historical Library.

David Davis. Illinois State Historical Library.

Leonard Swett. Illinois State Historical Library.

Dr. Ralph Isham. Illinois State Historical Library.

Dr. Charles Gilman Smith. Illinois State Historical Library.

Dr. Hosmer A. Johnson. Illinois State Historical Library.

Dr. Nathan Smith Davis. Illinois State Historical Library.

Dr. James Stewart Jewell. Illinois State Historical Library.

RELEASE

May 20, 1875, was Mary Todd Lincoln's first day in the asylum. Dr. Patterson wrote in the ledger that her case was "one of mental impairment which probably dates back to the murder of President Lincoln—More pronounced since the death of her son, but especially aggravated during the last 2 months." Otherwise, the Bellevue records are not very revealing.

Mrs. Lincoln was "cheerful," "contented," and "talkative" for the first five days of her confinement. Then she turned "rather depressed" and by the end of the month was "very melancholy" and no longer taking her daily carriage ride. She kept to her room most of the month of June. Patterson noted on July 2 that Mrs. Lincoln made an appointment to ride each morning but put it off when the time came. She had "a fit of crying" on July 5.

Three days later she surprised the Bellevue staff by agreeing to see a woman reporter from the *Chicago Evening Post and Mail*. "Mrs. L. seemed to be glad to hear of her Chicago friends," the asylum record book noted. Whatever news the reporter brought must have seemed encouraging to Mary, for on July 15 she announced to Dr. Patterson that she wanted to go live with her sister in Springfield. Patterson said he thought that Mary had not "felt kindly" toward her sister in the past, to which Mary replied hotly, "It is the most natural thing in the world to wish to live with

my sister—She raised me and I regard her as a sort of mother."
Patterson wrote in the record book after the conversation that the
"next moment she complained of her getting so agueish [?] in Jacksonville Florida and forthwith wanted to get immediately to St.
Augustine Fla. to live." Aside from general comments on Mrs.
Lincoln's mood, documenting little inconsistencies in her state-
ments or plans constituted the bulk of the doctor's notes on the case.
Just two days before the conversation about her sister, for example,
Patterson wrote that Mrs. Lincoln had promised to give a little boy
named Wilmarth some stockings purchased especially for him. The
doctor commented in his ledger that she bought the stockings in
Chicago before meeting the boy.[1]

Mrs. Lincoln's statement about the stockings seems little more
than a white lie, but what she said about her sister was rather
disingenuous. Mary had harbored unkind feelings toward Elizabeth
Todd Edwards for a long time, and Mrs. Edwards was, in fact, among
the many relatives from whom Mrs. Lincoln had cut herself off. The
statement came nearer the truth in another important respect:
Elizabeth Edwards had a motherly understanding of, and affection
for, her younger sister. In fact, if the sad story of Mary Todd Lincoln's later life has any heroes or heroines in it, Elizabeth Todd
Edwards is the prime candidate.

This will no doubt surprise those who know Mrs. Edwards only
from the standard biographies of Abraham or Mary Todd Lincoln.
Until now, history has glimpsed Mrs. Edwards only on two occasions when she did not show to great advantage, once on the eve of
Mary's marriage and once again on the very eve of Mary's death.

Elizabeth was five years older than Mary, and mothering became
her destined role when the girls' natural mother died in 1825. When
she was nineteen Elizabeth married a junior at Lexington's Tran-
sylvania University. Ninian Wirt Edwards was the son of Illinois'
territorial governor, Ninian Edwards, and a suitable mate for the
oldest daughter of prominent Lexington businessman and politician Robert Smith Todd.

The younger Edwards became a lawyer, businessman, and politician in Springfield, and his wife, thereby, a member of a local social
coterie as privileged as the one she had left in Lexington. After
moving to Illinois with her husband in 1835, Elizabeth found it easy
to continue her motherly role to the other Todd girls, who seemed

plenty willing to leave their stepmother and seek mates in Springfield. Frances, the child born between Elizabeth and Mary, was the
first to come. The Edwardses' charmed social circle soon brought her
to Dr. William Wallace's attention, and Frances married him in the
parlor of her sister's house. Mary was wed in the same parlor in
1842, and Elizabeth then sent for her sister Ann, six years younger
than Mary, who met and married Springfield merchant Clark M.
Smith.

Most Lincoln biographers know Mary's oldest sister as they know
many of the other minor characters in the Lincoln story, mainly
from statements dictated to Lincoln's old law partner, William H.
Herndon, in 1866. What Mrs. Edwards told Herndon has done little
to endear her to Lincoln's admirers. She said that she had known
Mr. Lincoln well and that "he was a cold man, had no affection, was
not social, was abstracted, thoughtful." At that early point in his
career, Lincoln "could not hold a lengthy conversation with a lady,
was not sufficiently educated and intelligent in the female line to do
so." She and Ninian admitted discouraging the marriage, in part
because of the social gulf which separated a Todd daughter from a
man of Lincoln's humble origins. And their objections mattered, for
Edwards was Mary's guardian in Springfield. Ninian and Elizabeth's opposition to the marriage—in keeping with his reputation
for hating "democracy . . . as the devil is said to hate holy water"—
and her frank description of Lincoln's character have made them
generally unattractive characters in most Lincoln biographies.

The second well-known episode came at the very end of Mary's life
when she came to the Edwards home to die. Mrs. Lincoln was so
physically miserable and mentally unstable by that late date that
her presence in any household would have tried the patience of a
saint. It certainly taxed Mrs. Edwards' patience, and her critical
comments on her sister's behavior in that dark period have seemed
of a piece with her hostility to Mary's brilliant marriage some forty
years earlier.

Mrs. Edwards' reputation has suffered considerably as well from
association with her husband's. Although they began as close Whig
allies (the two tall brothers-in-law were part of the famous "Long
Nine" delegation in the state legislature), Ninian Wirt Edwards
was to cause Abraham Lincoln many political problems over the
years. In 1843, for example, shortly after Mary and Abraham were

wed, Lincoln failed to gain the support of the Sangamon County Whig delegation for the nomination for representative to the United States House in part because his enemies depicted him as "the candidate of pride, wealth, and aristocratic family distinction." Such a charge, made against a man who had been so recently, as Lincoln protested, "a strange[r], friendless, uneducated, [a] penniless boy, working in a flat boat—at ten dollars per month," could stick only because he had married a Todd five months before. And the Todds, a Kentucky family, must have been known in Sangamon County, Illinois, mainly as a family associated with the aristocratic Edwards coterie.

Lincoln and Edwards parted ways politically in the 1850s when Ninian became a Democrat, a move which, David Davis reported, "deeply mortified" Lincoln. Edwards supported Democrat Joel Matteson for the United States Senate in 1855, when Lincoln tried unsuccessfully for the support of the coalition opposed to the Democrats and the Kansas-Nebraska Act. Mary never forgave one old friend whose husband opposed Lincoln's candidacy then, and without doubt Edwards' opposition did nothing to improve Mary's relations with her older sister.

Lincoln had a more forgiving nature and lent his brother-in-law $1,500 in 1860, despite Edwards' support of Stephen A. Douglas instead of Lincoln for president. After he won the election, Lincoln proved to be exceedingly generous in doling out the patronage to his wife's relatives. The Edwardses were suffering "pecuniary embarrassment" to the tune of $10,000 indebtedness. When Ninian's desire for an appointive office was made known to him, the president said, in the frank language of nineteenth-century spoilsmanship, that he would not deprive his brother-in-law "of a chance to make something, if it can be done without injustice." So, on August 8, 1861, Lincoln made Edwards a captain and commissary of subsistence. More than any other appointment Lincoln made, this one rankled the president's old Republican friends in Springfield, and Edwards did nothing to help matters when he awarded a government contract to the political friends of Joel Matteson. Edwards kept his official record "dryly correct" and Lincoln answered Republican allegations that his brother-in-law had made $15,000 from his office by saying that he did "not suppose Mr. Edwards has, at this time of his life, given up his old habits, and turned dishonest." But Edwards clearly did not care whether he caused Lincoln political headaches, and Lincoln replaced him in the summer of 1863.[2]

Ninian explained that he had in fact been able to retire $13,000 of debt since he took his government job, but he insisted that he and Elizabeth had done so by maintaining a strict economy, spending only $600 instead of $3,000 or $4,000 to live each year. And his rental properties had proven more profitable once the war began. Mary was not one to sympathize with the economic troubles of others, and her relationship with Elizabeth was much troubled by the time of the Civil War. In a letter written from Washington to a cousin on September 29, 1861, Mrs. Lincoln said:

> I received a letter from *Elizabeth* the other day—very kind and aff[ection-ate] yet very *characteristic*—said if *rents* and means permitted, she would like to make us a visit I believe for a season—I am weary of *intrigue*, when she is by herself she can be very agreeable, especially when her mind is not dwelling on the merits of fair daughters & a talented son in law, such personages always speak for *themselves*. I often regret [Elizabeth's] . . . little *weaknesses*, after all, since the election she is the only one of my sisters who has appeared to be pleased with our advancement.[3]

Even while gossiping about her sister's little weaknesses, Mary had to admit to her genuine kindness of heart. This does not fit well with the portrait of Mrs. Edwards derived from Herndon's notes. No one questions the veracity of Herndon's renderings of his famous interviews, but they are distinctly in *his* idiom. In his search for Lincoln's character, Herndon missed Mrs. Edwards' altogether, failing to uncover the spontaneous generosity and sincere motherly affection she showed toward her sister. Elizabeth was the sister who went to the White House to care for Mary after the death of Willie Lincoln on February 20, 1862. She remained for two months. Their relationship deteriorated afterward, but when trouble afflicted Mary again in 1875, Elizabeth was the sister who offered to help.[4]

Mary's resourcefulness in her suicide attempts immediately after the trial should have provided Robert and Dr. Patterson with a warning of her behavior as a patient at Bellevue Place, but they had apparently been fooled by her seemingly stoic acceptance of her lot afterward. Had they known about the single-mindedness with which she had conducted her campaign to obtain a government pension, they might have realized that she could concentrate on serious problems and orchestrate the efforts of sympathetic friends.

That orchestration apparently began after the visit of the Chicago newspaper reporter. Twenty days later Robert made one of his regular visits, with Mary's granddaughter. Afterward, Mrs. Lincoln asked to be taken to the post office to mail a letter to her sister, written at Robert's suggestion. Mary seized the occasion to mail a letter in secret to General John Franklin Farnsworth, who had lived in St. Charles, Illinois, about five miles north of Batavia, and who now had a law practice in Chicago. He was a Republican politician of a slightly more radical stripe than Abraham Lincoln, as was typically the case with Republicans from the northern part of the state. But he and Lincoln had got along well enough, and—something Mary was not likely to forget—Farnsworth had been present at Lincoln's deathbed in 1865.[5]

Mary was by 1875 an experienced hand at cashing in on her husband's old political associations. General Farnsworth came to Batavia the very next day and caused quite a stir at Bellevue Place. After talking with Mrs. Lincoln, he informed Dr. Patterson that Mary had asked him to help her gain her freedom. The general thought she looked better than when he last saw her. She had "been on the border of insanity for many years" and still did not entirely "talk like a sane woman." But, Farnsworth said, "She still would hardly be called insane by those who used to know her." Farnsworth saw immediately that the practical solution was the one rejected in the spring: "He thinks [the Bellevue Place record book stated] that if she were free and her property still under the control of Mr. Robt Lincoln she would not do much harm, but would do many outre things."[6]

On the same day that Farnsworth came, Myra Bradwell and her husband James B. Bradwell also visited Mrs. Lincoln, apparently in response to a letter like the one smuggled to Farnsworth. The Bradwells were Chicagoans, friends of Mary's, and—most important—legal experts, ardent feminists, and advocates of reform of the laws governing insane persons.

The judge, born in England in 1828, was raised in America. He lived in Illinois from 1833 until 1852, when, with his new wife, he moved to Memphis, Tennessee, to operate a school. He was admitted to the bar in Tennessee and returned to Chicago to practice about 1854. He served two terms as county judge of Cook County (1861–69—had he remained two more terms, he would have been the judge at Mary's trial). In 1875 he was serving his second consecutive term in the lower house of the Illinois General Assembly. He was the author of the law which made women eligible for school offices in Illinois and which allowed them to become notaries public.

Bradwell's remarkable wife, Myra Colby, was born in Manchester, Vermont, in 1831. Her family was active in the abolitionist movement. After a career as a schoolteacher first in Tennessee and then in Chicago's public schools, Mrs. Bradwell became involved with the women's groups organized for the home front effort during the Civil War. She played a major role in Chicago's sanitary fairs, enormous charity bazaars which raised money and supplies for the soldiers in the field and the wounded. As it did for many other upper-class American women, this work led to involvement in feminist causes after the war, in part because of the vexing obstacles, both legal and customary, they had encountered in their charitable work, and in part because of the expanded horizons in organizational, administrative, and financial management war relief work gave the movement's leaders.

For her part, Mrs. Bradwell began to study law after the war. She founded the *Chicago Legal News* in 1868, publishing the latest reports of midwestern case law. She also published the biennial session laws of the Illinois General Assembly. But she could not practice law herself, her application for admission to the Illinois bar in 1871 having been denied because of her sex. The Illinois Supreme Court and the United States Supreme Court upheld the decision. She would become the first female member of the state bar association only in 1892, two years before her death.[7]

How and when Mrs. Lincoln and the Bradwells became friends are unknown, but by 1872 Judge Bradwell was handling Mrs. Lincoln's will. Nor is it possible to state with precision what Mrs. Bradwell thought of Mrs. Lincoln's mental state. The records of her first visit to Bellevue Place indicate that Mrs. Bradwell "thought that Mrs. Lincoln was not quite right, but that she still ought to be at home and have 'tender loving care.'" When she came again on August 6, Mrs. Bradwell had a long conversation with the doctor in which, again according to the Bellevue Place record, "She told the doctor distinctly that she had no doubt that Mrs. Lincoln was insane and had been so for some time—but she doubted the propriety of keeping her in an asylum for insane." Myra spent that night with Mary, concluded she was better, and suggested she should be removed to her sister's home in Springfield.[8]

Although private, the records of those conversations with Myra Bradwell are secondhand. She stated more flatly in a letter in her own hand, written a few days later, that Mrs. Lincoln was "quite well & as I think not insane." This is not necessarily inconsistent with the Bellevue Place record, for Mrs. Bradwell added in the letter, "It never seemed necessary for her to be sent there, to me at least."[9] In other words, Mrs. Bradwell, like John Todd Stuart and General Farnsworth, did not think Mrs. Lincoln required involuntary institutionalization. Such a view still left room for the belief that someone else should handle Mary's financial affairs.

Mrs. Bradwell returned to Batavia on August 7, bringing with her a "Mr. Wilkie of Chicago." The Bellevue staff later learned, to their dismay, that Franc B. Wilkie was a reporter for the *Chicago Times*. The Bradwells had decided to bring the press in on Mrs. Lincoln's case, and things were rapidly coming to a head.[10]

Meanwhile, Mary had received an answer to her letter to Elizabeth Edwards, inviting her to stay in the Edwards home in Springfield. At Mrs. Bradwell's request, Dr. Patterson showed the letter to Robert on August 7. Robert wasted no time in writing to his aunt.

Mrs. Bradwell, Robert cautioned, "expresses herself in a very melodramatic way to Dr. Patterson that 'her dear girl' is not a fit subject for 'bolted doors and barred windows' but ought to be allowed to be under the care of 'some tender and sympathetic friend.'" With rare candor, Robert said he had kept Swett from using all the evidence against his mother, that she had nearly destroyed his marriage, and that she had once spoken of kidnapping his child. He explained that his mother's severed relations with her sisters had prevented him from calling on them for help. He described the freedoms his mother enjoyed at the sanitarium, the only restraint being a "white wire netting such as you may see often to keep children from falling out of the window."

"What trouble Mrs. Bradwell may give me with her interference I cannot foretell," said Robert. He understood that she was "a high priestess in a gang of Spiritualists and from what I have heard it is to their interest that my mother should be at liberty to control herself and her property." When Mary had expressed a desire to visit Elizabeth in late July, Robert had told his mother he had no objection himself but that she should write her sister first. Now he was having second thoughts, apparently because of Mrs. Bradwell's intervention.

> I have done my duty as I best knew and Providence must take care of the rest—If you have in your mind any plan by which my mother can be placed under care and under some control which will prevent her from making herself talked of by everybody, I hope you will tell it to me—I do not know who is willing to assume such an understanding, nor do I believe any one could succeed in it unless backed by the authority of the law, as is Dr. Patterson—He is a most excellent and kindhearted man & as she knows his authority, he has absolutely no trouble with her.

Given her freedom, Mary "would at once go to Europe," a distressing prospect in her present state of mind. Robert doubted that if she were in Springfield, "she would receive a call from any one of her sisters." "Keep this letter," he challenged his aunt, "& see if I am not correct, when the time comes."[11]

Before he heard from Elizabeth, Robert had an interesting caller: Myra Bradwell herself. From their conversation he learned that he had been "misinformed" about her spiritualism. She told Robert, as he recalled later, that she thought Mary was "not entirely 'right' but that she ought to be at large." Robert told her he had no objection to the proposed visit to the Edwards home, but in a later letter about the meeting with Bradwell he could not suppress a tone of self-righteous indignation: "How completly recovered my mother really is is shown by Mrs. B's saying she was to take out to her samples of dress goods she wants to buy—She has with her *seven* trunks of clothing and there are stored here *nine* more—I told Mrs. Bradwell that the experiment of putting her entirely at liberty would be interesting to those who have no responsibility for the results— They can afterwards dismiss the matter with a shrug of the shoulder." Myra Bradwell's intercession was causing Robert to become defensive and to grasp at arguments to prove his mother's incompetent status. He did not want Mary "making herself talked of by everybody" or purchasing trunkloads of useless clothing—less serious problems than the hallucinations and life-threatening behavior that had led to the insanity trial two and a half months before.[12]

The day after Mrs. Bradwell's visit, Robert received Mrs. Edwards' reply to his letter. Sprinkled with arbitrary commas in characteristic Todd fashion, the letter was generally apologetic in tone. Elizabeth regretted "that any act of mine, should have occasioned you annoyance." She had been surprised, she said, to receive a letter from Mrs. Bradwell suggesting Mary's visit and "made a mistake in expressing to her [Mrs. Bradwell], my views, upon the subject, of the treatment, I supposed would have been most beneficial to your Mother." Now, Elizabeth explained contritely, "After hearing all the facts from you—her position, and difficulties in your family—I do not see, that you could have pursued, any other course." Mrs. Edwards sought "atonement" and promised her nephew that he had nothing to fear in the future from her "instrusiveness."[13]

Robert's letter describing Myra Bradwell's call crossed Elizabeth's in the mail, and she answered it on August 12. "When your poor Mother proposed a visit to me," she said, "I felt I must respond in a kind manner: supposing that if the visit, was permitted, she would be in charge of a responsible person, and taken back again for a continuation of treatment." "Visit" is an ambiguous word, and Elizabeth had assumed that it meant something on the order of "holiday," whereas Mrs. Lincoln and Mrs. Bradwell equated it with "release." In keeping with the contrite tone Elizabeth had assumed since Robert wrote her, she now gave the impression that she had never envisaged anything resembling a long-term arrangement. She assured Robert that the "peculiarities" of Mary's "whole life, have been so marked and well understood by me that I have not indulged in faintest hope, of a permanent cure." Mary's recent tragedies had "only added to the malady, [letter torn] apparent to her family for years, before the saddest events occurred." Mrs. Edwards was "unwilling to urge any step, or assume any responsibility" in her sister's case. Elizabeth's own "present feeble health," she now pleaded, was "causing such nervous prostation, as would render me, a most unfit person to control an unsound mind."[14]

Robert seems to have been stalling for time. While Elizabeth's second letter was on its way to him, he wrote Mrs. Bradwell a note, telling her that Dr. Patterson had asked him to forward to her

Elizabeth's letter inviting Mary to Springfield. The doctor "had already some days [ago] sent the letter to me to be transmitted to you and the delay is caused by my accidental neglect or forgetfulness, for which I beg to be excused." In truth, Robert had probably been thinking of little else, having written two letters to his aunt on the subject in the week preceding the receipt of Mrs. Bradwell's reminder. No doubt, he wanted to sound out Mrs. Edwards before resisting the Springfield scheme.[15]

When he received his aunt's second letter, Robert seized the opportunity to block Mary's release. "I regret beyond measure," he wrote Mrs. Bradwell disingenuously on August 14, "that my Aunt is not able to aid me, as she says that her health is such that she cannot assume the responsibility—I had hoped for a possibility of benefit from my Mothers apparent desire to renew her proper relations with her sister." Then Robert unleashed his counterattack. On visiting his mother on the thirteenth, he "could not help observing with pain, a renewal in degree of the same appearances which marred her in May and which I had not noticed in my last few visits." The only cause he could assign for this decline was "the constant excitement she has been in since your first visit." He now felt "compelled to request that you visit her less often and not at all with persons with whom I am not acquainted and especially that you do not aid her in corresponding with persons other than her relations." Robert told his mother much the same thing the next day. "I am dreadfully disappointed," he wrote, "that Aunt Lizzie writes me that she is not well enough to have you visit her just now but I am going to try to arrange it with her very soon—There is nothing I want so much as to have you with her—for I am sure nothing would do you more good."[16]

This was not Robert's finest hour. Despite some bland assurances to his mother, he had resisted the Springfield scheme from the start, or at least as soon as he learned of Mrs. Bradwell's involvement in it. But he had succeeded in blocking it, at least temporarily, and he now left for a vacation. If he thought his troubles were over, he was terribly mistaken. They were only beginning.

Franc Wilkie's article based on his August 7 interview with Mrs. Lincoln, appeared in the *Chicago Times* on August 24. The headline told all: "MRS. LINCOLN. Her Physicians Pronounce Her Entirely Sane." In quest of scientific facts by means of personal observation, "the reporter had engaged Mary in conversation on a wide range of topics, pleasant and painful" and had found "not a sign of weakness or of any abnormal manifestations of mind." She had remembered meeting Wilkie in Washington back in 1862, when he was a war correspondent for the *New York Times*. She spoke of Tad and the assassination with no difficulty. She "especially dwelt on the friendship which existed between Mr. Seward and Mr. Lincoln and herself. It was the habit of the secretary [of state] to dine with Mr. Lincoln and herself informally, two or three times a week."

In regard to the more important current issue, Wilkie asked Mrs. Lincoln about her behavior the preceding May, and she attributed "any eccentricities she might have manifested" upon her return from Florida to having been suffering "from fever, and her nervous system was somewhat shattered." She now feared that the presence of insane persons in the sanitarium "might . . . unseat her reason, in time." Wilkie "departed thoroughly convinced that whatever condition of mind Mrs. Lincoln may have been in previously, she is unquestionably compos mentis now, and ought not to be deprived of her liberty."[17]

Mary could not have asked for more had she written the article herself. She in fact despised and distrusted William H. Seward, a "wicked" man whose appointment to her husband's cabinet she had opposed from the start. In 1866 she accused Seward of circulating malicious rumors. She thought him "capable of any meanness," including keeping for himself gifts sent to her from Europe.[18] But Mrs. Lincoln knew that the *New York Times*, when Wilkie worked for it, was a Seward organ, and she was obviously careful to cater to Wilkie's factional preferences in politics. The result was that Wilkie told the story as Mary and Myra Bradwell wanted it told, whatever the facts. Not a single physician—certainly no one in the staff at Bellevue place—doubted Mrs. Lincoln's insanity. She had no contact with the other patients at the sanitarium. And there was no evidence that she had been physically ill when she returned from Florida.

Dr. Patterson had almost as much at stake in this controversy as Robert. On August 15 he wrote Judge Bradwell a letter very like Robert's to Mrs. Bradwell. The doctor could see only harm for Mary in discussing "*with her* the question of her removal from this place." These were questions "which should not be determined by an insane mind." Since Robert was to be away from home for a couple of weeks, Patterson wanted Mrs. Lincoln let alone "at least until his return."[19]

Bradwell responded on the nineteenth, asking, "who was it but yourself that told Mrs. Lincoln and also myself that she was in a condition to visit her sister, . . . and that you had written a letter to her son Robert to that effect?" The judge's letter grew warmer:

> Mrs. Bradwell, to carry out the expressed wish of Mrs. Lincoln, went to Springfield to see Mrs. Edwards to see if she would take her sister, and was assured by her that she would do so if brought by her son, and [Mrs. Bradwell] saw him day before yesterday. No, Doctor, if you have the good of Mrs. Lincoln at heart, I am sure that you will see that she is taken to her sister. It is in accordance with your letter, I am satisfied, that Mrs. Lincoln does not require to be confined in a house for the insane, and that it would be greatly for her good to be allowed to visit her relatives and friends. She pines for liberty. Some of the best medical men in America say that it is shameful to lock Mrs. Lincoln up behind grates as she has been, and I concur with them. I believe that such confinement is injurious to her in the extreme, and calculated to drive her insane. Are you not going to allow her to visit her relatives to see if it will benefit her or will you take the responsibility and run the risk of the American people saying hereafter that it was the restraint of your institution that injured Mrs. Lincoln and proved her ruin? Should you not allow her to visit Mrs. Edwards, and insist on keeping her in close confinement, and I should be satisfied that the good of Mrs. Lincoln required it, as I certainly shall unless there is a change in her condition, I, as her legal adviser and friend, will see if a habeas corpus cannot open the door of Mrs. Lincoln's prison house.[20]

Judge Bradwell's letter for the first time revealed the outlines of the brilliant strategy devised by the Bradwells to spring Mrs. Lincoln from Bellevue Place. They knew better than to attack Robert. Mary was the martyred president's widow, but Robert was his son, and as far as the general public was concerned, there was little to choose between them. No, the Bradwells would attack Dr. Patterson, a vulnerable target in a society exposed to the sensational literature of wrongful confinement. The letter hardly mentioned Robert and said nothing of his views of the Springfield scheme. The nature of the "visit"—its duration, its legal status in light of the court decision, indeed its very nature beyond anything but an innocent social call—was left entirely to speculation. Only the problem of personal restraint was mentioned; nothing was said of the court's financial restraints on Mrs. Lincoln.

To these ardent feminists, Mrs. Lincoln may have been the victim of a male judge, male jury, and male doctors, but the Bradwells said nothing of this. Moreover, their strategy left the heavy fighting to the judge. It might have been too easy for the public to dismiss such arguments from Mrs. Bradwell as emanating from a meddlesome nuisance, as Robert did—at first.

As tempers on both sides flared, only Elizabeth Edwards remained fair-minded and uncalculating. In a letter written on August 13, she expressed her delight at Mary's changed attitude toward her and her other estranged relatives and urged Robert not to show his mother her letters about her mental state, being "unwilling to excite her by intimating any thing unpleasant, when she seems disposed to be amiable." In a postscript marked "Private," Elizabeth broached to Robert "a most painful subject":

Insanity, although a new feature, in our family history, first appeared within my knowledge, in the case of my own daughter, at the early age of thirteen—for six months, she was so decidedly flighty, as to be closely guarded—her back from irritants is scarred its length—At the birth of each child, the same symptoms were shown, and severely felt, particularly by her husband, and myself—At no time, has she ever been natural in her demeanor—God pity those who are the victims—and who are the anxious sufferers in such terrible afflictions!

More a sufferer from the trials of coping with insane relatives than Robert had ever dreamed, Aunt Lizzie therefore proved especially charitable toward Mary.[21]

Elizabeth grew even more sympathetic with Mary after Myra Bradwell visited her in the wake of Robert's letter stating that Elizabeth could not handle the responsibility of a visit from her sister. Mrs. Bradwell was persuasive and Mrs. Edwards reconsidered her position, telling Robert on August 17 that "it may be that a refusal, to yield, to her [Mary's] wishes, at this crisis, will greatly increase her disorder." Mrs. Bradwell had shown her Robert's letter to his mother, "which satisfies me," Elizabeth wrote, "that you misapprehend my intention, while willing to receive, I shrank from the responsibility, after your statement of her condition. . . . I now say, that if *you will bring* her down, *feeling perfectly willing*, to make the experiment—I promise to do all in my power, for her comfort and recovery—I would wish her to have a suitable white person, one wholly competent for the situation, brought with her—further arrangements when I see you."[22]

Perhaps because of Robert's absence from home, the battle was left to be fought in the newspapers. On August 23 the *Chicago Post and Mail* carried a "Startling Interview" with Judge Bradwell. "Mrs. Lincoln was found partially insane about three months ago by the Cook County Court, but it did not commit her to a public asylum or any other. The conservator appointed to control her movements, however, removed her to A PRIVATE HOSPITAL for the insane at Batavia, kept by Dr. Patterson. There she was placed under a restraint that was virtual imprisonment."

That was the newspaper speaking, not Judge Bradwell, and the paragraph shows how successfully the Bradwells conquered the press. The paragraph did not mention that the conservator was Robert Todd Lincoln and, in keeping with the Bradwells' strategy, focused instead on Dr. Patterson's "virtual imprisonment" of Mrs. Lincoln. Contrary to the *Post and Mail*, the court definitely required Mrs. Lincoln's commitment and did so because she was "insane" not "partially insane." And the decision to send her to Batavia was simply choosing a small private sanitarium over the grim cells of the state hospital for the insane.

Claiming (falsely) to be "the only paper whose correspondent has ever interviewed" Mrs. Lincoln at Bellevue Place, the *Post and Mail* also published an interview with "the courteous and humane Judge." (Mrs. Bradwell did not engage in this public strife.) "She is [no] more insane today than you and I are," the judge declared flatly for the first time in public. "There is NOT THE SLIGHTEST TRACE OF INSANITY or of a weak mind about any of her writings," business or friendly, Bradwell added as proof. Would she be allowed to visit her sister? the reporter asked.

"We would hope so," responded Bradwell. "Dr. Patterson HAS SIGNED A CERTIFICATE of her fitness to go; but she has not got it, and I have not, but he told me he had signed it. Mrs. Edwards wrote to her that she could come and live with her, and it is expected that when Robert Lincoln returns from the East, about the middle of this week, he will go to Batavia and accompany his mother to Springfield." Bradwell then added what the newspaper made into an all-capitals subheading: "DR. PATTERSON IS A VERY PECULIAR MAN," and concluded with these dark specualtions: "I know that some letters she has sent have not been allowed to reach her friends, and some that have been sent her have not reached her. You can't tell what motives may tend to keep her there. Human nature is human nature. But if she is not soon out, there will be startling developments not to be mentioned now. Let her get out of danger first." All of this sensational innuendo focused on Dr. Patterson, leaving an opportunity for Robert to rescue Mary and take her to Springfield.[23]

Once again, the Bradwells had brilliantly steered the newspapers onto a course likely to help Mary and to put Patterson on the defensive. The rights of the insane to their mail constituted a sensitive issue long ago given prominence by Illinois' most famous asylum inmate, Elizabeth Packard. She had testified in 1867 before a committee established by the legislature about the despotic powers of the state hospital's superintendent. His ability to censor the patients' mail she singled out for particular denunciation: "Now I maintain that such laws as deprive American citizens of their natural inalienable constitutional rights, are unconstitutional laws, except as punishment for crime. No kind of disease can abrogate the post office rights." Five years later she lobbied successfully for a law in Iowa which removed all restraints from patients' outgoing mail and gave the power to screen incoming mail to a supervisory visiting committee rather than the hospital superintendent. It also provided that the names and addresses of the committee members be posted in every inmate's cell. Establishing the postal rights of the insane was perhaps Mrs. Packard's most lasting success, and the Iowa law was copied by other states later in the century.[24]

The Bradwells had worked with Mrs. Packard in the past, and they were most likely aware of the postal issue. Dr. Patterson was on the defensive again. On August 28, he wrote the *Chicago Tribune*, denying that he had "'certified' to the recovery, or mental soundness, of Mrs. Lincoln. This is not true. She is certainly much improved, both mentally and physically; but I have not at any time regarded her as a person of sound mind. I heard all the testimony at the trial, May 19, and saw no reason then to doubt the correctness of the verdict of the jury. I believe her to be now insane." Patterson did admit that he had earlier responded favorably to the Springfield proposition: "The proposition having . . . been made that she should go and live with her sister . . . , I at once said that if she would do this in good faith, and thus secure a quiet home for herself, I should favor it, 'unless her condition should change for the worse.' This was written to Mr. Robert T. Lincoln in a letter addressed to him on the 9th inst. And this is all there is of the 'certificate' said to have been given by me of the 'recovery' or 'mental soundness' of Mrs. Lincoln."

To maintain that Mrs. Lincoln was still insane but that she could try the Springfield experiment, however, not only undermined Robert's position but also called into question the verdict of the jury. Medical "science" provided the doctor with just the doctrine he needed to do that skillfully. "It is well known," Patterson noted in a jargon-filled sentence, "that there are certain insane persons who need what in medico-legal science is termed interdiction, which does not necessarily imply restraint." "If the time should show," he added, "that Mrs. Lincoln needs only the former, without the latter, all will rejoice to see any possible enlargement of her privileges."[25]

The maddeningly "professional" stance of the learned medical scientist talking down to the multitudes conspired with the slack standards of Chicago journalism to leave "interdiction" unexplained. But it was a good idea, known to Dr. Patterson, probably, from Isaac Ray's landmark *Treatise on the Medical Jurisprudence of Insanity*. First published in Boston in 1838, Ray's book had appeared in its fifth edition in 1871 and constituted a nineteenth-century classic. One chapter dealt with "interdiction," that is, the control of an insane person's property without putting the person in an asylum. "Restraint," Ray had insisted, "is a measure entirely distinct from that of interdiction, and neither should be considered, as they sometimes are, necessarily dependent on the other." Some people had thought all along that this was what Mrs. Lincoln needed.[26]

For now, however, serious consideration of that compromise option was lost in the polarizing struggle over Mrs. Lincoln's personal freedom. Patterson predicted that if the Springfield experiment were tried, "such is the character of her malady [that] she will not be content to do this, and . . . the experiment . . . will result only in giving the coveted opportunity to make extended rambles, to renew the indulgence of her purchasing mania, and other morbid mental manifestations." And he felt compelled, as well, to defend Bellevue Place from charges that it was a prison. He described the freedoms Mary enjoyed—to ride and walk about the grounds and to receive visitors. The "light ornamental screen," a natural enough precaution immediately after her suicide attempt, had now been removed from her window.

As for the habeas corpus threat, Dr. Patterson stated calmly that "Mrs. Lincoln has been placed where she is under the forms of law, and, if any have a grievance, the law is open to them." If Patterson kept up with the literature of his profession, then he probably knew it was safe to scoff at this threat. Isaac Ray had found that in 1867, for example, only two persons had been discharged from the Pennsylvania Hospital for the Insane by habeas corpus remedy, and neither of them on grounds that they were not in fact insane. Of 1,300 patients in other public and private hospitals in Pennsylvania, not a single one had been released on a habeas corpus writ. In fact, of the 5,000 patients received in twenty-seven years at the Pennsylvania Hospital for the Insane, only 3 had been discharged by writs of habeas corpus. And in Illinois, where a jury trial preceded the commitment, such a discharge was even more unlikely.[27]

Still, Dr. Patterson did not present a merely defiant pose. Although he claimed that the Bradwells' interference had already worsened Mrs. Lincoln's condition, he was "still unwilling to throw any obstacle in the way of giving her an opportunity to have a home with her sister." In response to the letter, Judge Bradwell released his letter and Patterson's previous one to the press.

By protecting his flank, Dr. Patterson had exposed Robert to attack. Now only Robert stood in the way of his mother's release, and thanks to the press, everyone knew it. When he returned to Chicago, therefore, Robert had to act quickly. On September 2 he asked Patterson whether his mother's condition had changed. She was worse while the Bradwells were visiting, the doctor answered, and better after the visit ceased. Robert also asked about the "safety" of the Springfield visit. Dr. Patterson had to admit that he had put Robert in a trap by his initial response to the Bradwells back in early August: "Inasmuch as Mrs. Lincoln has had the promise that on certain conditions she can go and live with her sister, and as those conditions, so far as I know, have been complied with, I suppose the experiment ought to be made."[28]

Robert's initial response to Patterson's advice was to ignore it and get another doctor. He immediately sought the opinions of two of the most eminent psychiatric authorities in the United States, Andrew W. McFarland and A. G. McDill. Up to this point in the crisis, Robert's inclinations seemed clear. Of all the principals involved, he thought the worst of Mary's condition. Dr. Patterson knew, or felt he knew, precisely how serious Mary's illness was. He thought her insane but not dangerously enough so to keep a screen on her window. He apparently believed the evidence from the trial and from conversations with Robert and Mary, some of which showed that her illness was not of recent origin. As hopeful as the medical profession of that era tended to be about insanity, it was never very hopeful about cases not caught in the early stages. She could be made better—had been, in fact—but she probably could not be entirely cured. The degree of her illness was such, the doctor hinted, that it perhaps required interdiction rather than restraint. Patterson knew this and had immediately agreed to the Springfield scheme—without consulting Robert's wishes in the matter. By releasing Mary to Springfield, the doctor, unlike Robert, could relieve the potential for a messy crisis in his professional life—one he certainly knew to be brewing when the Bradwells showed up in Bellevue Place with a newspaper reporter.

Robert, who had the ultimate responsibility in the case, both moral and legal, just as clearly saw that the potential for crisis in his own family life would increase if Mary were allowed to go out in public again. He had a horror of seeing his mother "making herself talked of by everybody." Thus Robert's immediate response to the Springfield scheme was to discourage it with his letter to Mrs. Edwards. Thinking he had nipped the potential crisis in the bud with Mrs. Edwards' response that she did not want the responsibility of her sister's care, he had left for a vacation in the East.

The crisis had instead grown worse in Robert's absence. Patterson was no help at all, and Robert quickly called in McFarland and McDill. McDill was the superintendent of the Wisconsin State Hospital for the Insane. McFarland, after a long career as the head of similar public asylums, was now the proprietor of Oak Lawn Retreat, a private sanitarium. Fearing the prying eyes of the press, Dr. McFarland proceeded from Jacksonville to Chicago in "the strictest secrecy, remarking to people who saw me at the depot that I was 'going East.'" He apparently registered at the hotel in Chicago under an assumed name and went to Batavia by train for a day's visit.[29]

On September 8, 1875, McFarland wrote Robert after an interview with Mrs. Lincoln, "protracted, confidential, and such as to possess me of all the facts and features of her case." The doctor doubted "the safety" of Mary's visit to Springfield "unless she was, all the time, under the care of some discreet and responsible person." Even under those conditions, he could "see no good results likely to follow beyond gratifying an ardent desire to go." He feared "that a desire for further adventure will take possession of her mind, as soon as beyond the control of the present guardians of her safety, that may be attended with hazard if gratified." McFarland's opinion was that "all the steps taken" to date had been "absolutely necessary" for Mary's "interests, her safety, and her hope of restoration." What was being done by way of restraint at the moment was "no more than her helpless and irresponsible state of mind render unavoidable." It pained him "to add, that there are features of her case that give me grave apprehensions as to the result unless the utmost quietude is observed for the few ensuing months, beyond which all reasonable hope of restoration must be abandoned, unless success within that period is achieved."[30]

Robert now had the letter that he seemed to want. McFarland's advice was so clear that Robert did not even bother to arrange to have McDill, whose schedule did not allow him to consult on Mrs. Lincoln's case at the time Robert suggested, give a second opinion.[31] To date, Robert had used such letters—like the earlier one from his aunt—to buttress his opposition to the Springfield scheme, even while he told his mother and Mrs. Bradwell that he was hoping it could be worked out. His course to this point had been almost perversely legalistic if not downright obstructionist; when the document reinforced his own inclinations and interests, he used it.

Now he did not. Two days after McFarland wrote his letter, Mary Todd Lincoln was released from Bellevue Place. The heart of the son conquered the head of the lawyerly conservator. His mother went to Springfield and Elizabeth Todd Edwards' tender loving care.

THE EXPERIMENT

On the morning of September 11, 1875, Mary Todd Lincoln arrived in Chicago on a 9:00 train. Robert met her at the railway station and then accompanied her that afternoon on the 3:40 train to Springfield. The Lincolns rode in a private car belonging to the president of the railroad. The trip must have been rather awkward, but no one left a recollection of it.[1]

The Lincolns were accompanied by Anna Kyle, who was to be Mrs. Lincoln's nurse and companion. Robert had chosen her on Dr. McFarland's recommendation. She lacked refinement and culture, the doctor had admitted, but he had commended her "qualities of willingness, good disposition, sagacity and presence of mind . . . qualities . . . most needed in the present instance." She was to receive sixteen dollars a month, paid by Robert from his mother's estate.[2]

Anna, like many of Mary's servants, did not last long on the job. Within a week of their arrival in Springfield, Anna wanted to leave. She did not fit in well with the servants in the Edwards household and was replaced by a young woman from Bellevue Place named Amanda. She would last a month in the difficult position.[3]

Mrs. Lincoln's impedimenta caused little problems as well. From the start, Robert had wanted to keep her baggage train to a minimum. He arranged to send three trunks with her and to store the rest, eleven trunks, at Bellevue Place. By September 15 she was writing to exchange a trunk in Springfield for one Robert controlled.[4]

But these were minor irritants in what was otherwise a successful experiment from the start. Aunt Lizzie, as Mrs. Edwards always signed her letters to Robert, told him things were going well and that friends who called at the Edwards home found Mary "looking . . . well, and in every respect acting in the most agreeable manner." Elizabeth took her sister's willingness to receive company as a hopeful sign.

Unlike her difficult husband, who had given Robert's father several headaches and was soon to have the same effect on Robert, Mrs. Edwards was an exceedingly pleasant person who sought always to avoid conflict or confrontation. She usually tried not to dispute Robert's word but only to describe actions of her sister which refuted the dire predictions of Robert's rather gloomy letters. Seemingly innocent accounts of social callers were, in fact, refutations of Robert's belief that his mother "would [not] receive a call from any one of her sisters." He had challenged his aunt to keep his letter containing that prediction and "see if I am not correct, when the time comes." Elizabeth met the challenge without gloating.

Just four days after her arrival in Springfield, Mrs. Lincoln accompanied the Edwardses' daughter on a visit to the wife of Jesse K. Dubois, one of Abraham Lincoln's old political cronies. "I will certainly indulge the hope," Mrs. Edwards concluded her letter to Robert about the visit, "that ere long every one will be thoroughly convinced of her entire recovery." Again, she seemed to be describing Springfield society but she may in fact have been conveying a message to Robert.[5]

He apparently did not take the hint, and when Elizabeth wrote him a week later, she asked him to send letters to her and to his mother in separate envelopes, as Mary would otherwise ask to see both letters. And Mrs. Edwards advised Robert to "avoid as far as possible, any allusion" to his "belief in her insanity." No doubt it made Mrs. Lincoln testy.

Minor squabbles still arose over Mary's living arrangements. Robert and his aunt had agreed on a figure of $100 a month for Mrs. Lincoln's board, when Mary insisted on paying board. In fact, Mary had suggested $150, but Elizabeth advised Robert, who as his mother's conservator would be sending the payments to the Edwardses, not to tell Mrs. Lincoln that they had agreed on a lower figure. Elizabeth once again sought to avoid needless conflict, and she knew her sister well. Although Mary could be niggardly about some things, she had always been generous toward relatives with whom she was on good terms, and considering herself to rank in society well above "the very middle classes," Mary probably thought a small rent would reflect poorly on her economic and social status.

Servants continued to cause problems as well. When Amanda decided to return to Batavia, Mrs. Edwards put an end to the troubles by arranging to have her own servants take care of her difficult boarder. Mary's niece slept in an adjoining room and took care of Mrs. Lincoln at night, as she took a special interest in her aunt's case anyway. Nothing more was said about the need for a trained attendant. Mrs. Lincoln took daily carriage rides, dined occasionally at the Smiths' (another sister and brother-in-law), and took tea sometimes at her sister Frances' house. She "received every visitor, with a manifestation of cheerfulness and pleasure" which greatly "surprised" Elizabeth.[6]

More than a month passed, while Mrs. Edwards observed her sister's "mental condition." On November 5 Elizabeth told Robert that she now had "no hesitation, in pronouncing her sane, and far more reasonable, and gentle, than in former years." Like the Chicago reporter who had interviewed Mary at Bellevue Place, Mrs. Edwards was swayed by Mary's explanation for her bizarre behavior in the previous spring: poor physical health, fever, and the free use of chloral. As far as Elizabeth could tell, her sister seemed "capable of taking care of her interest." Mary had convinced her that she had added to the principal of her estate from its income every year. "To a person of my plain practical ideas," Aunt Lizzie wrote, "it is surprising to look upon unnecessary purchases." Elizabeth had been so often startled by "the extravagances of persons, of small means, as to judge leniently, of those who can afford."

When it came to discussing financial matters, Elizabeth misjudged Mary's candor and Robert's acute sensitiveness. It is doubtful that Mary had added to her capital. Did she tell Elizabeth that she had cashed a $1,000 bond in May? Did Mary herself know that the source of additions to her capital had probably been Robert's investments made with the money returned secretly by Chicago merchants? When Elizabeth explained to Robert that she could not judge Mary's financial necessities and that Mary was far too independent-minded for her to exercise any control in this realm, she mentioned a seemingly innocent anecdote: "I quite agreed with her, that her dust-soiled veil bonnet & shawl, were too shabby for her to wear in visiting or church-going—she stated, that she had no fresh substitutes in her trunks. You understand her sensitive nature, and know why, I hesitate to presume to oppose what I really think, she is entitled to enjoy." This graphically disturbing depiction of Mrs. Lincoln, going about in soiled clothes while trunks full of the finest goods sat unused, was bound to upset Robert.[7]

In the week after Mrs. Edwards wrote this letter, Mrs. Lincoln began "pressing this matter [of financial independence], until the unpleasantness is such," Elizabeth said, "that I am constrained to make this plea." The "only alternative in this case, for the sake of peace and quietness, will be to yield your Mother the right to control her possessions." Yet neither Elizabeth nor Ninian was really prepared to see Mary that independent, and Mrs. Edwards hastened to tell Robert, "She assures us, that she will pledge herself to place her bonds with [Springfield banker] Mr. [Jacob] Bunn, to be undisturbed during her life." Elizabeth added, none too tactfully, that Mary had, "some time since, . . . mentioned that she had left a will with Judge B.—had set apart $20,000 for little Mamie, leaving the remainder of her property to you. I cannot believe that she would ever divert it from you—and should she in resentment do so by will—you can well understand that your interests would not be injured."[8]

Instead of reassuring the suspicious Robert, this letter mostly upset him. Talking of his mother's will implied that his interest in his mother's case was financial and that his real fear was loss of his inheritance. Mentioning the need to replace her soiled clothes merely conjured up in Robert's mind the troubling picture of his mother going out in public in ridiculous rags. And to a lawyer of Robert's incisiveness, the Bunn scheme seemed impractical. "It would probably be impossible," he pointed out, "for my mother to do anything which she could not immediately undo." If that were true, then the "question is simply whether she shall at once control and be able to dispose of all her means and whether you and my mother's sisters feel fully confident there is no danger . . . she would not after a comparatively little time find herself destitute of the means which will probably for many years be necessary to her happiness and without which she would be very wretched."[9]

The Edwardses had attempted to soothe Robert's fears about his mother on other scores as well. "With regard to Spiritualism," Aunt Lizzie reported, "she is wholly reticent—I would infer that she had no ideas upon the subject, and that it would not be an acceptable subject to one of her timid nature." Elizabeth assured Robert that Mary had not, as Robert suspected, given some of her silverware to a spiritualist named Mrs. Farwell, but had actually given it to a charitable home. As for Mrs. Lincoln's purchasing mania, Mrs. Edwards could recommend only philosophic resignation, "It has always been a prominent trait in her character to accumulate a large amount of clothing, and now that she has the means, it seems to be, the only available pleasure." The same was more or less true of Mary's "roving propensity," Elizabeth cautioned. "If you determine, to become indifferent, to what you cannot prevent—you will insure yourself, a greater degree of repose of mind, than you have known for years." The important thing to keep in mind was that "there is no evidence of derangement at this time, that would justify confinement in an asylum."[10]

Ninian Edwards, on Mary's behalf, asked Robert "whether if she can establish before Gov. [John M.] Palmer, Gov. [John L.] Beveridge, [Shelby M.] Cullom, Mr. [Ozias M.] Hatch and Mr. [Jesse K.] Dubois, or either of them or before the County Court of Cook County that she is now a fit person to have the care and custody and control of her property you will consent that said Court shall enter an Order fully restoring her to all the rights and privileges enjoyed by her before you were appointed her conservator." He mentioned the Bunn scheme as a substitute and noted that the generous banker offered his services "without any charge." Edwards had consulted Mrs. Lincoln's brother-in-law Clark M. Smith and her cousin John Todd Stuart before writing. Unlike his wife, Ninian took Mary at her word when she assured him she had "no idea of leaving here this winter—she may wish in the future, to make occasional trips but expects to make Springfield her home." When Robert expressed doubts about the wisdom of removing all restraints, Ninian quickly retreated, avoiding responsibility for the advice given in his letter. "If you will refer to my letter . . . you will see that I consulted with

Mr. Stuart and Mr. Smith, only as to whether I had better write to you in accordance with your mother's request."[11]

Robert, obviously shaken by the pleas from Springfield, decided to consult Stuart, Swett, and David Davis again, as he had the previous spring. The ensuing correspondence introduced an important political theme in the crisis.

Readers familiar with the existing secondary literature on the case of Mary Todd Lincoln may well have wondered why this book has as yet mentioned no political themes, for there is a political interpretation of the case. A popular book, *The Trial of Mary Todd Lincoln* by James Rhodes and Dean Jauchius, weaves a tale of political conspiracy into the case, suggesting that David Davis and other Liberal Republicans maneuvered Robert into committing his mother in order to ruin his promise as a politician with the magical vote-getting name of Lincoln. Robert was a staunch adherent of the more conservative wing of the Republican party, the faction which stalwartly supported Ulysses S. Grant.

This political interpretation of the insanity trial rests mainly on the simple fact that Robert Todd Lincoln's political career never amounted to much. But the Rhodes-Jauchius explanation of that ignores chronology and every scrap of written evidence available.

A brief glance at the chronology of Robert's career proves that the insanity trial did not hurt him in the least, in this respect. Indeed, just two years after he committed his mother, Robert Todd Lincoln was offered a position as assistant secretary of state by Rutherford B. Hayes. Lincoln turned him down because he thought he should continue to build his fledgling law practice, launched with Edward Isham in 1872. In 1880 Robert supported the drive for a third term for Ulysses S. Grant and was nevertheless offered the position of secretary of war in James A. Garfield's cabinet. This time he accepted, but Robert really had no taste for public life. What kept him from rising higher was neither his pro-Grant stalwartism nor any stigma from the insanity trial; it was mainly his own detestation of political life, a loathing Robert himself once described as "almost morbid."[12]

Robert was nevertheless a thoroughly partisan man who watched political developments closely. What he saw around the time of his mother's trial he did not like. It had not pleased him to see the Democrats gain control of the United States House of Representatives—for the first time in his whole adult life—in 1874. Among other things, he feared that this might endanger his mother's pension.

In his letter of November 15, 1875, asking for John Todd Stuart's advice, Robert confided his apprehension that "the continuance of the pension" was "at least precarious." The "composition of the House" was "such that it would be stopped except by reason of the politics of the Senate," and in 1876, a presidential election year which promised a close contest, the composition of the Senate might change significantly. His fears about the pension were not without foundation. The vote to grant his mother a pension back in 1870 had followed strict partisan lines.[13]

The Edwardses always thought Robert's worries about his mother's finances were needlessly exaggerated. Whatever happened to her capital, they figured, she would still have her $3,000 annual pension from the government—far more money than the Edwardses had lived on in their financial crisis of the early 1860s. Robert feared otherwise, but he never told his aunt and uncle. Therefore, this episode is doubly revealing, not only of a previously unknown reason to fear for Mrs. Lincoln's financial security but also of Robert's intensely private nature.

He unburdened himself more to David Davis than perhaps anyone else. Writing this man who had been like a father to him since 1865, Robert answered the arguments of his aunt and uncle. Among the last deliveries of goods to Mary before her departure for Batavia had been four new bonnets. (Little did Elizabeth know how sickening to Robert had been her casual mention of Mary's soiled bonnet.) All the bonnets were now in her trunks in Springfield, unworn. To Robert, that indicated "that no radical change has taken place since last spring." Only "opportunity" was "wanting to develop the same trouble" again. Elizabeth's clumsy assurances about Mary's will led Robert to assure Davis that he had no interest in his mother's property beyond preserving what was essential for her comfort the rest of her days.

On other points, Robert differed rather sharply with his aunt's account. The controversial silverware, for example, was now in the possession of "a Clairvoyant woman" who owned a house a few blocks from Robert's, and three different people had told him so. He scoffed as well at his aunt's belief in Mary's indifference to spiritualism. "She hardly thinks of anything else," Robert insisted, "and almost her only companions are spiritualists."[14]

Robert certainly did not care and probably did not know that persecution for spiritualist religious beliefs was one of the themes of Elizabeth Packard's reform crusade. But if one did not believe in spiritualism and if, by spiritualism, one meant not so much mystical religion as the work of mediums and clairvoyants, a belief in the essentially fraudulent nature of the enterprise would be entirely natural. At least that had been the way Robert's father had seen it. Mrs. Lincoln's interest in spiritualism dated back to the death of Willie early in 1862, after which she occasionally attended seances. Abraham Lincoln sometimes went along to protect her and to figure out how the mediums' tricks were done. He even got the head of the Smithsonian to expose the mechanical devices by which one medium, a man who went by the name of Colchester, produced mysterious noises in a darkened room. Mrs. Lincoln, like many other bereaved widows in wartime America, proved more susceptible to the lure of contacting loved ones, lost to untimely deaths, in the spirit world.[15]

Exposés may have generally weakened the wartime spiritualist surge by 1865, and Mrs. Lincoln's most capable biographer claims that Mary "emphatically repudiated it" in later life. Mary told Mrs. Gideon Welles on July 11, 1865, "Time, my dear Mrs. Welles, has at *length* taught & convinced me, that the loved & idolized being, comes no more, and I must patiently await, the hour, when 'God's love,' shall place me, by *his* side again." A more emphatic denial came in 1869, when Mrs. Lincoln told her friend Sally Orne, "I am not EITHER a spiritualist—but *I* sincerely believe—our loved ones, who have only, 'gone *before*' are permitted to watch over those who were dearer to them than life." In the best intimate biography of the Lincolns, historian Charles B. Strozier notes that she "eventually repudiated the more extreme claims of the spiritualists—for example, that during a seance one actually converses with the dead—and retreated to a more religiously legitimated, though still rather mystical idea."[16]

Robert no doubt exaggerated when he said his mother's only associates by the 1870s were spiritualists. He certainly proved to be dead wrong about Mrs. Bradwell and admitted it. But some of Mrs.

Lincoln's associates were spiritualists. General Farnsworth, for example, was an ardent spiritualist with a keen interest in seances. And witnesses testified under oath that Mrs. Lincoln claimed to receive messages from the dead. The Indian spirit who pulled wires in her head and removed her scalp may have had his origins in "Little Pinkie," the Indian maiden who had been the spirit-world contact of Nettie Colburn Maynard, a medium who presided over several seances attended by Mrs. Lincoln in Washington ten years earlier.[17]

If Robert exaggerated his mother's interest in spiritualism, he only exaggerated; he did not make it up. And it was perfectly natural for him to assume his father's role, as he and David Davis had done financially after the spring of 1865, as her protector from frauds, charlatans, and sharpers who might exploit the interest to get at Mrs. Lincoln's estate. Such an active role as his mother's protector was less alien to Robert than his aunt's fatalism: "if I let it alone," he told Davis, "it would not let me alone."

Robert revealed to Davis, as he would to no other person, his chagrin at Mrs. Edwards' having invited Mary to stay in Springfield at Mrs. Bradwell's instigation without having checked with him first. Robert now felt that the Edwardses' troubles, though admittedly great, had been brought on themselves.

Robert also asked Leonard Swett to see Judge Wallace about Mrs. Lincoln's finances. The judge would not entertain an application for her relief until one year after Robert's appointment as conservator for the simple reason that the statute which governed the case provided "that no application shall be entertained for the removal of any conservator appointed for any person under the provisions of this act, within less than one year from such appointment, unless for neglect of duty or mismanagement of his trust." Apparently, however, the judge would agree to anything Robert and his lawyer recommended—short of full relief. Robert, with Swett's help, came up with a list of options:

1. To remove all restraints upon travel and residence.
2. To pay her to be expended by herself without scrutiny of any kind her whole income in monthly installments . . . [of] about $700.
3. To have a competent person make an estimate . . . of what monthly

sum can be paid her during her life so as to leave nothing at her death and if Judge Wallace will consent, to pay such sum to her monthly. . . .

4. In addition to 2 & 3 or to 1 & 3 to deliver to as being necessary for her comfort all of her personal effects which consist of Clothing and Jewelry.

Robert himself had reservations about the third option because of the uncertainty of the continuation of Mrs. Lincoln's pension.[18]

David Davis answered Robert's letter on the twentieth after taking a whole day to reflect on the problem. He agreed that the Edwardses had been "officious" and he blamed Elizabeth's invitation to Springfield for bringing on the current crisis. Her "advice of indifference to you," he added, was "to say the least grounded in a total misapprehension of the relations between parent and child." Moreover, part of the problem was that Elizabeth "does not believe that Spiritualism has anything to do with it, while you & I know differently."

Nevertheless, Davis advised, Robert could not "now send her [Mrs. Lincoln] back to Batavia & Mrs. Edwards must be relieved of the trouble." Therefore, Robert should "remove restraints on travel and residence and . . . pay her monthly, the amount of her income." If Mary spent "no more than her monthly income, it is no matter," Davis said. True, if she contracted debts beyond this "with persons, who do not know her to have been adjudged insane, it is not clear that they could be recovered, because of her being discharged from the asylum & being left to go free & unrestrained," but "this must be risked." This freedom would constitute a genuine test, for the six months remaining "before she can be discharged & you relieved will develop her insane vagaries—if they still exist, which we all believe." Had Mary "remained undisturbed at Batavia there might have been a chance for her recovery," but Davis now feared that "the intermeddling will prove disastrous to her."

Davis dismissed the idea of a self-liquidating annuity because there was "no necessity for it, & the judge [Wallace] would hardly be justified in paying her more than monthly income." "If she is not insane," Davis pointed out, "she w[oul]d never expend as much as this [her income]." Strangely enough, Davis failed to comment on the obvious difference between this option and the others: it was a lifetime plan and the alternatives were plans only for the six months remaining in the court-mandated conservatorship. The self-liquidating annuity, for Robert, may have been less a practical financial blueprint for Mary's future than a personal declaration of Robert's lack of selfish interest in his mother's estate. Mrs. Edwards' tactless assurances about the security of Robert's inheritance had obviously bothered him a great deal. Perhaps Davis saw this and therefore did not probe the question very deeply.

Finally, Davis said he could see no harm in turning Mrs. Lincoln's personal possessions over to her. If she gave any of them away, it would be "a small matter." He was especially pleased to learn that Robert was consulting Swett. "Do nothing without his sanction," Davis warned. "He is a wise counsellor, & a sympathetick one."[19]

Ten days later Davis dropped Robert a note congratulating him "upon the birth of another child." While the crisis had been brewing in Springfield, the other Mary Lincoln, Robert's wife, had been ill with a difficult pregnancy. She gave birth to a daughter, Jessie, on November 6, 1875. Davis added the only note of humor in the entire documentary record of the case, telling Robert, "If I had a large family, I should be very happy, provided the children behaved cherubly—This is a very important *proviso*."[20]

Robert obtained permission from Judge Wallace to pay his mother the whole income from her estate, about $8,500 a year, but he remained wary of Davis' other recommendations. December therefore brought stalemate, degenerating into deep crisis. On the first day of the month, Ninian wrote to inform Robert that Mrs. Lincoln, still "in fine health and spirits" and "only agitated on one subject—the restoration of her right to control and manage her own property and bonds," was now "determined to employ counsel to have the order of court depriving her of their control set aside." Ninian had "told her that she can do nothing until one year from the 19th of May last" and had tried to assure her that her capital was safe in her son's hands. But she was not satisfied to have only "as much of her income as she wishes." As usual, Ninian left the decision up to Robert but added a nagging reminder: "we would all regret to have resort to the law."[21]

Mr. Edwards had no idea what Mrs. Lincoln did with the income her son sent her each month, and neither did Mrs. Edwards. Elizabeth professed surprise to hear from Robert that Mary had recently demanded more money. "I had supposed," Elizabeth said, "from her assurances, that she was *fixed* for the winter, that her shopping was over." Although Elizabeth did "not really know anything about her purchases," she "was exceedingly pained" to learn that a music box Mary had given to her sister Frances after Robert sent it to her "had been withdrawn from you." Mrs. Edwards assured her nephew that Mary's Springfield relative were intent "as far as possible to prevent any distribution of her [Mary's] money in our midst, and will not encourage any generous inclinations."

Otherwise, things in Springfield were fine, Elizabeth told Robert. Having acceded to Mary's insistence on paying $150 each month for her board, the Edwardses used the extra money to hire a third servant girl, who did Mrs. Lincoln's washing and rendered her every service. From time to time Mr. and Mrs. Edwards also hired temporary help for the grounds to free a servant so that Mary would always have a carriage at her disposal. Their boarder had been quite pleasant, and Elizabeth assured Robert, "I would gladly look forward to the pleasure of protecting her for life."[22]

Robert reminded Ninian that his appointment as conservator dated not from May 19 (the date of the insanity trial) but from June 14, thus making his term almost a month longer than Edwards had assumed it to be. If anything, this news only made things worse. Mary, still intent on employing "able lawyers to have all her rights restored to her," had contacted John M. Palmer, a lawyer and former governor of Illinois. Moreover, she repeatedly asked whether Robert had replied to Ninian's letter asking for complete release from the court's restraints. Edwards urged him to reply, but Robert merely sent the rest of his mother's trunks, which now occupied a whole room adjoining hers, and stalled for time.[23]

As Christmas approached, Ninian's letters grew more frequent and the crisis more grave. Robert finally expressed some resentment at Ninian's pose of neutrality; he needed advice. On the eighteenth, Edwards gave it, noting that he had previously refrained "because in several of your letters you said you would be governed by the advice of Judge Davis, Mr. Swett, Stuart and *others* of your fathers friends." He seemed miffed at not having been mentioned by name. Ninian's letter contained the outlines of an important compromise solution as well as a frank assessment of Mary's mood and plans and is therefore worth quoting at length:

Thus far you have done everything your mother has asked with the exception of restoring to her her bonds and you have the approbation of Judge Wallace written to me that you would give to her the entire income to do as she pleases with it. As the delivery of the bonds is the only point of issue I will confine myself exclusively to it. It is true that the 39th section page 689 of the Revised Statutes provides that "No application shall be entertained for the removal of a conservator within less than one year from the time of his appointment" and if the judge is unwilling with the consent of both parties to entertain such a motion within the year, of course nothing can be done until then.

If your mother could know this from him, she would probably not fret over it, nor find fault with you for not yielding to her wishes. As soon as she can legally do so, she says she will apply to have all her rights restored to her, and that she is a fit person to have the care and custody of her property. She says she will prove before the court how well she has managed it, how much she has given you, and how much she has added to the principal and that she has already within a few days past, requested you to invest $2,000.00 of her income in bonds. She says she will show to the court how much she would have lost if she had acceded to your request to allow investments to be made by you and John Forsyth. I wish if possible to prevent all this, and I would therefore advise as soon as it can be done for you to consent to what she proposes to do—that she shall by deed of trust place her bonds and monies in the hands of a trustee to pay over to her the income only and to hold the principal to be paid on her decease to those persons entitled by law to receive it. She has said she would do this and would consent that Mr. Bunn should be her trustee. Your Aunt and myself both think that all her property should at death go to you and your children. Judge Bradwell has at her request sent her the will she made two years ago and she has shown it to me. In it she left $20,000.00 to your daughter Mary, about $5,000 of the income to you until the year 1781 [sic] to be paid annually, and after 1881 the entire balance is left to you and your children. Whether she would do this now in a deed of trust I cannot say as she is so much exasperated against you. If she has to go to law, she will summons a good many witnesses from here and she is waiting for Governor Palmer to return for the purpose of seeing whether she can have her funds restored to her name.

I think she will consent that Mr. Bunn shall hold in trust the principal. When this is done, I think it is fair to say to you, that I believe she will go to Europe to remain there.

You mentioned in one of your letters that such a deed of trust couldn't be made. In this I think you are mistaken. C.C. Bunn is trustee under such a deed of trust for my daughter Mrs. Baker. I would under no circumstances, advise that her bonds should be given up to her, or placed

under her control, unless such a compromise is made. It is important
however that while she is with us that she should not know that I have so
advised. I have therefore written this in confidence. We fully sympathise
with you and believe that you have done what under all the circumstances you thought is best.

When you write send two letters one of which I may hand to her, as she
always asks to see them.[24]

Following his uncle's suggestion, Robert addressed two letters to
Springfield on December 21. He told his mother that the delay in
answering her request stemmed from his inability to get in to see
Judge Wallace. Robert doubted that the judge would "consider it
proper in his official position to write an opinion on a matter not
actually before him" in court, but there was "no harm in asking."
When he had spoken to Wallace about the matter in the past, the
judge had said "at once there was no question about it in his mind
and that he had several times so decided in cases before him."
Robert promised to go to the judge's rooms again the next day.

To his uncle Robert pleaded that he had "absolutely no power in
the matter" and that he was merely "an officer of the Court" charged
with carrying out "the directions of the Court in such matters as lie
in the discretion of the judge." "This matter of receiving and acting
upon an application for discharge, the Judge says does not lie in his
discretion but is governed entirely by the statute," Robert said. And
he argued that in "all the matters in which the judge has any power,
exercised through me, I have obtained his consent so far as I could,
in removing all the practical restraints which my mother has been
under."[25]

These spare legalisms were not entirely disingenuous. Robert had
acted as a potential shaper of the court's opinion, not merely its
passive agent, when he had outlined the possibilities for Davis in
November. But he did nevertheless delineate the most potent obstacle to the sensible resolution of the case sought by Edwards. The
law's inflexibility, more than Robert's, would shape the Lincolns'
lives until next summer. That Robert did not protest the law was a
function of his personal belief that his mother was in more danger
than almost anyone else believed, but the obstacles were no less
real. He had in the past occasionally ignored his own better judgment to bend the law as far in the direction of satisfying his mother's
desires as possible, and he might have been persuaded to do so again

were the law more pliable. But, as all good lawyers knew, the law was what the judge said it was, and Judge Wallace had spoken.

Robert, almost with a detectable sigh, also asked Ninian to draw up with Mr. Bunn "the particulars of a plan which seems possible to you and will accomplish the object with the authorities supporting it. I do not desire that any interest of mine or of my children in the ultimate disposition of her property should be covenanted and the only object I wish attained by any plan is her own protection." Robert was speaking of "covenants" and legal "authorities"—a legal trust, in other words, and not some friendlier agreement which might be dissolved as soon as one party to the agreement grew unfriendly. He did not comment on the absurdity of Ninian's pointing to the trust for his daughter as a model. That trust held Mr. Edwards' money for her and not her own money.

Indeed, there was plenty of reason to doubt the success of the Bunn scheme if it depended on Mrs. Lincoln's goodwill, for, like many other prominent citizens of Springfield, Jacob Bunn had once been the object of Mary Todd Lincoln's mercurial wrath. In the midst of the Old Clothes Scandal, Mrs. Lincoln had denounced Bunn in a sharply worded letter to her seamstress Elizabeth Keckley:

> There is a paper published in Chicago called the *Republican*, owned and published by Springfield men. Each morning . . . it has been thrown at my door, filled with abuse of myself. Four days ago a piece appeared in it, asking "What right has Mrs. L—— to diamonds and laces?" Yesterday morning an article appeared in the same paper, announcing that the day previous, at the house of Mr. Bunn (the owner of the paper), in Springfield, Illinois—the house had been entered . . . by burglars, and had been robbed of *five* diamond rings, and a quantity of fine laces. . . . Mr. Bunn who made his hundreds of thousands off our government, is running this paper, and denouncing the wife of the man from whom he obtained his means. . . . A few years ago he had a *small grocery* in S——. These facts can be authenticated.

Mrs. Keckley published the letter in *Behind the Scenes* in 1868.

This augury of failure for the Bunn scheme was known to Robert and anyone in Springfield curious enough to read the sensational results of Mrs. Keckley's betrayal of her mistress' trust. Robert still could not see how Mrs. Lincoln could establish any trust she could not later disestablish, but he had asked Leonard Swett to look into "the possibility of such a thing." David Davis would be in Chicago in a day or two, and Robert would ask him to consider the question as well. "The present means of restraint," he insisted, "is legally perfect and the question is can any other be adopted." As far as Robert was concerned, the question was "purely a legal one and her present legal status has to be considered in determing it."

But despite all his legalistic stonewalling, Robert had at last realized an important point. "You and I," he told Ninian, "agree entirely now on the goal to be reached and the only question is how to attain it." Edwards had said that he "would under no circumstances advise that her bonds should be given over to Mary" unless a trusteeship were established. Robert was given to expressing the problem in starker language: "I am thoroughly convinced in my own mind that my mother, would permanently ruin herself in a comparatively short time if allowed to do so & I have not the slightest desire to restraining her from anything but that."

Robert denied, incidentally, that he had ever given his mother investment advice and admitted that she had "always been exceedingly generous to me in every way both in money & otherwise." He even noted that "the delusion under which she hastened to Chicago last spring was that I was in some straits for money and she came expressly to give me everything she had."[26]

Now, of course, Mrs. Lincoln was striving to do just the opposite, to get back from Robert all of her estate, and John M. Palmer was supposed to help her. He returned to Springfield, where he was building up a large law practice after leaving the governor's office in January 1873, from his old home in Carlinville just before Christmas. A Liberal Republican on the brink of becoming a Democrat, Palmer had a role in Mrs. Lincoln's case, heretofore unknown, which helps to disprove the idea that a conspiracy of Liberal Republicans inveigled Robert into committing his mother. At Mrs. Lincoln's request, Palmer wrote Robert on December 21, saying, "She feels herself to be entirely competent to manage her own affairs and her conduct since she came to the city seems to justify a belief entertained by her friends that she is correct and my principal object in writing to you is to inquire whether your consent can be obtained to allow her to do so." In other words, would Robert allow "the proceedings of the County Court of Cook County to be set aside and her conservator be discharged?" Despite the somewhat peremptory tone of his request, Palmer added a reassurance to Robert that he

meant "no more than to urge the matter upon you as one that causes
her much uneasiness and in regard to which very much should be
risked to relieve her." He spelled out clearly that his letter should
not be construed as a threat of legal action: "She understands me to
represent her professionally but I write under the influence of motives of a different character."

Those motives included a sense of obligation to the memory of
Abraham Lincoln. After Lincoln's attempt to gain the U.S. Senate
seat back in 1855, when Palmer, an anti-Nebraska Democrat serving the state legislature, refused to vote for any former Whig and
thus helped torpedo Lincoln's chances, the Carlinville politico had
felt he owed Lincoln a special debt. In 1856, now a full-fledged
Republican, Palmer had attempted to make amends by pushing
Lincoln's nomination as vice-president on the national ticket.
Twenty years later, he was willing to help Lincoln's widow but he
was not about to be a party to further dividing the tiny remainder of
the great man's family by forcing a public examination in court of
the family's finances over the last decade.[27]

After Palmer read Robert's most recent letter to Ninian Edwards
(which Edwards apparently showed him after Palmer had written
the body of his letter to Robert), he added a significant postscript: "I
find you are naturally embarrassed in regard to this subject[.] I hope
you will regard this in the light of a Suggestion and answer me in
Such way that I may lay it before your Mother."[28]

The situation was deteriorating rapidly enough without serious
threats of recourse to law. The day after Palmer wrote his letter to
Robert, Mr. Edwards informed Robert for the first time of the depth
of Mrs. Lincoln's ill will toward her son. "Your mother," he wrote,
"for the last two or three weeks has been much embittered against
you and the more you have yielded the more unreasonable she
seems to be." Even Edwards seemed now driven toward Robert's
camp. Mrs. Lincoln was "threatening to withdraw all of her possessions in your house," he told Robert, but Mrs. Edwards was "pleading with her not to do so, urging the inconvenience and expense of
storing them elsewhere."

This was a far more serious matter than may appear on the
surface, for, as Robert had commented in an earlier letter, his
mother had been very generous toward him in the past. She had
showered him and his new bride—and later her first grandchild—

with gifts, pressing expensive presents on them and repeatedly urging them to take and use many of her old possessions for which she had no use in her peripatetic exile. The threat of legal action implied in contacting Palmer coupled with this vague mention of "possessions" conjured up visions of the ugliest kind of dispute: a suit to recover property that she might claim Robert had stolen from her.

Mrs. Lincoln, Ninian reported, did "not now believe she will consent to the compromise she requested me several weeks ago to propose to you," and he warned Robert to ask Davis what to do if Mary should ask unconditionally for full control of her bonds. Freed at last from his own reticence to give advice in this family feud, Edwards said, "I believe on reflection, and knowing her as I now do, and as in any event she will have her pension for life, I would give them up to her, provided nothing else will satisfy her." Thus Robert's stubborn secretiveness further exacerbated the conflict, leading Ninian to take a position Robert was bound to reject, because Ninian assumed precisely what Robert feared not to be the case, namely, that Mrs. Lincoln's pension was guaranteed for life. But Robert's secrecy was only part of the problem. Edwards was simply beginning to unravel, contradicting advice he had given just four days earlier, that he "would under no circumstances, advise that her bonds should be given up to her."

His new advice also apparently defied the law, a point which Edwards, though himself a lawyer, simply refused to reckon with. Both Ninian and John M. Palmer persisted in expressing no "doubt but that the court would be justifiable by consent in allowing the order appointing a conservator to be vacated." Intense fear of controversy "either before the courts or in the newspapers" was distracting Edwards' judgment. He told Robert that Palmer agreed "that she could make such a deed of trust as she proposed sometime since to make," and he tried to reassure Robert about it by saying, "If it should turn out that she was insane when she made it, it could be set aside on her decease."

Contracts and agreements made by a person adjudged insane would not be recognized in Illinois' courts, but Edwards' reliance of that legal axiom in this case was absurd. In the first place, would not Mr. Bunn therefore be reluctant to enter into an agreement that was destined to be set aside later as illegal (for Mrs. Lincoln *was* legally insane)? And in the second place, would not the setting aside of the Cook County Court's judgment be irrefragable proof that she was not legally insane and therefore the agreement would be incontestable? Moreover, Edwards never really addressed Robert's main concern. Robert had said repeatedly that he did not care about the disposition of his mother's estate at her death. What he cared about was the preservation of the estate *until* she died. Robert's lack of a confiding nature, of course, contributed to the irrelevance of Ninian's advice, for the Edwardses' continuing ignorance of Robert's fears about the political delicacy of the future of Mary's pension caused them to bank on this income source out of Mary's control. But Ninian's headlong drive to find a way out of the impasse before it exploded into scandalous court proceedings and newspaper allegations was simply making his advice useless to Robert. It ignored his fundamental concerns. It continued to impugn Robert's motives by tacitly assuming he wanted Mary's money at her death. It failed to address the legal issues in any systematic way. It was growing self-contradictory.

Moreover, Ninian surely gave Robert pause by virtue of his lack of candor. In the letter of December 22, Edwards wrote, "As I said in one of my letters I do not think she will remain with us a week after her bonds are restored to her." Actually he had never said any such thing in a letter to Robert, and the general tone of the Edwardses' previous remarks could have led Robert to believe his mother had given up roaming.[29]

It is little wonder, therefore, that Robert turned to Davis and Swett for advice he trusted. But in ignoring Edwards' advice, Robert not only overlooked a viable compromise solution but also failed to understand the desperate nature of the situation. Ninian was becoming almost incoherent because the situation in Springfield now had the makings of deepest tragedy. After passing a tense and gloomy Christmas, with Mary "impatient and unhappy" and the Edwardses finding it simply "impossible to reason with her on the subject" of her bonds, the Lincolns' family crisis came near finding its final resolution in violence in the new year. On January 14, 1876, Ninian W. Edwards wrote Robert an alarming letter:

I am sorry to say that your mother has for the last month been very much embittered against you and has on several occasions said that she had hired two men to take your life. On this morning we learned that she carries a pistol in her pocket. Gov. Palmer advises me to inform you of new threats and of her carrying the pistol. . . . If you think it best to come down, you had better not come direct to our house but advise me where to meet you. Please do not let her know that I have written to you on the subject. The information in regard to the pistol you can learn from others.[30]

The Cook County Court once again proved to be a poor predictor. The jury had declared Mrs. Lincoln insane but not suicidal or homicidal. On the night after the trial she had attempted suicide. Now she was planning her son's murder.

A NEW TRIAL

Until Robert received Mr. Edwards' letter of January 14, 1876, he seemed unaware of the severity of the crisis. To be sure, his flexibility in dealing with his mother's case was severely limited by forces beyond his control. The law, for example, did not seem to accommodate a full discharge, as he had told John M. Palmer two days before Christmas:

> I have tried to the utmost limit to which Judge Wallace, our County Judge, would allow, to satisfy every wish of my mother since she has been in Springfield. On the question of her discharge I have already written to my uncle Mr. Edwards the opinion as expressed to me sustained by the Judge of his power under the statutes. I called on him today and received permission to say to you that he will write to you his views on any points you may suggest. He said he would do so. I did this because what I have said heretofore seems to be taken as my opinion of his power instead of his own. I wish you would write to him (Hon. M. R. M. Wallace) and learn from himself.

Robert could not resist adding a stinging rejoinder: "If you are confident in your views that the question of vacating the proceedings of the County Court depend upon the consent of the conservator, will you not as I resign take my place as conservator and then act on your own judgment as representing my mother's interests?"[1]

Robert's interpretation appears to have been correct in law and in fact. The Illinois Supreme Court in 1868 had ruled in a case involving the lunacy statute: "The act confers power on the court by its action to deprive him [the insane person] of the custody and control of his property, to require its faithful care and proper application, and to require its custodian to report his proceedings whenever deemed necessary, . . . and even to remove the conservator and appoint another, when the interests of the lunatic shall require it." Replacing a conservator was mentioned but not abandoning a conservatorship.[2]

There were practical financial problems for Robert as well. Robert's sureties, Henry F. Eames and Edward Isham, guaranteed his bond as conservator at $150,000, twice the value of Mrs. Lincoln's estate, as the law stipulated. The stakes were high, and Robert dared not handle the bonds carelessly.

Within those constraints, Robert might well have assumed a more tractable position than he in fact did. But he did not really think his mother could be trusted with her estate. If Robert was not really ready to compromise yet, neither was the other side. Edwards almost studiously refrained from suggesting that Bunn *replace* Robert as legal conservator, and the reason for ignoring that obvious compromise must have been that Mrs. Lincoln would have no conservator she could not herself dismiss. In other words, she apparently would not submit completely to a conservatorship and Robert would not allow its abandonment. Neither would Judge Wallace, and Robert could thus buttress his resistance by invoking the impersonal mandate of the law.

Mrs. Lincoln had decided to grasp at the law too, and, at first, there were some lawyers who saw the case her way—Ninian Edwards, for example, and John M. Palmer. But she did not possess the patient personality capable of using the law to gain her ends. In part, this may have been the case because she came from a political family. When she was in trouble, she thought less of justice or the legal system than of influence. So Mrs. Lincoln, for some reason, no longer reached out to sympathetic legal experts like the Bradwells. Instead, she reached out to a man of political influence, John M. Palmer.

She also reached for a gun. But that was only the most startling manifestation of Mrs. Lincoln's independence and assertiveness.

Throughout her adult life, Mary Todd Lincoln had exemplified a paradoxical devotion to traditional female roles and a sprightly willingness to break out of the molds.

Like most American women in the nineteenth century, Mary Todd Lincoln lived her life outwardly within the confines of the female roles acceptable to Victorian society. Like more than 90 percent of American women in that time, she married. Like more than 97 percent of married women then, she never worked outside the home. Within those accepted roles of wife and mother, however, Mrs. Lincoln—like some other American women—exerted the force of a strong personality. She might well be seen, to borrow a term coined by a modern historian of women, as a "domestic feminist." The most important proof of this was her ability—probably with the cooperation of her husband—to limit the size of her family. But she was a domestic feminist in other ways as well. She married against her family's wishes. She shared her husband's interest in politics to the point of attempting to influence some presidential appointments during the Civil War. Though a very proper woman, she was by no means a passive or weak-willed person.[3]

Mary had proven herself to be willful enough, when greatly vexed, to attempt suicide—and now to contemplate murder. Mrs. Edwards, writing the day after her husband had told Robert about the pistol, attempted to calm her nephew's fears. "Your Uncle is perhaps unnecessarily excited upon the subject of the pistol," Elizabeth reported. "There may be danger to herself and others," she admitted, however, and she suggested that Robert "write to her, saying you have obtained such information from outside parties." If Robert were to write to Ninian at the same time, it would then give his uncle "an opportunity of investigating and demanding the weapon, without exciting her suspicions of our being the informant."[4]

The necessity of revealing this rather shocking behavior to Robert for his safety's sake made it pointless for the Edwardses to maintain their reticence about other aspects of Mary's behavior sure to bother Robert. Ninian admitted hearing "from others that she has a great many drapes made, and is still purchasing largely for her own use. She spends half of every day in such activities." She did her buying and hoarding in secret, having "everything she buys sent to her rooms."[15] Elizabeth confirmed her husband's tale, "There is no doubt that her chief enjoyment consists in purchasing and storing." And Mrs. Lincoln was indeed "very secretive, errand boys go to her room and the merchants disguise from me the extent of her mania." Summing up, Ninian said, "Except on the subject of the restoration of her bonds and her purchases, she is as rational as I ever knew her."[6]

Writing another letter about the gun on January 15, Mr. Edwards, obviously quite upset, speculated about where Mary might have obtained a pistol. The floors of the Edwards house now groaned under the weight of Mrs. Lincoln's many trunks and boxes, and one of those may have contained a pistol presented to President Lincoln as a gift. The crisis was fast reducing Edwards to incoherence: "Your Aunt still thinks that she [Mary] should have all her rights restored to her and especially if she would put her bonds in trust and that she ought not to be sent to an asylum. If this is done she would probably, be again reconciled to you. The danger is that she might insist on having her bonds, and they might be stolen."[7]

Death—even murder—were nothing new for the Lincoln family, and Robert reacted with a stoicism reminiscent of his behavior during the terrible aftermath of his father's assassination. He told his aunt and uncle that their letters caused "great concern," of course, but not for his own safety, rather "that something unforseen may happen." The doctors last spring, he said, "were very urgent in expressing their opinion that no one could foretell the possible freaks which might take possession of my mother—and that the ideas she then had rendered it necessary that she should be placed where no catastrophe could happen." Although the Edwardses pointed to her frustration at Robert's continuance as conservator of her estate, Robert noted that his mother had never herself asked him to restore her bonds to her. Nor had he ever received "a word in her letters indicating animosity" since his decision to send her trunks and jewelry to Springfield. He had "heard from Springfield last week that she is constantly making large and unnecessary purchases and *giving her notes* to various Merchants." Such behavior was "merely one of the evidences of the real trouble," and he could not see that sending her bonds to Springfield would "ease this great trouble." Robert reported that both Davis and Swett had expressed the opinion that he "would commit a grave and dangerous breach of trust to the sureties" of his bond if he allowed her estate to leave his hands "except to a successor in office." They also thought the Bunn scheme "could not be carried out," Davis calling such an arrangement "a mere nullity."

News of "the pistol business and her purchases" had convinced Robert that "the situation will as it did last Spring move from bad to worse." If it improved, he said, giving a rare glimpse of his own emotional state, "it would relieve me from an anxiety which is overwhelming." Robert lived "in continual apprehension" of catastrophe. He was willing now to state flatly that his mother's move to Springfield from the sanitarium had been against his judgment, and, he added, "She remains out of professional care contrary to my judgment."

Despite the obvious hardening of his position, Robert reassured his aunt and uncle that he would not return his mother to Batavia without their concurrence "in the necessity of so doing." They were on the scene, after all, and would see evidence of the necessity before he would. He refused to regard "the pistol business" as "serious," but he warned his aunt not be fooled by Mary's behavior. At "the height of my mother's mental troubles last Spring," he reminded Elizabeth, "she usually appeared to me personally to be perfectly calm & sane when I saw her in the evening, except that she consistently denied (usually) having been out of her room—She seemed ordinarily able to control herself before me but her conduct before others was utterly incompatible with any idea of her being sane." And he insisted that there had been "nothing unpleasant"—"aside from the idea of the place"—about Batavia. Clearly, Robert was trying to pave Mary's way back to the asylum.

After drafting letters to Elizabeth and Ninian embodying these tough ideas, Robert sent them, with the Edwardses' most recent letters, to Edward Isham. Robert asked him to send them on to Springfield only if they seemed "prudent." Otherwise, Isham could bring them back to Robert. The letters are still among Robert's papers—proof that he probably never mailed them. Only history and Edward Isham have been permitted a glimpse of Robert's darkest fears. With the help of Isham's advice, he proved willing once again to go easy on his mother.[8]

Even Mrs. Edwards was becoming somewhat exasperated at her sister's behavior. On February 7 Robert arranged to send his mother a number of possessions she had requested, including six paintings, a clock, two candelabras, and more than one hundred fifteen books, mostly multi-volume sets of the works of authors like Shakespeare and Dickens. Mrs. Edwards, perplexed by this new storage problem, now suggested that Robert, as his mother's conservator, should refuse the request on the grounds that the shipping and eventual storage in Springfield would be injurious to Mrs. Lincoln's possessions. After all, the Edwardses already had a library of "5000 volumes of the most varied literature" in their home. Moreover, the items Mary had asked for this time apparently consisted mostly of items in Robert's house, some of them gifts from his mother in earlier and happier times. Robert sent them anyway.

After the first week in February, Palmer received a letter from Judge Wallace and showed it to his client. Mrs. Edwards reported that Mary had been "much calmer, since she was informed, in a positive way, that she would entertain no hope of release until *May*." Indeed, Robert's recent warning was proving accurate, for at the very time Elizabeth was reporting greater calm, he was receiving a very agitated letter from his mother. It consisted of "more than a dozen pages . . . filled with demands for 'my this' and 'my that,' almost without end. Everything that we can recognize was a present at one time or another—many things neither my wife nor I remember seeing—many others (dress goods & the like) are worn out & forgotten." Robert pronounced the letter "plainly irrational" and the "emanation of an insane mind." And he forgot his earlier prudence, complaining to the Edwardses that he had "with great trouble obtained from the Probate judge the permission from time to time to relax in various ways the legal restraints imposed upon her." This had "worked harm instead of good." "I do not propose to go any further," he declared with some bitterness, and in fact it was now "a serious question . . . whether we will not have to take the back track."[9]

Even the customarily stolid Robert had at last flown off the handle. When he reexamined his mother's letter, he discovered that "on one of the crossed pages [Mrs. Lincoln had a habit of jamming the final pages of her letters with vertical lines of writing which crossed the horizontal ones] . . . she asks for a number of things" which were at her old residence in Chicago. They were of little value, but, Robert had to admit, she had stored them there herself and they had never been gifts to her son and daughter-in-law.[10]

After the flurry of excitement over Mary's attempt to harass Robert about her "possessions," the situation calmed down briefly. Faced with Judge Wallace's decision and Palmer's reluctance to take legal action, Mary at last lapsed into a stoic acceptance of her situation reminiscent of the days immediately following her trial. Ninian reported her "very happy and contented" in early April; she had not "said one word" about Robert or her bonds "since she was told that they could not be restored to her until the expiration of a year."[11]

In late April the crisis heated up again. Ninian reported on the eighteenth that Mary had "employed Governor Palmer in the case." She was planning a visit to Kentucky with Frances Wallace and a departure to Europe after that, and Edwards advised Robert to let her go and to let her have her bonds (again, he emphasized the security of her pension).[12]

Palmer reentered the fray rather gingerly. Now he was asking Robert whether he would be willing to be discharged as conservator at the expiration of the year stipulated in the statute. "I am conscious," Palmer hastened to add, "that letters like this annoy you but she insists that I write and I cannot refuse." After reminding Palmer that the term expired on June 14 rather than May 19, Robert said "that unless my duty to my mother, backed by the strongest evidence, forbids it, I shall gladly aid her in procuring her discharge."[13]

When Ninian Edwards saw Robert's letter to Palmer, he had a brainstorm. Why did Robert not hide his role as conservator and make his payments to his mother through Bunn? Palmer thought it possible for Bunn to hold the bonds, and if Mary demanded possession of them, Robert could get an order from Judge Wallace authorizing Bunn to return them to Robert. Edwards admitted to being surprised that Mary agreed to have Bunn hold the bonds, but he had been firm and "told her she would not be allowed to carry her bonds about her person."[14]

Robert asked his sureties about the idea. Eames, the cautious banker, requested a day to think it over. In the meantime Robert asked why Bunn would not simply succeed him as conservator. There was never any answer from Springfield to that question, and eventually the sureties refused to agree to the secret arrangement.[15]

Meanwhile, Palmer wrote Swett, admitting that it was "impossible for anyone to say with any certainty what Robert Lincoln ought to do" about his mother's case. She was greatly agitated, and Palmer said that he wrote Robert only in the interests of peace, trusting Robert's tactful answers "will quiet her for awhile." He was "very well satisfied that a custodian for her property is essential for its safety." The Edwardses thought otherwise, but they were "very distressed at her importunities." Palmer agreed with Swett "that her property would probably be lost if placed in her possession." Palmer thought Robert ought "not to commit himself to any absolute promise. His last letter to me was very judicious."

Now Mrs. Lincoln's own counsel, apparently after a meeting with the shrewd and persuasive Leonard Swett, had joined his voice to a nearly unanimous chorus of opinion. Except for Mary and Robert, the persons involved were now agreed that whereas Mary no longer needed restraint in an asylum, she nevertheless could never be trusted to handle her own financial affairs. The Edwardses, whose views altered with the degree of severity of the crisis in their own household, thought Mary's financial security guaranteed by the government pension and premised their occasional recommendations that she be given her bonds on that assumption. And at times, they admitted she should never be given the bonds outright.

Although Robert persisted in his belief that his mother still required treatment in a sanitarium, he had resolved, even in one of the most trying periods, not to demand her return to Batavia without the consent of the Edwardses. That, obviously, was never going to be given, and he, therefore, was reconcilable to the idea of some sort of conservatorship for life. And Mrs. Lincoln, who thought she deserved to control all of her own property, had more than once agreed to the Edwardses' suggestion of a sort of conservatorship or trust—as long as Robert was not the conservator.

The case of Mary Todd Lincoln was nearing its close. Had these people not reached a meeting of the minds—and, especially, had Palmer proved more adversarial and less obliging—the approach of June 14, 1876, would have brought sharply renewed crisis. As it was, prospects were improving. Only the legal details needed working out, and one last person, nearly everyone seems to have agreed, had to give his blessing to the solution: David Davis. Palmer told Mary that he would write Davis and "invoke his assistance to my putting her affairs in a satisfactory shape."[16]

Davis said that he would advise Robert not to contest his mother's application for discharge of her conservator, and Mary was "very happy" to hear it. She promised to "deposit her bonds with Mr. Bunn or with some person whom her friends would consider responsible and that under no circumstances would she use the principal." Mr. Edwards recommended obtaining the requisite court order to restore Mary's bonds to her after June 14 without employing counsel and "without serving the notice required by the statute which of course can be done by Robert's waving it." He felt certain Mary would become reconciled with her son after she had her bonds.[17]

The crisis was settled in substance outside the law, but the law would exercise its power to rule the parties' lives until the date prescribed by statute. Robert agreed not to oppose the petition. Edwards would present Mrs. Lincoln's petition to the Cook County Court. Only he, Robert, Swett, Judge Wallace, a clerk, and the jury would be present.[18]

At two o'clock on the afternoon of June 15, 1876, the brief hearing began. Edwards, despite decades of experience as a lawyer and despite knowing that no opposing counsel would be present, was nervous. An eye infection added to his bewildered misery. He adjusted his eyeglasses and began to read the petition:

> Your petitioner, Mary Lincoln, respectfully represents unto your honor that on the 14th day of June, at the June term of 1875 of the county court in and for said county that Robert Lincoln, whom your petitioner prays may be made defendant to this petition, was appointed under the provision of chapter 86 of revised statutes of said state now in force, her conservator, your petitioner showeth to your honor that she is a proper person to have the care and management of her own estate. Your petitioner therefore prays that her said conservator may be removed and that your honor may enter an order fully restoring her to all the rights and privileges enjoyed by her before her said conservator may be required to restore to her all the money, estate, title, and pension papers, United States bonds, leases, and all other effects with which he is chargeable as her conservator.

Swett responded, saying "that the friends of the petitioner had been anxious to restore her to the management of her estate some time ago, but as that could not be done under the statute until the expiration of a year, they had deferred making the application until this time." They "had conferred together upon the matter, and now asked for a jury to pass upon the case."

At that point Judge Wallace selected a jury of twelve men, one of them a doctor, and Edwards was sworn in as a witness. He made a statement, which the clerk took down in shorthand and later put in the form of an affidavit:

> Mrs. Lincoln has been with me for nine or ten months, and her friends all think she is a proper person to take charge of her own affairs. [The Judge asked him to speak louder]. She has been with me about nine months, and her friends all of them recognize that she is a fit person to take care of and manage her own affairs. That she is now in such condition that she can manage her own affairs. She has not spent all that she was allowed to spend during the last year, and we all think she is in a condition to take care of her own affairs.

Ordinarily, the conservator was allowed to give ten days' notice, but Robert waived his right.[19]

The jury retired and returned quickly with the following verdict: "We the undersigned in the case wherein Mary Lincoln, who was heretofore found to be insane, and who is now alleged to be restored to reason having heard the evidence in said cause, find that the said Mary Lincoln is restored to reason and is capable to manage and control her estate." Unlike the illustrious jury at her first trial, this jury contained no men of prominence. With no opposing counsel present and with the result certain to be freedom rather than the opposite, the judge knew that the decision would be easy for an ordinary jury and would not require the weight of community prestige. The members included a doctor, R. M. Paddock, and D. J. Weatherhead, S. F. Knowles, Cyrus Gleason, W. J. Heren, D. Kimball, R. F. Childs, William G. Lyon, C. H. Chapin, H. Dahl, W. S. Dunham, and William Roberts.

Robert Todd Lincoln had already submitted the final accounting of his conservatorship. He charged no fee for his services as conservator, though he could have. The estate, augmented by over $4,000 in saved interest, now equaled $81,390.35, a "snug sum," the *Chicago Times* reported, "amply sufficient to enable her to live in an elegant and comfortable manner." Robert surrendered the bonds immediately and Edwards telegraphed Mrs. Lincoln right away: "All right. We will send them."[20]

Mrs. Lincoln was so pleased by the jury's verdict as described in the Springfield paper that she had reports of it sent to the *Chicago Times* as well as newspapers in New York, Philadelphia, San Francisco, and other cities. She wanted the record set straight.

After the trial, Edwards was "ashamed and mortified" by his muddled and repetitious affidavit. He wrote Robert about it no fewer than three times in the same day, begging him to get the editor of the *Chicago Times* to explain that Edwards had signed the statement only because he thought it was for Robert's private use. He wanted the newspaper to point out that the repetitions were caused by Judge Wallace's having asked him to speak louder. As usual in a crisis, Edwards had been rattled, and as usual he was concerned about appearances.

To the very end as well, the legal system still vexed and confused even the experienced Illinois lawyers present in Judge Wallace's courtroom that June day. In his hurried letters explaining the incoherence of his statement in court, Edwards said that he had "used the language contained in the law and the petition." He thought "the Jury was summoned 'to try the question whether she was a fit person to have the care, custody and control of her property.'" "They were not called upon," Edwards said emphatically, "to try the question of her sanity, and I regret very much that the verdict stated that she was 'restored to her reason.'" Edwards knew very well that a "person may be insane and yet capable of taking care of his property."[21]

If Edwards had done even rudimentary research on the case law, he would have known better. The Illinois Supreme Court had commented on the statute as recently as September 1872. In regard to the very sections Edwards was interpreting, Justice William K. McAllister had said: "The tenth and eleventh [sections of the statute] provide for the restoration of property and removal of disabilities, when the insane person is restored to reason, . . . and which fact is also to be determined by a jury."[22]

The petition, it is true, had not mentioned Mrs. Lincoln's being "restored to reason." It asked only for the discharge of her conservator. Edwards was not the only person surprised about the language of the final verdict declaring Mrs. Lincoln "restored to reason." Mary herself was much excited by the declaration that she was "restored to reason," Edwards said. Presumably, she had not desired such a verdict because it implied that she had lost something she felt she had all the time.

As usual, the spare documentary records available for nineteenth-century trials provide inadequate proof of precisely what happened in the courtroom that day. Robert's official waiver of notice, written in his hand and filed with the Cook County Court, is headed:

> In the Matter of the
> Petition of Mary Lincoln
> to be declared to be a
> proper person to have the
> charge of her property

Ninian Edwards' affidavit, in the hand of the clerk of court (who misspelled the affiant's name "Ninnian"), is headed:

> In the matter of the
> restoration to reason
> of Mary Lincoln

The jury's verdict, which declared Mrs. Lincoln restored to reason and a fit person to manage her own property, is not in the same form as the May 19, 1875, verdict declaring her insane. The earlier verdict appeared on a printed form, signed by the jurors with six blanks filled in by hand and personal pronouns adjusted for a female. The later verdict is handwritten.[23]

The legal point at issue was important. The Illinois Supreme Court had noted in 1872 that the lunacy statute made void "all contracts made with such idiots, lunatics, insane or distracted persons . . . after the verdict of the jury [declaring them insane]" and made "all bartering and trading with them, by which any valuable thing is obtained, swindling, and visited them with the same penalties." Thus by law, if Mrs. Lincoln were not declared restored to reason, then presumably her son would have retained this recourse to recovering her property. In 1856 the Illinois Supreme Court had ruled: "When insanity is established to have existed, it will be presumed that it continues, until the presumption is overthrown by proof, which must be made by the party who alleges a restoration to reason." From all appearances, then, restoration of Mrs. Lincoln's bonds to her would have been meaningless without the second verdict, and anyone who entered into a contract or even a simple sale would have run the risk that a court could declare the transaction "swindling."[24]

The statute appears fairly clear on the point at issue as well. Paragraph 37 stated that "when any person, for whom a conservator has been . . . appointed . . . shall be restored to his reason, . . . such person may apply to the county court . . . to have said conservator removed and the care and management of his property . . . restored to him." Paragraph 39, from which Edwards quoted in the petition to the court, required the judge "to cause a jury to be summoned to try the question whether said applicant is a fit person to have the care, custody and control of his or her property." But paragraph 37 had stated that the property would be restored only when the person was "restored to his reason."[25]

This strange incident in the aftermath of Mrs. Lincoln's second trial does more than highlight Ninian Edwards' ignorance of the law. It also reveals the real doubts he harbored about Mrs. Lincoln's sanity; he desired an outcome which would leave Robert the chance to recover his mother's estate if she began to squander it.

Despite the somewhat muddled conclusion to the case of Mary Todd Lincoln, the ever sanguine Edwardses told Robert they were "in hopes she will in a very short time be reconciled to you." But Mary, at last completely unrestrained, unleashed the full fury of her vindictiveness on her son. On June 19 she wrote to him, saying, "you have tried your game of robbery long enough." She now demanded "*all* my paintings . . . my silver set . . . and other articles your wife appropriated." Six years before she had told Mary Harlan Lincoln, "*Anything* and *everything* [of Mary's household articles in Chicago] is yours—if you will consider them worth an acceptance. . . . It will be such a relief to me to know that articles can be used and enjoyed by you." But times had changed, and Mary now claimed to have met with two lawyers concerning a "list" of her stolen property.[26]

Robert showed this searing letter to his lawyer and confidante, and Swett drafted a blistering response, addressed to Ninian Edwards. "Before her recent mental troubles," Swett said, "Mrs. Lincoln was exceedingly kind to her children," showering them with gifts. Fortunately, he added pointedly, most of Mary's letters accompanying those gifts had survived. She was now demanding these things, threatening suits and "scandalous publications." Robert and his lawyer had had enough. The son had "committed acts of doubtful propriety" in returning to his mother what he had already returned. At Robert's request, Swett had not opposed the application to have her bonds returned to her—despite "great danger [they] will never be of any benefit either to her or her friends, and that too upon the distinction which you drew in your testimony and in your letter received today, that while she is not in her right mind, she is able to manage her business." As Edwards well knew, she spent most of her income on dresses and most of her time making and fitting them and then folding them in trunks never to be unfolded. That was "harmless" as long as she had the income. It kept her occupied and helped the merchants. Swett had long advocated letting her have her income and as much of her principal as would exhaust her whole estate by the time of her death. "Robert is her only heir," Swett went on, "and he has had enough to give him a start, and now let him for his own good work his own way." He was surely making $5,000 a year and did not need his inheritance. Swett was only warming up. Thunder followed:

> Now with such a son bearing patiently for ten years, after all his past sad family history the terrible burden of his mothers approaching insanity putting off any steps restraining her until seven of the most prominent physicians say to him professionally there is danger of her jumping out of her window every week at Batavia, permitting her to be restored the first day the statute permits it, mainly at your request, and when you yourself say that she is not in her right mind, giving her also, mainly at your request, every dollar of her principal and all the interest accrued, when it was his judgment that it would be better to pay it in monthly instalments—I say with such a son and such a mother, shall we, friends of the family, permit her to go about with a pistol, avowing her purpose to shoot him, or shall we permit her to break him down and ruin him by harassing and annoying him.

Robert would return specific items if his mother acknowledged them as having once been gifts, Swett said, but "he cannot return them upon the theory that they were improperly procured." He would "half acknowledge the charge by yielding them" under threats.

Then Swett made his own threat. "We both know," he told Edwards, "that the removal of civil disabilities from Mrs. Lincoln is an experiment." It was done "to err on the side of leniency towards her, if we should err at all." If Mary tried to ruin Robert, Swett swore, "I shall, as a citizen, irrespective of Robert, or any one, . . . have her confined as an insane person, whatever may be the clamor or consequences." He told Edwards to let Mrs. Lincoln know it, "kindly but firmly." Swett showed the letter to Davis, who approved it. Before Swett sent the letter, Robert received another letter from his mother, asking for some things already given to her and calling him a "monster of mankind."[27]

Leonard Swett was a formidable lawyer, capable even of swaying Mary's own counsel to Robert's side. Mary backed off, authorizing Edwards to tell Swett "that all she asks Robert to return to her are some paintings she left in his house for safekeeping, and her case of silverware." Edwards acknowledged that neither he, Mrs. Edwards, nor her other sisters believed Robert had acted from "Selfish motives." "I have never from considerations of policy expressed any opinion in regard to her sanity," Edwards noted, for he "knew that the words 'insanity and restoration to reason' were very offensive to her, and that it was not necessary, under the statute, that any verdict should be rendered by the jury, except that in the language of the 39th section of chapter 86 of the Revised Statutes of the State, it should be that she was a *fit person to have the control of her property* and before I consented to present her application to the court I exacted a promise from her that she would deposit her bonds with Mr. Bunn." Edwards had "reason now to believe, that the story in relation to the pistol was not true," and, as for the other threats, he "believed that she would never carry [them] into execution." Mary did spend her time and money as Swett had alleged and, moreover, had given her impoverished sister, Mrs. Wallace, $600 worth of materials for her home (something Edwards had never admitted to Robert before). But Mrs. Lincoln had promised Ninian "in the presence of her sister [Elizabeth] and niece Mrs. Clover, that she will neither bring any suits against Robert nor make any attacks on him."[28]

Mrs. Lincoln deposited her bonds with Mr. Bunn. Her trial—and Robert's—was over.

Elizabeth Packard. Illinois State Historical Library.

Dr. Andrew McFarland with a child. Illinois State Historical Library.

Isaac N. Arnold. Illinois State Historical Library.

Judge Marion R. M. Wallace. Illinois State Historical Library.

THE TRIAL OF ALEXANDER SULLIVAN FOR THE MURDER OF FRANCIS HANFORD.
HON. LEONARD SWETT, DELIVERING THE OPENING SPEECH IN BEHALF OF THE PRISONER.

Leonard Swett in a courtroom, from a Chicago newspaper woodcut.
Illinois State Historical Library.

Bellevue Place. Illinois State Historical Library.

Dr. Richard J. Patterson. Illinois State Historical Library.

Elizabeth Todd Edwards. Illinois State Historical Library.

Ninian Wirt Edwards. Illinois State Historical Library.

The Edwards home. Illinois State Historical Library.

General John Franklin Farnsworth. Illinois State Historical Library.

John M. Palmer. Illinois State Historical Library.

CONCLUSION

Free at last, Mary Todd Lincoln remained in Springfield only until summer's end. Although Elizabeth continued to argue that her sister should at least make Springfield her headquarters, Mary said that the town held too many sad memories. She departed in September 1876 with a new favorite, Edward Lewis Baker, Jr., a grandson of Ninian and Elizabeth and a sort of substitute for the grandchildren from whom Mrs. Lincoln was now estranged, one of whom, in fact, she had never laid eyes upon.

She and Baker went first to Kentucky, visited Mammoth Cave, toured the sites of Mary's youth in Lexington, and made a pilgrimage to the cemetery where the ancestral Todds lay. Then they went to the centennial exposition in Philadelphia. Afterward, Mary spent a week in New York City and finally departed on the *Labrador* for Le Havre. Her ultimate destination was Pau, France, where, Mary assured her sister, she had friends who would be kind to her, including several members of the Orleans family, the deposed bourgeois royalty of France, whom she had met in Washington during the Civil War and later again in England.[1]

After Mary left, Elizabeth wrote Robert an apologetic letter. Mary, fearing that her son might attempt once again to control her movements, had sworn her sister to secrecy in regard to her time of departure. She left, Elizabeth explained, because "her resentful nature found it necessary to place the ocean between you and herself." She predicted that Mary would weary of her self-described and self-imposed "exile" and return ere long to the United States, if not to Springfield.

Elizabeth admitted that it was "utterly hopeless" to think of Mary's recovering from her buying mania. When in the past she had let slip exclamations of surprise at useless purchases, it "invariably called forth angry words" from Mary. Elizabeth reckoned that her sister had already added six trunks to those Robert had sent down to Springfield the previous spring, and Mary had gone on a spending spree in New York before her departure. Aunt Lizzie summed up her feelings this way:

> I often wonder Dear Robert, if the course, I have been constrained to pursue has at all dissatisfied you—The truth is I only, from the beginning of this unpleasant matter, wished to do my duty, depending upon the judgements of others for guidance. It may yet turn out, that all parties have been too indulgent—if so, the consolation will be, in having erred on the side of humanity. I am still of the opinion that she will not expend her income, and also believe that a sense of loneliness will cause her return, sooner than she contemplated—the improvement in her social feeling, was quite manifest, during the stay here—and among strangers, she will yearn for home ties.[2]

Mary showed no evidence of yearning to see her son, and Robert quickly lost touch with her. When asked about his mother a little over a year later, he could say only that she was "somewhere in Europe" and that he did not "know her present address."[3] He could, of course, always get it from his aunt, who maintained contact and continued her role as intermediary between embittered mother and chastened son.

When Mary's letters began to speak almost immediately of apparently serious health problems, including rapid weight loss from her "great bloat" to one hundred pounds by early 1880, Elizabeth urged her to seek medical help and to return to America. But Mary still feared that Robert might interfere with her freedom if she returned, or so at least Elizabeth thought. By the spring of 1879 Mrs. Edwards was worried enough to suggest that Robert write his mother in France, but Robert was "afraid a letter from me would not be well received." "If I could persuade myself otherwise [he continued], I would write to her at once & not think I was making any concession, for I have not allowed her anger at me to have any other effect upon me than regret that she should so feel and express herself toward me. As to interfering to control her in any way, I assure you and I hope you will so write to her, that under no possible circumstances would I do so." In a rare moment of revealing candor, Robert reflected, "If I could have foreseen my own experience in the matter, no consideration would have induced me to go through it—and the ordinary troubles and distresses of life are enough without such as that—I therefore hope that . . . you may be able to convince her . . . that not only I have no reason to think that such interference is now or will hereafter be proper but that whatever I might think hereafter, I would under no circumstances do any-thing."[4]

Reassurances that Robert would not interfere, however, proved less influential than physical decline in bringing about Mrs. Lin-coln's return to America. After injuring herself in two falls, Mrs. Lincoln finally left her hotel in Pau and boarded *l'Amerique* for home on October 16, 1880. En route to New York the ailing widow would likely have lost her life in yet another fall had Sarah Bern-hardt, a fellow passenger, not firmly caught hold of her clothing as she was about to stumble down a steep stairway. Mrs. Lincoln thanked her for saving her life, but the Divine Sarah later realized that she had "just done this unhappy woman the only service that I ought not to have done her—I had saved her from death." Mary finally made it to Springfield in the company of Lewis Baker.

Mary's invalidism, combined with her not altogether sound men-tal condition, made her third and last stay at the Edwards home a nearly unbearable trial even for the loving Elizabeth. Mary wore a money belt day and night, apparently even when she slept. She accused her sister of stealing from her. She spent several hours of each day bent over her trunks full of exotic fabrics, the ones from her last European trip basted together to look like dresses so that she could escape paying the required customs duties. She kept the shades down and the room so dark at all times that after visiting her, Mrs. Edwards could hardly see to write a letter. Mary slept on only one side of her bed in order to leave "the President's place" beside her. Some said that she asked her infrequent visitors whether they did not hear the president's voice.[5]

Robert, of course, did not interfere, but reconciliation was not quick in coming. He moved to Washington in 1881 to become secretary of war in the Garfield administration and finally came to visit his mother in May 1881, while on an official trip for the War Department. "Little Mamie" paved the way back to Mrs. Lincoln's heart, and Robert brought his daughter with him. Later, when Mrs. Lincoln went to New York for medical treatment, Robert and, astonishingly, his wife apparently visited her there several times. At last the Edwardses predictions of reconciliation were vindicated.[6]

Mary Todd Lincoln died on July 15, 1882. Despite her sixty-four trunks of goods, the Edwardses could not find a dress to bury her in and telegraphed Chicago for white silk. They found $3,000 in gold in the top drawer of her dresser. Robert found disposing of the useless goods in his mother's trunks a bitter experience, but he was generous in distributing valuable things to her beloved sister Elizabeth.[7]

Four decades passed before anyone took any interest in the case of Mary Todd Lincoln. Then in the 1920s a distinguished Congregationalist minister who turned to Lincoln biography late in his life, William E. Barton, grew suspicious. He was among the earliest defenders of Mrs. Lincoln's reputation, but his historical work was not exactly hagiographic, either. Barton absorbed something of the iconoclastic style of the twenties and relished the demolition of historical myths by facts gleaned from grubby court houses. He was apparently the first researcher to seek documents bearing on Mary Todd Lincoln's insanity trial, but how he would use them if he could find them was by no means predictable.

Most of Barton's previous work with original sources had been aimed at solving genealogical problems, so he naturally employed the methods of the genealogist: he went first to the court house in Chicago where Mrs. Lincoln's trial for insanity occurred. The older clerks around the Cook County Courthouse expressed doubts that the papers in her case would still be on file in Chicago, but Barton was persistent and clerks eventually found the documents. When he at last saw them, they "had every appearance of not having been disturbed for many years." The judge of the court in Barton's day was Henry Horner, a Lincoln collector who would later become governor of Illinois. Horner had the original files "impounded with the clerk of the court so that they may not be lost" in 1925, but he supplied a few photostatic copies to "responsible persons who have promised that no publicity will be given them."[8]

Judge Horner's action was not illegal, for the judiciary has the inherent right to protect the records of its office. Nor was he necessarily overly protective or secretive. Robert Todd Lincoln was still alive in 1925 and Judge Horner feared that making the papers public "might embarrass some members of Mrs. Lincoln's family who are still alive." The president of the Chicago Historical Society and the executive secretary of the Abraham Lincoln Association received photostatic copies, and they agreed that there was no need to make the documents public at that time.[9]

But Judge Horner's protectiveness proved sufficient to supply William E. Barton's appetite for sensation. In *The Life of Abraham Lincoln*, published in 1925, Barton referred to the court documents in a brief passage which stated that the authorities had not acted "hastily or through prejudice" in Mrs. Lincoln's case. The "loose papers" documenting her case, he said, "were conveniently lost or mislaid" and he had found them "more by special providence than otherwise." But the minister's next book, *The Women Lincoln Loved* (1927), published a year after Robert's death, declared that "no little care was taken to hide the records" of Mrs. Lincoln's insanity trial. Thus in the space of two short years, Barton had escalated his accusation from carelessness to conspiracy as an explanation of his difficulties in the Cook County Courthouse.[10]

Mrs. Lincoln's family chose to maintain a conspiracy of silence. Katherine Helm, the daughter of one of Mary's half sisters, Emilie Todd Helm, published *The True Story of Mary, Wife of Lincoln* in 1928. The book revealed little about Mrs. Lincoln's insanity, in part because Miss Helm's mother never saw Mrs. Lincoln again after 1863. William E. Barton had something to do with Miss Helm's reticence as well. Scheming perhaps to protect the potential revelations in his own book, he told her "to leave out the clouded part of Mary Lincoln's life, except perhaps a brief summary." "Why not make your book," he suggested, "frankly the life of Mary Todd Lincoln as those who loved her knew her." In truth, Katherine revealed privately, her mother thought her half sister was insane and experienced only "intervals of apparent sanity" after President Lincoln's assassination.[11]

Four years after the appearance of Miss Helm's book, Paul M.

Angle and Carl Sandburg reproduced some of the Cook County Court documents in *Mary Lincoln: Wife and Widow* (1932), ending for a time any talk of mysteries surrounding the official record of Mary Todd Lincoln's insanity.[12]

In the succeeding years new mysteries arose. William E. Barton had written as though the records had been covered up in order not to cloud Mary's reputation. He had himself doubted that she was ever really restored to reason. Barton's lingering curiosity about the case soon infected W. A. Evans, a physician who followed Barton's suggestion that he investigate Mary's "mentality." "Curiosity, and interest in the mysterious and unexplainable," Evans said, "have made people anxious to read of Mrs. Lincoln." The book, *Mrs. Abraham Lincoln: A Study of Her Personality and Her Influence on Lincoln* (1932), used the court documents uncovered by Barton, but Evans grew intrigued by the "dearth of letters" written by Mrs. Lincoln in the period 1875–82. He also found a suspicious lack "of the vague collection of opinions and data that we call local tradition about Mrs. Lincoln" in the period 1865–75. Evans found "remarkable" the "paucity of any record or source material for the years 1872 to 1874" and chose to interpret the lack of a substantial documentary records as itself evidence that "her aloofness had become pathologic." In the end, the doctor concluded that Mrs. Lincoln was insane.[13]

For over two decades, despite the somewhat artificial atmosphere of mystery about the case, the view of Barton and Evans that Mrs. Lincoln was insane, just as the court had said she was, reigned supreme. Then in 1953, Ruth Painter Randall published the best-documented biography of Mary Todd Lincoln ever written, and her diligent research as well as her rather ardent defensiveness of Mrs. Lincoln's reputation served to reopen the case before the bar of history. Mrs. Randall entitled her chapter on Mrs. Lincoln's trial " 'Without Taddie': Insanity?" And the question mark at the beginning of that chapter may have been as important for future work on the case as the careful documentation that followed. That little piece of punctuation seems to have fixed mystery forever as a part of the story of Mary Todd Lincoln's later life.

Before Ruth Randall, suspicions about the case had been different. It had seemed as though men like Henry Horner, hoping to protect the Lincoln name, had made the record of Mrs. Lincoln's insanity difficult to obtain. After her biography, it seemed as though the record had been obscured in order to do damage to Mrs. Lincoln's reputation, to clinch the legal verdict of insanity by thwarting reexamination of it, and to hide the callous proceedings which had branded her a "lunatic" in the law.

Mrs. Randall argued that the "verdict of 'insanity' . . . was a legal term, not a psychological one." Mary did not lose her mind altogether, Randall insisted; she was rational and normal on many subjects. She managed to find agreement on that point even in Dr. Evans' book:

> She was [Ruth Randall wrote] irrational within a limited area and it is well to note what Dr. Evans says about that: "This complex of mania for money, extravagance, and miserliness—paradoxical as it appears to laymen—is well known to psychiatrists. *It is present in many people who are accepted as normal.*" . . . Dr. Evans also stated that Mrs. Lincoln when she was declared "sane" at the second trial had just the same degree of irrationality as she had when the jury found her insane.

Thus by reading closely and carefully, Mrs. Randall found it possible to maintain respect for Evans' technical medical expertise without actually giving way to his ultimate conclusion about Mrs. Lincoln's mental health. Randall did not have available to her the literature, only recently produced, which exposes the prejudices of male doctors, but she managed nevertheless to blunt the assertions of the twentieth-century heir of Mrs. Lincoln's old medical enemies.

Mrs. Randall also made two important discoveries of original sources. She found about a hundred letters, unknown to Evans, which Mrs. Lincoln had written after her release from the sanitarium. These, Randall insisted, were the work of "a keen and normal mind." She also discovered a letter which Robert wrote late in life, said Mrs. Randall, in which he admitted having attempted "to collect and destroy those letters of Mrs. Lincoln, which, to use his own words, revealed 'the distressing mental disorder of my mother.'"

Suggesting that part of the historical record had been deliberately destroyed was certain to create a greater aura of mystery about the case. Mrs. Randall also noted that Mrs. Lincoln's letters to the Bradwells had "vanished," and she referred as well to other relevant letters "which have been preserved (though not all of them can be quoted here)."[14]

Oddly enough, Mrs. Randall's defense of Mrs. Lincoln was accomplished in part by accepting for Lincoln's wife a passive Victorian female stereotype which did not entirely fit her subject. Within her allotted sphere, Mary Todd Lincoln could be quite aggressive, and Mrs. Randall's tendency always to rush to her defense sometimes caused her to ignore Mary's provocative behavior. Thus in her treatment of the Old Clothes Scandal of 1867, Randall particularly took Thurlow Weed to task for an editorial which accused Mrs. Lincoln of financial chicanery in the White House that barely stopped short of stealing the spoons. Mrs. Randall called the article a smear and attributed it to Weed's fear that the way he had enriched himself by means of political favors from the Lincoln administration might itself be investigated. This incident was a typical one from Mrs. Randall's point of view, for she always saw Mary as the passive victim of unfair criticism.

In truth, Mary Todd Lincoln could on occasion dish out punishment on a par with what she received. In the Old Clothes Scandal, for example, her letters pleading for sales generally chastised Republican politicians "for whom my noble husband did so much" because they had "unhesitatingly deprived me of all means of support and left me in a pittiless condition." She even singled out New York politician Abram Wakeman as a likely customer because he "was largely indebted to me for obtaining the lucrative office which he has held for several years, and from which he has amassed a very large fortune." Mrs. Randall failed to point out that Wakeman was a political disciple of Thurlow Weed; that Mrs. Lincoln gave her letters to a Democratic newspaper, the *New York World*; and that Weed's scathing editorial was an answer to the attack in the *World*.[15]

Such defensiveness tipped the historiographical scales in a new direction and set the scene for a dramatically altered tone in treatments of Mrs. Lincoln's insanity trial. *The Trial of Mary Todd Lincoln* (1959) by James A. Rhodes and Dean Jauchius called the verdict completely unjustified and blamed the backward laws of a bygone age for this travesty. The book also hinted at dark political motives behind the "kangaroo court." Rhodes and Jauchius, in other words, capitalized on the new aura of mystery about the case, beginning their book this way:

> There are probably many valid reasons why historians have given such scant attention to this peculiar and coldly brutal treatment of Lincoln's aging widow. Certainly, one of them is that the transcript of the trial has long since disappeared. The exact circumstances of its disappearance are now known. It is known that the son who used as the instrument for bringing his mother to trial and subsequent incarceration in an asylum expressed intent to do away with certain records pertaining to the action.[16]

A second book on the case, Homer Croy's *The Trial of Mrs. Abraham Lincoln*, appeared in 1962. Croy took as his premise not only the curious absence of a substantial documentary record for that crucial period of Mrs. Lincoln's life but also the notion of deliberate tampering with the evidence:

> The reason the story of the sanity trial of Mary Todd Lincoln has never before been told in factual form is that the legal papers were destroyed, and it was almost impossible to come by the facts. Even the docket number of the case disappeared. The shorthand notes taken by the court stenographers disappeared, as well as all loose papers. . . . William E. Barton, the father of Bruce Barton, came up against this dead wall when he was investigating the case. He was shocked to find that the official records had been tampered with, in some cases stolen. He communicated with the oldest clerks of the court, but they had never seen, or heard of, the papers. With their help he was able to find some secondary papers that had evidently been overlooked. However, since he worked in this field, many Lincoln letters, sealed for years, have been made available to writers in 1947.[17]

The letters made available in 1947 had absolutely nothing to do with Mary's trial. They were the Abraham Lincoln Papers at the Library of Congress and contained mostly letters written to the White House during the Lincoln administration. Sensationalists, who had long since laid claim to the subject of Lincoln's assassination, were about to gain control of another subject, his widow's insanity trial.

These developments occurred largely outside the mainstream of professional writing on American history. Not a single person who had investigated or written on the case was a professional historian. And interest in the case had not been dictated by changing currents of intellectual life in the universities. These books were not written out of a new interest in the generally neglected subject of women's history. Nor were they stimulated by new literature on the history of the treatment of the insane in America or by new interest in American legal history.

These books touched on all these themes, of course, but they led a life apart in the world of Lincolniana. Even the best of them, Ruth Painter Randall's able biography, appears to have been stimulated mainly by the circumstance of Mrs. Randall's being the wife of the distinguished Lincoln biographer James G. Randall. All of these writers, in other words, worked within the dominant pro-Lincoln tradition. As this tradition grew increasingly sympathetic to Mary Todd Lincoln as well as her husband, interpretations of her insanity trial moved from the assumption that the jury was right to hints that Mrs. Lincoln may not have been insane at all. The odor of mystery which had long surrounded the case had moved from Barton's sniffing secretive attempts to cover up evidence of Mary's insanity to allegations that someone suppressed the record in order to protect whoever conspired to send her to a sanitarium.

Of course, it was Robert Todd Lincoln who sent his mother to the sanitarium, but writing within the confines of the pro-Lincoln tradition made it awkward for historians to exonerate one Lincoln (Mary) by indicting another (Robert). Rhodes and Jauchius avoided the dilemma by depicting both Mary and Robert as victims of a Liberal Republican political conspiracy. But there was no real evidence for the political conspiracy and such a solution clearly would not work.

Ishbel Ross, author of *The President's Wife: Mary Todd Lincoln, a Biography* (1973), betrayed the impasse to which writing on the subject of the insanity trial had come. Her account of the trial achieved balance only through self-contradiction. On the one hand, she said of Robert that "history seemed to vindicate him," and, on the other hand, she said that the Bradwells' belief that Mary "was able to handle her own affairs and live as a free woman" was "a judgment that was confirmed in the years that followed" her release from the sanitarium. She noted that Robert had destroyed many of his mother's letters and that the Bradwell correspondence had "disappeared," but she attached no significance to these facts. In sum, Ross left a lot of questions unanswered.[18]

The only answers available within the tradition of Lincolniana, presumably, lay in Justin G. and Linda Levitt Turner's *Mary Todd Lincoln: Her Life and Letters* (1972), the most comprehensive compilation of Mrs. Lincoln's letters ever put together. The brief but extremely able text which stitched the original documents together in this book naturally came essentially to Mrs. Randall's conclusion about the trial, for she had done about all that could be done with the available documentation. The Turners faulted the "doctors and lawyers in that era" for failing to "distinguish between areas and degrees of incompetence" and dwelt on the idea that Mrs. Lincoln, "interestingly and oddly enough, refused to testify to her own madness" in her letters.

Since they also wrote within the dominant tradition of Lincolniana (Mr. Turner was a major Lincoln collector), the Turners were more restrained in the section of their book which dealt with the legal conflict between mother and son. They tended to exonerate Mary but they shied away from blaming Robert. They were perhaps least circumspect in discussing the many letters Mary wrote about getting her income from Springfield to Europe in the period 1876–80. These letters, the Turners claimed, "displayed an astonishing degree of perspicacity and control." Mary had a long history of eccentric behavior in financial matters, and "it was chiefly because of her inability to handle her finances that she was sent to a mental institution." Therefore, the Turners concluded, this "correspondence becomes an even greater source of wonder. Or perhaps one should wonder at the confinement."[19]

By the early 1970s, then, the literature on the trial of Mary Todd Lincoln was at a dead end. The known documents in her own hand and the official court documents had yielded about all they could. And the unconscious boundaries of the Lincoln tradition in American historical literature had been reached, causing that literature to stop a little short of blaming Robert for railroading his mother into an asylum for the insane. In other words, the historical record in the Lincoln repositories had proven too spare to answer questions about the trial more satisfactorily.

Readers now know that by 1879 Robert wished he had never

committed his mother. Would it not prove utterly damning if the spareness of the historical record were his fault? Did he wrong his mother and then ashamedly see to the suppression of the historical record that would have told a more enlightened age the full story of her case? Did he destroy the papers that would have documented his sordid work and tarnished his reputation in history?

Robert's record in archival matters contained much that might feed fevered suspicions. To him as the sole surviving son of the greatest man of the age came one of the most important collections of documents in American history, the Abraham Lincoln Papers. Historians begged Robert to let them see the collection. Historical institutions courted Robert, each hoping to become the repository of that national treasure. He refused for a long time to give them up. Suspicious-minded persons began to wonder what was in his father's papers that Robert did not want the public to see.

Well after the turn of the century, Horace Gedney Young, an Albany banker and one of Robert's wealthy golfing cronies, claimed that he saw Robert burning some of Abraham Lincoln's papers. The president of Columbia University, Nicholas Murray Butler, confirmed the story, saying that he rushed to Robert's house after Young alerted him to save what remained. The story has been authoritatively refuted, for the papers of Abraham Lincoln were already deposited at the Library of Congress when the event was supposed to have occurred. Yet Young was a friend of Robert's and Butler confirmed the story. The president of Columbia University had nothing much to gain by fabricating such a story and much to lose in the way of public esteem if he were proved a sensation-seeking fraud. In short, Young and Butler probably did see Robert burn some papers. His father's public papers were already at the Library of Congress. What was Robert burning?[20]

And where were Robert's own papers? The Library of Congress was interested in them, too, and in 1947 sent a diplomatic query to Robert's surviving daughter. It apparently brought no response.[21] Abraham Lincoln's son was secretive and shunned the public eye. He hated to see his name in the papers. He hated to have his photograph taken. Did he have something to hide?

Robert Todd Lincoln Beckwith, the grandson of Robert Todd Lincoln, believed that Horace Young had witnessed the destruction of all of Robert's papers. James T. Hickey, the indefatigable curator of the Lincoln collection at the Illinois State Historical Library, and a friend of Beckwith's, thought otherwise. Even as a boy, Hickey had discovered numerous Lincoln documents in Illinois courthouses long thought to have been exhausted of their supply of such valuable materials. A gentleman farmer like Beckwith, Hickey struck up a friendship with the last male descendant of Abraham Lincoln, who understandably avoided most other curators. Hickey was willing to wait and he was not discouraged by talk that Robert's papers no longer existed. Mr. Beckwith had no objection to letting him search the old family estate—Hildene—in Manchester, Vermont, but his sister Mary still lived there and wanted no such intrusions. She died in 1975 and Hickey subsequently made an anxious trip to Vermont.[22]

Robert Todd Lincoln had built Hildene as a summer home in 1904. He loved the rolling, verdant New England countryside and the cool summers so unlike the boiling prairies of his youth in central Illinois. He quickly began calling Hildene his "ancestral home." Robert felt comfortable there also because he had built precisely the house he wanted. Downstairs, the handsome mansion contained Robert's bedroom and private bath, his office, a den, and a private porch. This was the private wing of the private house of a very private man. Robert, by then a wealthy businessman, conducted Pullman Company business in the mahogany-paneled office which was lined with built-in shelves and files.[23]

When Hickey searched the house, he checked the office first. It contained some business papers, but no private ones. Sixty trunks in the attic proved to contain no papers. The file boxes where Robert kept his incoming correspondence had been found empty upon his death back in 1926; Robert had almost certainly burned most of those letters. Mr. Beckwith continued to insist that there were no papers, but Hickey could remember having read somewhere a statement by Robert indicating that he had removed all the papers from his other offices and residences to Hildene and burned most of them but that he "kept his letter press books" containing onion-skin copies of his own correspondence.

When he entered Robert's bedroom, Hickey's attention focused on a double-locked closet visible from Robert's bed. He opened it to find—amidst old coats, shoes, and ski equipment—shelving with forty letter books and a bundle of papers tied in a pink ribbon and marked "MTL Insanity File."[24] Robert was a private man but a meticulous recordkeeper. That he set up a file on his mother's case should come as no surprise. That he retained it for fifty years, on the other hand, seems completely out of character. He had no compunctions about destroying certain kinds of letters and papers. Yet these most private documents he left intact. For all his painful dislike of invasions of his privacy, Robert in the end proved willing to let history learn about the most controversial episode in his life.

That bundle of papers, the Insanity File, made this book possible. The letters in the Insanity File filled the gap in the documentary record that had so troubled all writers on the subject from Barton's day to this. With its discovery it seemed possible at last to tell the whole story of the trial of Mary Todd Lincoln.

But documents do not tell stories, historians do. And if this book were to avoid the hazards of earlier works on the subject, it was necessary to examine the case as something more than a newly discovered piece of Lincolniana. The case of Mary Todd Lincoln needed to be understood in the context of legal and social history. Examined in that light, the case of Mary Todd Lincoln becomes a tragedy different in outline from what the earlier literature had described, a tragedy which requires a new understanding altogether.

Certainly the least understood aspect of the case heretofore was the role of the law. Only Rhodes and Jauchius, despite writing the most wrongheaded book on the case, realized that the legal system deserved some attention. Yet neither they nor any other writer save one bothered even to read the statute governing Mrs. Lincoln's case. Had they done so, they would have seen right away that Mrs. Lincoln was not a victim of primitive laws less advanced than those of the modern era. She benefited from some legal safeguards, a mandatory jury trial, for example, which she would not have enjoyed in the twentieth century. Conversely, all the protagonists in the case were eventually victims of the law when the requirement that a conservatorship last one year perpetuated a financial relationship which everyone was willing to scrap before the law allowed.

Most people agreed by September 1875 that "interdiction," that is, outside supervision of Mrs. Lincoln's estate without institutionalization, offered the best solution to the case. General Farnsworth figured it out in a matter of hours, after one interview with Mary in Bellevue Place. Dr. Patterson also realized it before Mrs. Lincoln left his care. Mr. and Mrs. Edwards changed their minds on the question from crisis to crisis, but, as the principal architects of the Bunn scheme, they surely thought her incapable of handling her estate. If they had known of Robert's fears for the political safety of Mary's government pension, they would probably have been even more convinced of the wisdom of interdiction. And Ninian's unhappiness at the verdict of restoration to reason stemmed from his fear that such a legal declaration would prevent Mrs. Lincoln's friends and relatives from intervening to prevent irresponsible extravagance. Even Mrs. Lincoln's chosen counsel, John M. Palmer, whom she retained to regain control of her estate, quickly came around to the view that she needed a financial custodian. And the Bradwells were conspicuous for their absence from the scene after Mrs. Lincoln's release from the sanitarium—a possible sign that they saw no wisdom in going farther and releasing her from financial restraints as well. Mary herself agreed to let Bunn hold her capital and send the income to her in Europe. Robert resignedly agreed not to block this compromise as well.

But the solution had to be reached outside the law because Mary would not accept her son as her conservator, and Robert could not find anyone willing to assume his legal liability as conservator. The inflexibility of the law thus perpetuated the crisis unnecessarily. Did Mrs. Lincoln prove them all wrong by living independently after June 1876? The Turners have so argued:

> Even for a "border-line case," Mary Lincoln, in her letters to Bunn, displayed an astonishing degree of perspicacity and control—the more so when it is realized that she was dealing exclusively with money, the one area in which she had been demonstrably irrational. When one considers further that it was chiefly because of her inability to handle her finances that she was sent to a mental institution, the Bunn correspondence becomes an even greater source of wonder. Or perhaps one should wonder at the confinement.[25]

But Mary's letters to Bunn are proof of nothing except her obsession with money. The very fact that she had to write Bunn about her finances stemmed from the control he held over her capital, a control that everyone who knew Mary felt necessary for her continued financial security. In other words, she was not put to the essential financial test after her trial. Her estate was thereafter managed by others.

John Todd Stuart had recognized interdiction as the proper solution even before Mrs. Lincoln's trial and commitment. In a letter mentioned at her trial, Stuart told Robert: "I have carefully examined your two letters, and the facts, which you detail, in connection with those comeing under my observation and related to me while at Chicago [,] leave no doubt of the propriety of the appointment of a conservator for your mother. I am not so sure about the necessity of *personal restraint* but is it not probable that if a conservator was appointed that she would consent to remain at some private Hospital?" A conservator was not a cure for dangerous hallucinations, and Robert almost certainly would not have agreed to such a solution in May 1875 anyway, but even if he could have been brought around to the position he took in June 1876 and even if Mrs. Lincoln's mental health would have improved on her own, it is not at all clear that such a solution was possible.[26]

Here again the law may have provided an obstacle. As the June 1876 trial revealed, Mrs. Lincoln apparently had to be declared "restored to reason" before she could regain control of her property. It is not at all clear what options were available at the May 1875 trial, but the distinction between interdiction and restraint was not as well drawn in American law as Dr. Patterson had indicated in his letter to the newspaper.

The nineteenth-century bible on the subject was Isaac Ray's *Treatise on the Medical Jurisprudence of Insanity*, first published in 1838 and reissued in larger editions in 1844, 1853, 1860, and 1871. The book remained the standard work for many years after that and was occasionally cited in Illinois Supreme Court decisions. An edition published in 1962 noted that "it is only within the last few decades that any comparable contribution to the literature of forensic psychiatry has been made" and that the modern era has "not even yet fully caught up with the reforms he advocated."[27]

Written in the era of optimism over the curability of insanity, Ray's book noted a shameful anomaly: "While nations are vying with one another in the excellence of their public establishments for the accommodation of this unfortunate class of our fellow-men, and physicians are every year publishing some instance of an unexam-

pled proportion of cures, we remain perfectly satisfied with the
wisdom of our predecessors in everything relative to their legal
relations." Ray hoped to rid the jurisprudence of insanity of the
"marks of the crude and imperfect notions that have been entertained of its pathological character."

Among these was the notion of restraint, "a measure entirely
distinct from that of interdiction, and neither should be considered,
as they sometimes are, necessarily dependent on the other." The
statutes of Illinois certainly seem open to interpretation on this
point, and the Illinois Supreme Court never ruled on the point, but it
may be that Illinois failed to distinguish between them.[28]

The statute governing Mary Todd Lincoln's case was an 1874
revision of the state law "in relation to idiots, lunatics, drunkards
and spendthrifts." Chapter 86 stated:

§1. For whom conservators may be appointed.) *Be it enacted by the People
of the State of Illinois, represented in the General Assembly*, That whenever any idiot, lunatic or distracted person has any estate, real or personal, or when any person by excessive drinking, gaming idleness or debauchery of any kind, so spends, wastes or lessens his estate as to expose
himself or his family to want or suffering, or any county, town, or
incorporated city, town or village to any charge or expense for the support
of himself or his family, the county court of the county in which such
person lives shall, on the application of any relative or creditor, or if there
be neither relative or creditor, then any person living in such county,
order a jury to be summoned to ascertain whether any such person be
idiot, lunatic or distracted, a drunkard or such spendthrift; and if the
Jury return in their verdict that such person is idiot, lunatic or distracted, or drunkard, or so spends, wastes or lessens his estate, it shall be
the duty of the court to appoint some fit person to be the conservator of
such person.

The determination of lunacy was governed by the preceding chapter 85 of the Illinois statutes, also an 1874 revision of existing law.
Paragraphs 1, 4, and 5 were the most important for Mrs. Lincoln's
case:

§1. Insane and distracted persons.) *Be it enacted by the People of the State
of Illinois, represented in the General Assembly*. That when any person is
supposed to be insane or distracted, any near relative, or in case there be
none, any respectable person residing in the county may petition the
judge of the county court for proceedings to inquire into such alleged

insanity or distraction. For the hearing of such application and proceedings thereon, the county court shall be considered as always open. . . .

§4. jury trial, &c.) At the time fixed for the trial a jury of six persons, one of whom shall be a physician, shall be impaneled to try the case. The case shall be tried in the presence of the person alleged to be insane, who shall have the right to be assisted by counsel, and may challenge juries as in civil cases. The court may, for good cause, continue the case from time to time.

§5. Verdict.) After hearing the evidence, the jury shall render their verdict in writing, signed by them, which shall embody the substantial facts shown by the evidence, which verdict may be substantially in the following form:

STATE OF ILLINOIS

ss.

_____County,

We, the undersigned jurors in the case of _____ (naming the person alleged to be insane,) having heard the evidence in the case, are satisfied that said _____ is insane, and is a fit person to be sent to a state hospital for the insane; that he is a resident of the state of Illinois, and county of _____; that his age is _____; that his disease is (or is not) with him hereditary; that he is not (or is) subject to epilepsy, and that he does (or does not) manifest homicidal or suicidal tendencies. (If the person be a pauper, the fact shall also be announced in the verdict.)

The above was precisely the form of verdict used in Mary's trial.[29]

The statutes seem not to have allowed any other solution than the one arrived at. Mrs. Lincoln was no idiot, she was very likely a teetotaler like her husband, and she was a spendthrift only in the dictionary's definition of the term—not the law's. Illinois law defined a spendthrift as a person who "spends, wastes or lessens his estate" by "excessive drinking, gaming, idleness or debauchery." Mary Todd Lincoln did not waste her money that way, she had not yet exposed herself or Robert to "want and suffering," and she did not require support by the overseers of the poor.

Chapter 86, regarding the appointment of conservators, seems to have followed chapter 85, on the determination of lunacy, immediately for this reason: the Illinois code assumed that the appointment of a conservator would have to follow the determination of lunacy for any person possessed of an estate. Chapter 86 had grown out of the Illinois Lunatic Law of 1823, which in one brief paragraph had described the procedure for declaring a propertied person insane and having a conservator appointed to "have the entire care of the estate" of the person.[30]

Chapter 86 did not provide for a separate action from chapter 85. The court could appoint a conservator for insane persons with estates, but the jury had to declare the person insane first and the verdict prescribed by the statute joined that declaration with fitness "to be sent to a state hospital for the insane." Chapter 86 began with the "idiot, lunatic or distracted person" as given and then described what to do in case that person had "any estate." In Illinois law, it seems, an insane person was by definition a person fit to be sent to a state hospital for the insane.

In Mrs. Lincoln's case, after the verdict was rendered, the court ruled: "Whereupon, upon the verdict aforesaid, it is considered and adjudged by the Court that the said Mary Lincoln is an insane person. And it is ordered . . . that a summons be issued to the said Mary Lincoln commanding her to appear before this Court and show cause, if any she has or can show, why a conservator should not be appointed to manage and control her estate." In other words, once Robert gained the verdict of insanity, the law moved inexorably to interdiction.[31]

The court documents provide further evidence that the conservatorship was dependent on the insanity verdict and, hence, on restraint. Robert's "APPLICATION TO TRY THE QUESTION OF INSANITY" was a form printed by the State of Illinois.

A clerk filled in the blanks with the particulars of Robert's "petition" that (handwritten portions are italicized) "*his mother, Mary Lincoln, widow of Abraham Lincoln, deceased*, a resident of Cook County is insane, and that it would be for *her* benefit and for the safety of the community that *she* should be confined in the Cook County Hospital or the Illinois State Hospital for the insane." The petition listed the witnesses who could prove Robert's allegations and then went on:

> and that the said *Mary Lincoln* has property and effects consisting of *negotiable securities and other personal property* the value of which does not exceed the sum of *Seventy-five thousand* Dollars, and that the said *Mary Lincoln* is absolutely non compos mentis and incapable of managing his [her] estate, wherefore your petitioner prays that a Warrant be issued for a jury of *twelve* good and lawful men, to determine the truth of

the allegations in the foregoing petition contained; and also, that a subpoena be issued for the witnesses named, . . . and that said *Mary Lincoln* be declared an insane person after due hearing and proof, and that a Conservator be appointed to manage and control *her* estate.[32]

Sending the person named in the petition to an asylum and appointing a conservator were actions linked in law so routinely that they appeared together on a printed form issued by the state.

A handwritten document, undated, provided the official court record of Robert's appointment as conservator. In its first sentence, the document linked the insanity verdict and the conservatorship: "This day came Robert T. Lincoln who has heretofore to wit on the 19th day of May A.D. 1875, filed in this Court his petition for the appointment of a Conservator of the Estate of Mary Lincoln, who has been by the verdict of a jury in this Court declared to be insane and incapable of managing and controlling her Estate." No other court document of May 19 exists to match that description except Robert's "APPLICATION TO TRY THE QUESTION OF INSANITY." The petition for a conservator and the application to try the question of insanity seem to have been one and the same.[33]

Even if this interpretation of the Illinois statutes is in error, it is at least true that the varying degrees of interdiction which Isaac Ray recommended were unknown to Illinois law. "It is to be regretted," the reformer had said, "that in cases of insanity, where the mental disorder does not seem sufficient to warrant so extreme a measure of complete interdiction, while it occasions reasonable doubts of the ability to manage property with ordinary prudence, our laws have established no inferior grades of restraint." Ray admired the French *code civil* which allowed a court, even in cases in which it rejected interdiction, to "debar the defendant from appearing in suits, making contracts, borrowing, receiving payment for debts or giving a discharge, alienating or pledging his property, without the aid of a council which shall be appointed in the same judgment."[34]

In Illinois law, on the other hand, insanity was more nearly an all-or-nothing proposition. This codified regnant popular opinion which believed that there were sane and insane persons and that the latter should be in asylums. But doctors at the time, like Patterson, knew better and had some influence on the laws. Clearly, some other powerful factor was at work in shaping the law, and that was doubtless the individualistic assumptions underlying American jurisprudence. These tended to rule out mixtures of government and individual control of property. The radical individualism of American law frowned on paternalistic councils which could oversee, guide, regulate, or approve a partially competent individual's handling of his private property. American law would protect the individual's right to complete freedom more fiercely than European codes, guarding that person's sacred liberty with a jury trial in Illinois. But once American law was satisfied that an individual could not be trusted with full liberty, that person tended to lose all individuality in the law and become an inmate in a cell. Such language constitutes an exaggeration, to be sure, of the nature of Mrs. Lincoln's confinement but points accurately to the legal or philosophical underpinnings of the confinement—something which led even Isaac Ray to use the phrase "perpetual imprisonment" to describe what in fact often proved to be only a temporary stay in a mental institution.[35]

In a less individualistic society, then, Mary Todd Lincoln might not have enjoyed the protection of a jury trial with its guarantees of public knowledge and the right to defense counsel. But she might have escaped any period of confinement and almost certainly would have enjoyed more physical freedom while a court-appointed council oversaw any contracts or suits in which she might have become involved. This, too, added a tragic dimension to the case.

Beyond employing the cliché that insanity is a term no longer used in psychiatry, the previous literature on the case has not done much better in illuminating the medical side of Mrs. Lincoln's case. Here the problem was more directly one of lack of documentation, but some attention to the historical literature on the treatment of the insane might at least have suggested a refreshing abandonment of the temporally provincial idea that mental medicine must have been primitive or barbarous in Mrs. Lincoln's day. In truth, mental medicine in that day performed adequately, if one can judge from statistics on rates of cure. Experts on mental medicine testified to Mrs. Lincoln's insanity without a single dissenting voice. Mrs. Lincoln was treated by the premier method of the day, "moral treatment," by a prominent doctor of mental medicine at an asylum which regularly released patients as cured and improved.

The principal problem with this medical evidence is not so much its primitive backwardness vis-à-vis modern medicine as its taint of prejudice against women. That factor, also ignored by previous writers male and female alike, definitely renders the verdict of medical expertise suspect. A particularly unhappy circumstance was the inability of Dr. McDill to examine Mrs. Lincoln and the consequent fact of her examination in the summer of 1875 only by Dr. McFarland. This important examination, previously unknown, came from a specialist in diseases of the mind, and was, unlike some before her trial, based on a long personal examination of the patient. But McFarland's gloomy prognosis was, unfortunately for history, the work of Elizabeth Packard's oppressor, a man with a well-documented history of insensitivity to the problems of important female patients.

And the Insanity File provides no new clinical information on the nature of Mary Todd Lincoln's mental illness. The alienists of her era used three broad categories to describe types of insanity: mania, melancholia, and dementia. Not a single one of these terms appears in the official, legal, or medical documents from Mary's case.[36] But the Insanity File provides a resolution of the medical quandary without recourse to modern speculation on her symptoms or reliance on the word of men trapped in their era's demeaning assumptions about women. Mary Todd Lincoln was insane in the spring of 1875 by her own unconscious confession. On two occasions she admitted that her behavior was bizarre but explained it by her use of chloral and by physical illness. But Dr. Danforth testified under oath and after months of close personal medical examination that Mrs. Lincoln's behavior was not caused by physical illness, and medical science lets the historian know the harmless properties of chloral hydrate.

Finally, the Insanity File introduces a whole new cast of protagonists in this tragedy and allows a better understanding of the role played by each. This should provide a valuable corrective to the tendencies of the literature on the case, which was fast heading in the direction of such extreme defensiveness of Mary that it was bound to put at risk the reputations of just about everyone else involved. Mrs. Lincoln was indeed a much maligned woman, but an habitual sympathetic approach to each event in her unhappy life can only make Robert malign, the Illinois legal system malign, mental medicine malign, and many of her old friends and relatives malign. History is rarely so simple as that.

The real danger of falling into such a distorting dichotomous scheme lay in continuing to treat the case of Mary Todd Lincoln as a piece of Lincolniana. A broader institutional and social approach to the problem helps avoid the pitfalls. Moreover, new evidence allows a reappraisal of the roles played by the individuals involved in the case.

Among these, Elizabeth Todd Edwards certainly stands out as the most charitable and fair-minded person involved in the whole case, and she should no longer suffer the depiction inevitable in reading William Herndon's notes from her interview. Elizabeth's affection was genuinely motherly, not blind to her younger sister's faults but tolerant of them and loving withal. For her part, Mary returned the affection in kind. She could be remorselessly belittling to people she disliked, but for Mary, Elizabeth was ever after the summer of 1875 "very dear" and "precious"—"my dearly loved sister."[37]

To Ninian Edwards must go the credit for devising the plan which eventually resolved the crisis. Because of his own daughter's unfortunate mental condition, in part, he proved to be rather well equipped to come up with solutions outside the law. He was otherwise erratic, touchy, and poorly informed on legal aspects of the case.

David Davis never liked Mrs. Lincoln, and he found it easy to side with Robert consistently, continuing the fatherly role which began as executor of Abraham Lincoln's estate back in 1865.

Leonard Swett played a far larger role than heretofore imagined and amply demonstrated that his high legal reputation was well merited. More than anyone else except Robert, he was responsible for Mrs. Lincoln's commitment. He also wisely devised the actuarial proposal which proved Robert's lack of personal financial interest in his mother's case (as did Robert's own conduct as conservator, which increased his mother's capital without fee). Moreover, his tough final letter to Ninian Edwards about Mary's threats to regain her property from Robert put a firm and final end to the crisis. He proved to be more than an able legal servant and fulfilled the role of friend, especially when he agreed to handle getting Mary to the courtroom personally.

Swett also used his fabulous persuasive powers on John M.

Palmer, whose role in the case was previously altogether unknown. Palmer's willingness not to press his client's case allowed a quiet resolution that a fiercer lawyer, like Swett himself, might have rendered impossible.

Robert Todd Lincoln's role remains the most difficult to assess. Certainly he held the direst view of his mother's mental state, a darker view than that held by almost anyone else. But it did not always dictate his actions in the case. He repeatedly deferred to the milder judgments of others, Mr. and Mrs. Edwards, for example, and his law partner and David Davis.

But if he occasionally erred on the side of severity—and it was only occasionally—the Insanity File at least allows readers the first glimpse of some of the pressures under which he labored in the crisis, a marriage temporarily broken up by his mother, rumors that his mother wished to kidnap his child, his own wife's difficult pregnancy, and eventually threats of murder and assassination. If his 1879 letter to Mrs. Edwards was an admission that he had erred in committing his mother, the Insanity File surely makes the error more understandable. If his head was obstinately wrong about Mary's ability to enjoy personal physical freedom, his heart at least led him to ignore his better judgment time and time again.

Robert Todd Lincoln's heart is an organ rarely mentioned in biographical treatments of him, but he clearly had one. His greatest fault was not his coldness but his secretiveness, his infuriating reluctance to explain his motives, inner feelings, and judgments. His incredible refusal ever to reveal to the Edwardses his doubts about the continuance of his mother's pension seems downright perverse. Even though he surely knew that Ninian was a man of limited abilities and erratic judgment (and a Democrat to boot) and that Elizabeth was too warmhearted to possess objective judgment, he should have told them, for they repeatedly pointed to Mary's pension as the guarantee of her future financial security. He was, after all, willing to place his fate in their hands by promising no retrograde movements in his mother's case without their endorsement.

Robert's reticence, however, was not perverse. It was constitutional. It was one of those qualities which children mysteriously absorb from their parents' behavior, in this case, Abraham Lincoln's inability to be demonstrative, Abraham Lincoln's reticence, Abraham Lincoln's secretiveness, Abraham Lincoln's shut-mouthed nature. Robert's father was blessed with a marvelous sense of humor which made all but his closest associates overlook that trait, but Robert was not. He consistently denied to history any substantial record of the inner man. It would be interesting to know about Robert's own later periods of severe mental stress. In 1906, for example, he admitted suffering "a nervous break-down" after the death of a close friend—reminiscent of his mother's prostrations after family deaths—but, of course, he revealed little else about his mental state.[38]

Perhaps Robert should be forgiven even his silences. In the end, he decided to tell history the whole story of his mother's insanity trial. Of course, he was constitutionally incapable of doing so in the normal fashion. He chose a much more indirect route. He decided to save the papers on the case for posterity. He repeatedly culled his own and his father's papers. He destroyed the letters his mother wrote in 1875–76, her most troubled years. The nineteenth century was not finicky about correspondence burners. Privacy was not only a right then but an obsession. With Robert the quest for privacy reached the proportions almost of a personality disorder. But once in his life, at least, he overcame it. No assessment of his role is adequate without realizing that he kept the Insanity File even as he burned other family letters about matters that he felt were nobody's business but his own. The Insanity File contains more letters critical of Robert's course than letters supporting it. Except for his mother's letters, it seems complete. It is not what the papers in the file say about Robert's position in the crisis that has the greatest importance. It is the very existence of the file which counts. He did not fear having the case of Mary Todd Lincoln reviewed before the bar of history.

APPENDIX/NOTES/INDEX

APPENDIX

Letters and Fragments by Mary Todd Lincoln, Discovered in the Insanity File

The Insanity File contains, in whole or in part, twenty-five letters written by Mary Todd Lincoln to her daughter-in-law Mary Harlan Lincoln. There are also six letters from Mary Todd Lincoln to James B. Bradwell about her will.

The letters to Mary Harlan Lincoln predate the crisis of 1875–76 by five years or more, but they exist today because of that crisis. Robert Todd Lincoln and his wife obviously saved them as proof that the various possessions Robert's mother began demanding in 1875 and 1876 were in fact gifts to them. The younger Lincolns were always ready to acknowledge Mary's generosity to them, and they were probably not unwilling to surrender the items she demanded. The principle involved may have rankled Robert and his wife a little, but even that would not have stood in the way of their returning the objects. The possibility of legal harassment over unreturnable items like fabrics used for clothing or baby clothes long since discarded surely was the cause for saving the letters. A new Old Clothes Scandal, this time involving legal suits of mother against child, was enough to give the publicity-shy Robert and Mary

Harlan Lincoln nightmares. Leonard Swett used the existence of the letters to great advantage in squelching Mary Todd Lincoln's vindictive threats and accusations of thievery after her second trial.

The nature of the letters which exist in the file reveals precisely how Robert and his wife treated his mother's letters. While their relationship to his mother was normal, they saved her letters, probably as cherished mementos. When the letters became necessary as possible evidence in a courtroom, they sorted them systematically. But at some time Robert also apparently destroyed those parts of the letters which had no evidentiary value and which, to his way of thinking, showed the disordered state of his mother's mind. Thus in some cases only a torn page with news of a box sent from Europe by Mary exists, the rest of the letter having been removed and destroyed by Robert in that period when he sought with some thoroughness to destroy any of his mother's letters which revealed her insanity.

In the end, the letters did not have to be used as courtroom evidence, and they became accidental repositories of evidence of another kind: historical evidence of the relationship between Mary Todd Lincoln and the tragic remnants of her family. Robert or his widow allowed them to be used for that historical purpose once— when Katherine Helm, the daughter of Mary Todd Lincoln's half sister Emily, was doing the research for *The True Story of Mary, Wife of Lincoln*, published in 1928. Katherine, it must be said, did not use them well. She selected only a few of the letters for inclusion in her book, and those few she butchered. She corrected Mary's grammar and changed the style of her sentences. She eliminated lengthy descriptions of clothing for Mary Harlan Lincoln and her daughter Mamie, making Mary Todd Lincoln appear less materialistic. She left out Mrs. Lincoln's spiteful remarks on U. S. Grant, his family, and friends. She excised Mary's other gossipy criticisms of people she met in Europe. Katherine even eliminated Mary's bitter references to the city of Chicago. She did not include evidence of Mrs. Lincoln's attempts to escape customs duties on the goods she sent to her children. She removed from the record most of Mary's mentions of money and expenses.

Justin G. and Linda Levitt Turner were trapped into giving Katherine Helm's dishonesty a gloss of scholarly respectability.

When they compiled their definitive *Mary Todd Lincoln: Her Life and Letters*, they had access to the text of the letters only through Miss Helm's book. Of necessity, therefore, they perpetuated her dishonest editing in their attempt at comprehensiveness in reproducing Mrs. Lincoln's letters. Evidence abounds, for example in the Barton Collection at the University of Chicago, that Miss Helm's intentions were such that her editing could not be trusted, and it would have been better had the Turners offered a cautionary note.

Happily, the letters survived to tell their full story. To be sure, one must remember always the ones that did not survive. History will never know what Robert chose not to let posterity see. However, since his avowed purpose was to eliminate evidence of his mother's insanity, it can be assumed that the letters show Mrs. Lincoln at her best.

At her best, Mary Todd Lincoln was both good and bad. Her generosity with respect to members of her own family was boundless, and it extended to those persons whom members of her immediate family chose to add to the family. Mrs. Lincoln clearly loved her daughter-in-law and welcomed her into the family with genuine affection and sympathy—and with showers of presents.

These early letters make it seem almost impossible to believe that Mrs. Lincoln could ever have so serious a disagreement with her daughter-in-law that they would sever relations for six years or more. Yet there are some hints of future trouble. Mary Todd Lincoln was so possessive that her affectionate embrace almost crushed her daughter-in-law. When she bought Robert's wife material for a new dress, she expected her to get a seamstress and wear the finished product without delay. If she picked out a hat for Mary Harlan Lincoln to wear with the dress, she must wear it and furthermore give a report in a letter. If fashionable people in Europe were wearing plaids, Mary Harlan Lincoln should wear plaids regardless of what was being worn in "horrid Chicago." Mary Todd Lincoln knew how a proper home should be decorated, and she expected her daughter-in-law to decorate her home in that fashion.

If the mother-in-law said that the daughter-in-law was not to see Mrs. Samuel T. Atwater socially, that request was tantamount to an order. Yet, only a short time before, Mary Todd Lincoln had herself written Mrs. Atwater, the wife of a successful Chicago insurance agent, two very friendly letters insisting that she pay her a visit. Such sudden changes in Mrs. Lincoln's affections were to prove tragically possible even in the case of her own family.

Mrs. Lincoln's affectionate possessiveness likewise nearly suffocated her beloved and lovable son Tad. She was so protective and so demanding of his time, that at the age of twelve he still could not read and write. Mary's letters about Tad's schooling are without doubt defensive in tone. She was clearly worried that Robert would think she was neglecting his little brother's education.

Mary had an occasional kind word in her letters for Robert, but he is not often mentioned. As the oldest child—no longer a child—and as a man who had spent many years away from home, Robert had learned to be self-sufficient. Therefore, he figured most often in the letters as a financial agent and errand boy. The emotional distance and the fiscal role which he carved out for himself, and which his mother to some degree reinforced, by this time make it easier to understand how he came to view her in 1875. Financial responsibility for his mother and an ability to appraise her mental state coolly were part and parcel of his own sense of identity.

On the whole, there was a good relationship among mother, son, and daughter-in-law as long as there was an ocean between them. When Mary Todd Lincoln drew physically closer, trouble arose. To her credit, Mrs. Lincoln dimly perceived this. If her self-imposed exile had an unpleasant side to it as a self-indulgent pose of martyrdom, it also had a cannily charitable side to it as well. Mrs. Lincoln had trouble getting along with people, and something inside her told her it was best for all concerned if vast physical distance allowed her to escape the seemingly inevitable conflicts that arose from physical intimacy.

Even from a distance, Mrs. Lincoln's materialistic obsession with money, clothes, household furnishings, and jewels perplexed her son and daughter-in-law. Mary Todd Lincoln repeatedly fished for acknowledgments of gifts sent, and Mary Harlan Lincoln's failure to do so on occasion may have stemmed from a simple physical inability to keep track of so many boxes containing so many things. Surely it also stemmed from embarrassment and inability to embody in these material things a gratitude equal to the amount of love Mary could freight them with. Material things had different meanings for mother and daughter-in-law. And what was the solidly responsible Robert, the son of a lifelong advocate of high protective tariffs, to think of his mother's slippery attempts to evade customs duties?

Mrs. Lincoln lavished on her grandchild some of the finest baby clothes that European seamstresses and lacemakers could produce. The flannel petticoats, dainty dresses, shawls, hats, and embroidered cloaks eventually "frightened" Mary Harlan Lincoln, to use Robert's precise word. Apparently the clothes were much too elaborate for Chicago standards and too expensive for any child. In a revealing moment, Mary Todd Lincoln protested that an embroidered cloak was not too elaborate "for people in *our station* of life—The very *middle classes* in Europe, dress their children quite as much & as I do not consider ourselves in that category, I will not care what the mean & envious say." She added a little hotly, "I will send no more be assured."

In all her letters, those printed here and elsewhere, Mary Todd Lincoln seems emotionally transparent. When working for her pension, she appears nakedly and anxiously greedy. Her defensiveness about Tad's education seems obvious. Her evasiveness about embarrassing financial circumstances is easy to see. She seems almost emotionally simple. And one cannot help thinking that doctors and even laymen must have been able to analyze her mental state as accurately as they could anyone's. The letters betray little of the mental condition which led to the crisis of 1875–76, but they do reveal that Mrs. Lincoln had a revealing personality. The letters do not contain evidence of spiritualist tendencies, hallucinations, or even financial irresponsibility, but they do contain evidence that should allow confidence in what others said about Mrs. Lincoln in regard to these important matters. It is little wonder that opinion on her mental state was so nearly unanimous.

A NOTE ON THE LETTERS

Editorial insertions, where needed, have been enclosed in square brackets. Underlinings in the correspondence have been reprinted by means of normal typographical conventions: words or letters underlined once have been set in italic type; words or letters underlined twice, in small capitals; words or letters underlined three or more times, in full capitals. Otherwise, the spelling, punctuation, and paragraphing of the correspondence are followed exactly.

Nice, France
Feb 22^d '69

My dear Mary:

Your letter without date, has just been received— However as you mention writing about ten days after your return to Chicago, I will know *when* to place it. I should like to have thought of you (being still in my estimation, a bride,) as enjoying & appearing in that capacity, in Wash[ington], this winter[1] It would most certainly & naturally gratified your Mother, to have had you with her—and you assuredly have displayed your sweet womanly nature—in deciding to return to your husband. I hope the *winds* of C[hicago] will deal gently with you & you will pass your time pleasantly. You must write me what you think of the evening dress &&& I wrote you, that by degrees I was picking up your coral set. Next winter— I may get you a carved set— at present they are *not at all*, worn—This climate is beautiful, *beyond* description I wrote you quite a lengthy account a few days since— How much I wish you were here, to enjoy it with me. I have promised Taddie, I would return to him the 4th of April[2]— I am studying over the subject, whether I shall go on to Italy & remain until the 1st of April—which would give me *no* time to see anything or come down next October & remain 5 or 6 months— I am inclined to think— I will do the latter. I have promised Dr Smith[3]— to go up to Scotland in July— which being Taddie's— month of holyday, I will take him with me, return to Frankft in Aug— place Tad— again in school— (the 1st of Sept go to Switzerland— from thence to Italy— by northern route & remain at least 6 months— there is so much to see— I do not feel that I can travel & *sight see*— in the *month of April*— that brought so much misery on us all— (I hope Robert, will not fail to have my thousand bond in F[rankfur]t— when I return there— the 1st of April—) between one thing & another— it takes an immense amount of money *here* & indeed every where— I hope Congress— will give me a pension— but *I do not* expect it— I send him Dr H's bill for Taddie— I have received the checque for Dr H— and will send it to him— Taddie, writes me, he has outgrown all his clothes. Gloves— here are 40 cts— of our money will you send me, your number also R's— When I go to

Rome— I should like to have your photographs— to have a pin in cameo— Do write, my dear girl, more frequently I have sent you a small box, by a surgeon to the Baltimore. It contains a *liquer case* & a few other things

Always yours—

M L

I will send Dr. Hohagen's bills, *he* has just sent me *to R.*— another time

Frankfort.

March 22^d [1869?]

My very dear Mary:

After a most tedious journey from Nice, of constant travelling for 3 days— I arrived here this morning. Of course, I sent immediately for my Taddie, & he has just left me for an hour, I feel that I cannot refrain from writing you— for your most welcome letter of March 1st has just been read.[4] It pains me beyond expression, to learn of your recent illness & I deeply deplore— that I was not with you, to wait upon you. Let me urge upon you, my dear child, to take good care of your precious health— *even* the *thought* of you, at this great distance, is a great alleviation, to the sorrow, I am enduring. When "Mrs Grants' sudden! "beauty & attractiveness," shall have ceased to BEWILDER the vacillating & *time serving*, American people, and they will have ceased to remember— "*the great contrast*," then perhaps I may quietly return to you, as it is, nothing can please me, in what is beyond doubt— most necessary at the present time— to me— both to my peace of mind & health— *this* change of scene— My thoughts have been constantly with you, for months past— and oh how I have wished day by day, that you could be with me & enjoy the air and the sunshine, of the lovely climate I have just left. It would have been utterly impossible for me, with my present health & sad state of mind, to have taken the least interest, in *Italian* cities, this winter. I return to find my dear boy, much grown, in even so short a time & I am pained to see his face thinner, although he retains his usual bright complexion. He is doubtless greatly improving in his studies, yet I am very sure— the food he gets at his school— does not agree with him. *This*, you may be sure, is a most painful belief to me— When I am here— I can always give him, his dinner— as he has their permission to be absent. His presence has become so necessary, even to my life. In two days time, he will have his Easter vacation for ten days, & he is urging me to take him *somewhere* at that time— and if I was not so fatigued, I would gladly consent to do so, but I suppose, it will end, in my acquiescence, with his wishes.

I wish my dear Mary, you would gratify me, by taking any lace or muslin waists you may see— as of course, I shall never need them again— Also take any lace of any description— for it is all yours— or any thing you see— Every thing is only getting soiled, by being laid aside— There are also needle worked kchfs with "M L"— worked in them, which are pretty— do oblige me by considering me as a mother— for you are very dear to me, as a daughter. *Any thing & every thing* is yours— if you will consider them worth an acceptance. One lace waist, which I never wore was particularly pretty— composed entirely of lace— do make use of it & other things, as they are entirely yours— There is a white crape shawl— very rich & new— which I hope you will accept, it will be pretty, in the evening air there is a needle worked white flounced muslin dress with narrow flounces— it was never done up— *do* have this made over for yourself— in Europe— those dresses are so much worn— you will find the cape of it— *near by*— perhaps. My mind was so distracted with my grief, in that house, *375*[5]— I cannot remember, where any thing was put. It will be such a relief to me to know, that articles, that were costly, can be used & enjoyed by you— There are some spring silks— to be made up— which I think would be pretty for you. Remember, every thing is yours and feeling so fully assured as you must be— of my love— will you not, my dear girl, consider them as such? I have scarcely the least recollection of any of the articles— I know you have all you wish, but remember *everything*, in that upper room, will never be worn by me & is yours— to do with— as you please, Oh! that I could be with you! for with the lonely life, I impose upon myself, separation from those I love so much, at this trying, heart rending time, is excruciating pain— if when we meet, I find you restored to health, I will feel in a measure compensated for the dreary absence. I am glad you enjoyed your visit to Springfield— They are all so pleasantly situated— so hospitable— & so fully prepared to receive you with the greatest affection— Do make the promised visit to Mrs. E[6]— in the summer— and go to the sea side— and *rest quietly for a month*— no less time. Let me beseech you, dear Mary, to take care of your health— My headache now aches for the tears I have shed, this morning, in thinking of you, & you sickness. And our loving boy Taddie, with his *great, good* heart— loves you so devotedly. I shall try & think of you, as with your dear Mother, *at present*— whilst it is, so cold in Chicago I know they will be careful of you I have the loveliest white Paris hat to send you— with the Sweetest white & green wreath— Flowers are altogether worn on these hats— a lovely apple green & white silk— for a costume a green malachite set of Jewellry & one or two other things, I found in Italy— all simple and not very expensive— but very pretty. If I only could meet with an opportunity, *now* of *sending* them— I never see, any thing, that is *particularly* pretty— that I do not wish, it was yours. My spirit is very willing, but my purse, not very extensive. I think it is time, the *generous* American people, would let me alone— I am sure, *they*, do not disturb my thoughts. I can fancy entre— nous— that the present *inflated* dynasty, will not be very much enjoyed by your Mother in W[ashington]— Perhaps *E.H*[7]— will now add, *Mrs Grant*— to her group of "loveliest ladies." When I think of the wickedness, of *that woman*, my breath is almost taken away. It is, just such characters, who stem the tide. I am pained to hear of Bettie Stuart's death[8]— She was a most amiable woman. And *her* father— is a very dearly loved Cousin. A most affectionate relation Did you see Mrs. Lizzie Brown[9] in Springfield a very sweet woman— I am wearying you, with a very long letter. I shall, dear Mary, await most anxiously, news from you— If I do not hear soon, I shall imagine every trouble. If you will write to dear Taddie— you will gratify both him & myself very much— Tell Bob, I draw on the 17th of *this* month, $1,000—francs— at Nice. Do write immediately— with much love to all.

Always, most affectionately yours

M. L.

[FRAGMENT]
 ... I hope dear Mary you will imm[ediately]—get the *box* from the bank—near the Tremont House—either of the partners, will give it to you— the contents is yours—also at 375—is a new set of plaited silver—very neat for you—you will find it, (the set) in a large bas-ket—all the ornaments you can find take—the books too—also the large horn chair[10]—if you like shells—you will find plenty of them—

in a large red bowl—they were gathered together, in my own happy, S. home—when life was very different to me—from what it is now—broken hearted as I am, take all the bed linen—quilts && you may find some blankets & some sofa cushions—life is so changed to me—I care for none of these things—I shall never want them again—Some day when I am more composed—I will write you of other places—I visited in Scotland[11]—after I *last* wrote you I am sick of journeying & sight-seeing [part of letter missing]

. . . will be pretty, the figure is not very large & it is beautiful papering—buff ground & gold figures—papering is a great improvement—makes a house look home like— Use it all the different patterns—if you need it—You never see a place in E—which is not papered—Will you be able to decipher this scrawl—do write, I have so little to comfort *me*

Aug 20—[1869?]

Dear Mary—

If you have need of any narrow thread lace— which you will certainly require— you will find some among my lace— which has never been washed— also about my dress waists. It is a great pity, that you were *so cautious*, in giving me the *recent infor*mation— otherwise I should have had a good opportunity of making selections in Paris— as it is— I will do as well as I can *here*—so do not make any *little* dresses at all— I will go out in a few days— to make a search for SMALL clothes

My very pleasant & affectionate friend arrived in town since I wrote the first part of this letter— Mrs Orne[12]— she came from Hambourg— in search of me— & has rooms at the same hotel where I am now stopping— we are together all the time She is a very lovely woman & will remain here some time— she says to be with me— I feel quite made up.

Cronbeig [Kronberg],
Germany
Sept 4th '69—

My dear Mary:

After I last wrote you, the weather became so warm in F——that I concluded to come out to this mountain retreat. Mrs Orne & family, went on to Wiesbaden; *she* writes me she will join me here, in a few days. I have been here now a week & as the house I am in, is perched on the highest on the Taunus range— 15 miles from Frankfurt, which we can [see] plainly, you may imagine the air is very pure & delightful & the view unsurpassed— My room opens out on a balcony & in full view are the ruins of two castles with a little village at the foot of each castle— (in ruins) of the 11 & 12th centuries on *the other side*, of the high mountains, about two miles distant from this, are the ruins of quite the oldest castle in Germany, dating back 800— years. I am so pleasantly situated here, that I think I shall remain until about the middle of October— I suppose, dear Mary, you are just settling *yourselves* at housekeeping, feeling tired enough I dare say, at the close of each day, superintending the arrangements. Dear child, I wish I wish I was there to assist you, but alas a wide & stormy ocean separates us— you must be very careful of yourself, but I hope even now, your Dear Mother, may be with you to enjoin ALL THAT caution upon you. Robert, I am sure, will be quite as exacting in that respect, as will be necessary. *Twenty six* years ago my beloved husband, was bending over me at the birth of *your* husband, with all the affectionate devotion, which a human being is capable of, it appears *so short* a time since, and now, my son, will be enacting over the same scene— with HIS darling little wife— Such *are* time's changes— When I left F—— I left some *baby* work, in the hands— of two different parties— 2— *very* handsome long dresses— are promised me *made & tucked entirely* by hand— 3 weeks hence— 4 others— with needle worked waists & long tucked skirts— cannot be completed before the 10th of Oct— And when you are sick— *have them*, write me *immediately* & often. Tad comes out, to pass the Sabbath with me— In place of the *front* vacancy, in his mouth— a tooth— is coming. May the choicest blessing rest upon you, my dear child.

Always affectionately

yours—

I have a very pretty thibet baby shawl *already* to send you—

Cronberg, Germany
Sept 9th 1869—

My dear Mary:

As this, to day, (Thursday afternoon) was Taddie[s] vacation, in his delight at finding two letters from Robert & yourself to me— he has just brought them out— as he returns to town in an hour or two— I have concluded to send you a short note— "As to Mrs Grund,"[13] she is one of the kindest hearted women in the world, she is eccentric as you can readily perceive, we all know how to take her— She was prepared to find you very charming, and it appears that she has not been disappointed— Like *that miserable* LITTLE humbug Mrs Atwater[14] she is *not* deceitful. Mrs. G—— is a little masculine in manner— but she has seen an immense deal of good society— and moves in a fine circle in Europe (to my knowledge— She is also intelligent & most amusing, in fact a good hearted woman of the world— You will find her always *the same*— Do oblige me, dear Mary— *not* to see Mrs Atwater, when she calls to see you— She acted a most perfidious part to me & it was a great piece of impudence— that she ventured near you— please oblige me by never going *near her*— Mrs Orne, of whom I wrote you, left here on yesterday for Baden— will return on Saturday she is very amiable & good— knows every one— She *too* amuses herself ENTIRELY BE-TWEEN OURSELVES, over the Grant's— I wrote R. of the *promised* influence of G—— for my pension, when Congress meets, so *we* must not say a word. The day I *get* THAT pension!!— the monthly rent of *375*— shall be handed to you & when the lease expires—R—— can sell the house & invest— we can *only hope—3* months will tell When I return, I shall bring you some lovely parlor ornaments & a beautiful *inlaid*— table— which I purchased 6 months since— They are *pretty* enough *believe me* to keep— If I get my pension— I shall claim the privilege of handing you about two thousand— five hundred— for your parlour furniture—I went to housekeeping myself once— with a husband— I loved better than all the world beside & a baby (alias R) and with not a great deal in my house so I know by experience— what it is to wait patiently— Two of the handsomest baby dresses— I am having made— will be completed in about ten days— also some little shirts— 4 other dresses— will not be finished until 10th of Oct— I wrote you however all about it— Did you receive a *small* box— about a foot square in July— it was directed to State Depart— Also another one sent from Dundee The first had a little *rose* hat in it— Taddie is impatient to be off & sends much love— You are continually in my thoughts & do write, if only a line—

Always
Your

When Mrs Atwater calls you can very conveniently excuse your self— on some little plea— will you not do it, for *my sake*— dear Mary?

I have just received the thousand florins from Robert

Frankfurt a. Maine
Oct. 16*th* '69

My dear Mary:

Your very sweet & welcome letter of the 25th of Sept was received this morning. On that day & on the previous one my thoughts were much with you and as I was moving back to town, I had no opportunity of writing to you, as I fully intended doing. Taddie, has been absent for the last four days, on an alternate walking & riding voyage— with his Professor & the pupils in the school— You may be sure, I miss his cheerful presence very much, he is such a darling boy. In a long letter from Paris, from my dear friend Mrs Orne— to day she dwells so much on Taddie— she became so fond of him. *She* writes me most encouragingly— says that her brother Charles O'Neil[15] has just written her— that the Phil[adelphia] members of Congress— just so soon as it meets— will make it their especial business that I shall be *well* remembered— by Christmas— with your kind father and other influential friends in the Senate— I am sure there will be success— She proposes soon to return to Germany & then we will be together again— from here she goes on to Dresden— and if I have good news from W[ashington]— Tad & myself may join her there for a week or two at Christmas. You must not allow yourself my darling child, to have gloomy thoughts, regarding your safety. I am afraid you have been too much alone— With your good Constitution, the care that will be taken of you— an excellent physician— you can but do well With Bob— I had two physicians & with Taddie two also & instruments were if they should be required on hand. As dearly as I love you and with the *long* distance between us— I will not allow myself to be seriously uneasy— yet believe me it will be a great relief to me— when it is all safely over— which I earnestly trust it may be— when you receive this letter[16]— and the comfort of having your Mother with you— and when that precious baby is about three weeks old— you will receive some of the prettiest baby clothes— which are all finished & quite ready to be shipped—

I have written most hurridly My dear Mary. Hoping and fondly believing you are doing well— & with much love to baby & others, I remain always

Most affectionately
Yours—
M.L.

[FRAGMENT]

. . . I hope to start your things from Hamburg— *next* Saturday— *Oct. 23^d* —they will go to Wash[ington]— as if for your Mother— under the *present* circumstances— this will be best— Bob— can make it all right with your father regarding the *mean* Custom House duties— I have added this morning a *brown* cloth sack— to your suit when it is very cold— & a very warm plaid brown shawl— to throw around you at any time— house— carriage or *railroad*— I am sure by next March— you will want to exhibit your baby in Wash[ington]— When you get well please have my velvets cloaks— dresses shawls camel hairs—2—removed to your house or any other thing that is woollen I have *such* a *terror* of moths—when they get in—it is almost impossible to destroy them. There is also a large & very fine fur carriage rug at 375— I prize it very much, as it so often covered my dear husband— please guard that carefully— in the box— by the front room door up stairs— is a box of woollens— 2— elegant sofa cusions. I hope you will make yourself very comfort-able— be sure & have the rent of this month handed you— for your own particular use— Also the Nov rents of the 2 houses[17]— you must receive into your own hands— I only wish it was more I hope *some day*—I may be able to do better by you. Heaven bless you, my dear child—

With much love
M.L

[FRAGMENT]

Dear Mary, in case you have not sufficient bedlinen, you will find all that you want in that way, as well as linen pillow cases— wrapped round furs, clothes && in the different boxes— get out all that you want— but when you remove the sheeting && *take good* care *not* to displace the *camphor*, and wrap plenty of your HORRID Chicago papers—round each article to keep out the *moths*— do not stint yourself of bed changes   In a box near the front room door, I think you will find some blankets— you will need them all & they save money— I am sure you will require this bed linen that I am speaking of— There is some of the more common kind that will do for the servants— I have a box of 12 bottles of cologne for you, how provoking that you should not have it— at this time. it will do for the *next.* I have some of the nicest things to send you—needle work—linen covers for your pillows for the day laid over the others—will send them with the baby articles. I wish you would send me in a letter one of the smallest corals beads— next the clasp— *I had one*— but cannot find— it is to match *the color*— you will understand— so do not forget. In a basket— you will find some fancy things, that look pretty in a house— you will find a nice pair of plaited castors. You will I am sure—when you remove the sheeting, pillow cases from the clothes— carefully wrap up every thing thickly in paper you will need all you find. There are some engraving[s] in frames— I think you would like Did you not find it difficult to open & *close* the door— the latter— I hope you will *carefully secure* always— you will fancy me very particular but *you* will appreciate . . .

[FRAGMENT]

It is double— and well suited for a Chicago winter—There is also a New white Paisley shawl— which you may like—I wish you would send for Hammond— on Lake St— a clever & accomodating furrier— and have him alter the large ermine cape into a sack for you— also change the Russian collar I once sent you— into a collar & muff— it— the latter will look beautifully with your new brown suit— you must not expect to keep the house quite so closely, cease occasionally from admiring the baby—which I am sure will be lovely indeed— go out when you recover & take the fresh air— in the afternoon in the brown— in the morning with the plaid suit & shawl. I send you in the box— a *brown* jupon. and please ask your mother to accept the black & red jupon— stockings of the same & red under waist— I am having you a *brown* one knit You will find Mrs Sullivan—a very good dress maker— she will make up your plaid very nicely for you & come to your house to fit— which she does very nicely— all this time, your thoughts are far away, from your clothes— & with that sweet precious baby— How I longed to be with you on the anniversary, when you last wrote— the next I may be— a man has come whilst I am writing— with a very pretty baby shawl— in two or three days— I hope to see the little trunk of things off— I hope when they arrive dear Mary, you will be in good health & spirits to receive them— I hope by spring, I will be able to send you a handsome white embroidered cloak for the baby. How I shall long to see *you* & *it*, so soon as you are able— you must write me all about it— I shall be very nervous, until I hear tidings of you. Did I tell you that at the Hotel, where we stopped in Paris last summer— I saw 3 or 4 immense Saratoga-Carroll trunks— in the hall— with a disconsolate looking maid, keeping watch over them— they *all*— belonged to Mrs Col. Kinney— nee Carrol[18]— who had come on to Germany. leaving their maid & luggage behind— who said they had with them 5— others I hope— you will not have to practise such economy, should I be fortunate enough to get my pension— you will then certainly have monthly the rent of 375— and on occasion of little journeys to Wash[ington] or sea side— *both* rents monthly— Let us hope for the best . . .[19]

[FRAGMENT, November 1869]

. . . of my house this winter—If *we* have success—I will send you half a dozen pairs of lace ones in the spring & eight months hence— very handsome heavy ones— for parlors— your front bed room && I want you to write me too— how many parlors you have— how many windows to each— the length from floor— how many windows in upper front room & dining room. Is your house in a block? Write me all about it & *do not neglect* any question— this interesting sheet contains— write particularly *about all*—My health is so poor here in the winter— that I long to get away— but I cannot do so— without something is given me from Con[gress]— We can only hope— Make good use of the time I will be— & write me about BABY— *boxes— windows* height & depth & every thing. Last week, our darling Taddie— sent the baby— in a letter— a very *cunning* little gold ring set in blue— write *too if* you have received *that*— Certainly ill luck presided at my birth— certainly within the last few years it has been a *faithful attendant*. It appears— that *all* the Americans whom we know, are this winter in Paris— Do you ever see *Mrs Grund*— she is good natured & amusing— and her son, plays wonderfully well— on the piano. How they detest Chicago— What a world we would have to talk about— if we were together again! I am well aware, without my physician so frequently repeating to me— that *quiet* is necessary to my life— therefore *such* places, I must at present abide in— If I had remained in C— I should not *now* be living —

Frankfurt a Maine
[November/December 1869]

My dear Mary:

Although I wrote you three days since, I will write you again to day to enclose—these bills of lading— which you had best send immediately to your father. *The one*— from *here* to Bremen *is paid*— it is a receipt— I find that although the small trunk & little box— were sent from *here* on Oct 26*th* on the 5th of Nov—they had not left Bremen !! These Germans are the *slowest* people in the world. You must know— it is only about *ten* hours journey, between F & Bremen. I have also seen the man, who took charge of the little box— in *June* last— which he shipped from here— he, as well as myself wish you to write—just so soon as you receive *this*— whether you *ever* received it— in the event of your *not* having done so— enquiries can be instituted— Do not fail to write *imm*[ediately]— all, that I can remember in the box— was two fine embroidered kchfs — a white Shetland shawl— and I fear a set of green Malachite & coral bracelet— if you did not receive *these two* latter— in the larger box— which contained your green silk walking suit & striped blue & white foulard— Also— a very pretty white muslin waist trimmed with *blue*— Whenever you do not receive any thing of which I speak— I wish you would *imm advise* me— If you had done so— *two* months since— probably the box— before now — would have been recovered. About the box sent from Scotland — early in Aug. last I took such pains— to select in Edinburgh the handsomest & softest plaid— for a costume— also— a double shawl— the *exact* match— as well as a similar wide sash ribbon. Concerning the *June* box write me *at* once— do — and it may be— when you write again— you will have received the Scotland box— write me about both— You must cheer up & feel bright & young again— when you recover your strength— you must go out, at least *two* hours every pleasant day — Nothing gives me the

horrors so— as to mope in the house— attend operas & concerts in the evening it will do you good— You are a very young & we all think a most charming & pretty little lady
I am sure it will do you much good— to go to Wash[ington] in Feb & remain until April— I hope you will do so— It is always a dreary time, for a young Mother when her monthly nurse—leaves her— I do hope— your girl— that you value so highly— will *learn* that DIFFICULT lesson— to like Chicago, sufficiently to remain with you & nurse that precious baby, (Taddie & myself so long to see) a great while— If only that *terrible* Congress—will *reimburse* me a little this winter she shall have a walking costume *each* season— to promenade *our baby* out in—Write me, how you liked the baby clothes— the *emb flannels*— will be forthcoming in two or th[r]ee months— What a blotted scrawl to send you—I am suffering badly with Neuralgia— all over me— I would get *no* curtains—for any part These Germans are slow— but so they are sure about the work, to complete it, as I have *enjoined* upon them— the little delay can be endured— I suppose your letter of 14*th* of June in which the *announcement* was made — arrived here about a week after I left— otherwise, I could have secured what I wished in Paris— yet probably, *not so neatly* done— as *their* work is very much for *effect* & done with a sewing machine— Never purchase a needle work waist in the U.S. As I can get lovely ones her[e] for two dollars, of our American money—I am having 3 of the waists— of that kind— costing 8 fl— each, but at another place I found some at *3 fl*—quite as pretty (which I did *not* get)— You will have 6— *very* very pretty long dresses— which are being made— When I return to F. I will enclose in a letters, four 4 needle worked waists, which you can have put on long jaconet skirts— You must be a little patient— for I fear these dresses, will not reach you until the 1*st* of Nov. and I will try & get the new Consul— here to send them with *his packages* to Wash[ington]— which I believe do not undergo an examination in N.Y. In Europe they have become very indifferent about examining baggage— mine has seldom been opened— but in the U.S. alas— how different it is! The morning I left — Gov Fenton,[20] stepped in upon me & we had a very pleasant little interview. He is a courteous, elegant gentleman. I also found on my return, among my letters, cards from several of our distinguished Americans, who are now in Europe— Germany, is a great resort for them all, in the summer

season. I suppose if I *should* wander *southwards*— the coming winter, THE NEW ARRIVAL, must have some coral & I intend completing *your set*— with another bracelet— *parasol handle* & comb & cuff buttons   As I have dwelt so much upon "needle worked waists"—do not suppose that all I have ordered—will be made with them— 2 of the handsomest— & they *will be charming the gala suits*— Wrap the "baby buntin' " — in something modest & plain, until mine arrive— & do not stitch yourself at all— The sewing machine I give you is "Wheeler & Wilson's— and will do your sewing for a longtime— girls to work on them are easily procured, & they do a great deal in a day— There is a rose & white *tea set* with flower vases to match— which I think you would like at *375*— Never purchase *any thing*, which you can find there— My thoughts will wander to you all the time, and I pray Heaven, dear Mary, that you may be *easily* & *safely* delivered out of your trouble— Do not fail to write me— on the receipt of this

How did you like your coral serpent bracelet?— Did you receive the small box sent through Dr S—— office? Also one— a little previous? I will give you a breathing time of *a* week & write again— Hoping *very soon* to hear from you— with kisses for the sweet baby & best love to Robert, I remain always.

Most affectionately
yours
M L —

Frankfort A Maine
Nov 21st '69—

My dear Mary:

I am just recovering from a severe attack of Neuralgea— in my head & limbs— accompanied by great indisposition, which has been my faithful companion for more than two weeks— It has been so long since I have heard from you, that I feel that I must write you to day. I *do hope* by this time, that you have entirely recovered & that your dear baby, continues very well, quiet & sleeps well at night. You surely must have received the two boxes— by this time & I trust you are pleased with the contents. The two parasols— lined with pink & blue are for the nurse— when in the spring she *carries* Miss baby out— I have also a very warm woollen plaid cloak— red & white— to wrap the baby up in when you carry it *perhaps* to

Wash[ington] in— next March with the soft little white hood— I sent you— also a white embroidered cloak— which had just arrived from Paris— and was so cheap that I bought it— I will start them to you, some time in January. I have also a very pretty reception dress— ready made to send you at the same time— for afternoons in your Mother's drawing room in March & April— You see I am calculating— that you will pass the spring in Wash[ington]— as *you should do.* I will send *these things*— quite as soon as you care to have them— also one of the loveliest blue & white plaid woollen wrappers— you can receive any *one* in— it is very beautiful. The dress— is a silver gray, plush— which is very much worn— trimmed with *Marie Louise* blue— it is just as distingué— and as pretty as *can well be*— Bob will surely think you are more charming than ever, when you are arrayed in it— At the time you *receive this* letter, mention may be made in Con[gress]— regarding a pension for me— therefore— show the baby clothes to *no one*— until after THAT— or make no mention of the other things— I will send you— after it *is all over*— *one way or the* other— I hope by the time you receive this— I shall have a letter from you— telling me *all about the baby*— You will miss your nurse very much when she leaves you, as well as your Mother— I had supposed, the latter would have written me, whilst she was with you, regarding yourself & baby— My pen will scarcely make a mark, so I will close— Another thing my dear girl— I am *very anxious* lest the moths may get into my *velvets*— which I can *never replace fine shawls, flannels* && When you are able, will you kindly pack these things together— & take them to your house— they can be nailed in boxes with camphor— Excuse me for troubling you so much I cannot overcome my weakness— for my velvets & [illeg] shawls— I hope the moths can be kept out of *every thing.* Tell Bob— to send me all interest that is due me— & my DEC money— I am terribly in want of money— I hope Con[gress] will mercifully remember me— Write soon— to yours, Most affectionatly,

M.L.

I feel miserably *blue to day*, so pray excuse this scrawl—

Frankfurt a Maine
Nov 25th '69'.

My dear Mary:

Your letter of the 6*th* Nov.— is just received— as Taddie is just

carrying a few lines, to the P.O— I have just written to Dr Smith—
regarding the box sent the *1*st of *Aug*— from Scotland. I will also
write you. *Do have* enquiries made at the State Dept— *it must* be
there— Seeing so many beautiful plaids worn this winter, I have
often pictured you in your *complete* costume— There were also—
two or three pretty thin dresses— in the box— ribbon sashes other
things— and a *gem* of a book a straw hat— also a lovely fan bought
in Paris The box— was about a foot — half in length & the same in
height— The middle of June— just as we were leaving for Paris— I
sent you from Frankfort a small box— not quite so large— as the box
from Scotland— directed also to State D- from the Consular office
here— in it was some choice little things. two or three embroidered
handkerchiefs— I remember with your initials beautifully worked
in the corner— a *rose* coloured summer hat— & some other things, I
cannot now remember. Did you ever receive *that* box? Write me
about them both— and have *diligent search* made for them at State
D—— Write imm[ediately]— to your Mother to see after them
HERSELF— you certainly must by THIS TIME— have received the
two— boxes— one of them a small trunk— containing the baby
clothes & a few things for your self— I trust there will be no
difficulty and that they are now safe with you— I wrote you a few
days since regarding them— also concerning a few things— which I
will not start you until the 1*st* of Jany — I told you I had picked up a
white embroidered cloak— which is ready to be sent you then— but
it is not the embroidered cloak— that blessed baby IS to have in three
or four months— I am also having embroidered for the baby, two
long flannel petticoats— a [cash(m)ere?] sack & you are not to get a
short dress for the baby— *when it walks these all*— I will bring you—
I am worried— about the box containing the plaids— they are so
extremely fashionable this winter— *That box* must be found— It is a
great pity, you did not write earlier about it — As you are well
aware— I give you full liberty to take & keep for *ever & aye*— any
thing you see up in that garret— you will scarcely so far as I am
concerned— take particular care in guarding them from damage—
By this time, you must understand— Bob's teasing way. I would be
glad if *every* article was out of that garret— *Terrible, gloomy* Chicago, what good cause I *had* to remember *that place.* The picture
looks brighter with you & the baby in it! And those shocking servants—that infest *the place & are part of it*— I am sorry you are so

soon realizing, the discomforts of keeping house *there*— If you only had some of these faithful German servants— How much I wish I could be with you for with your young baby— I could help you very much— What a scrawl this is— The news of the missing box— makes me very anxious regarding the little box & trunk— I sent you— four weeks since—

Dr. Smith, is such a fearfully careles man— that I might have anticipated something going amiss— I have written him, quite Seriously on the subject, to have them looked up— The articles— I have to send you in Jany— are not fit— for *Wash*[ington] & *March*— Do write me— *just* so soon as you receive this— Always yours ·

ML

[FRAGMENT]

. . . I received a card to Bishop Simpson's[21] daughter's marriage & by a gentleman through the Consulate here— sent as handsome a white bridal fan— as I have ever seen— with a note of course with congratulations— There appears to be such difficulty, in any thing reaching its destination in America— please quietly find out— if it was received— the fan was mother of pearl & was very lovely & white satin—

[On reverse]   Friday morning.

I sat up so late last night, writing to yourself & Mrs Orne in Paris— that I suffered all night with Neuralgia— in the head & to day— write this in bed— I am *just* as anxious to go further South— this winter as you are— & must be to leave Chicago for Wash[ing-ton]— My health has become quite as bad— as it was last winter I hope you will go to Wash[ington] in *Feb* & remain *two* months. You are in *no state*— to be annoyed by housekeeping cares, entre nous— I will leave a very pretty . . .

[FRAGMENT]

. . . I wrote you a few days since, dear Mary, about the diamonds. A small wooden box, is on the table near me, in which I propose placing the cluster set. It is a very pretty set & I cannot but feel, that you will like it—In *after times* if you would like to exchange it for *the* solitaire you can do so—you know, *you* will always be, my FIRST LOVE of daughter-in-laws—I often tell Tad—that I can scarcely flatter my-self, he will ever Marry to suit me, *quite* as well as dear Bob—has

done. I send a *very handsome—gold chatelaine* chain to Bob—by Mr.
O'Neil—has he ever received it, it was sent six weeks ago—

Oberunsel, Germany
May 19*th* 1870

My dear Mary:

I have come out here to pass a day or two, with Taddie (his new
school quarters) as I leave most probably tomorrow for Bohemia— a
journey, which will require fully *twenty* hours to accomplish. The
first evening I shall stop, at the *very* old town of Nuremburg, so full
of interest & perhaps remain there a day, to see the old castles &
churches— This morning in *this* old village— 5 minutes by rail,
from Hombourg, I entered an old church— with dates of 1610— on
it— the Christs that are suspended on the walks around the town—
bear dates 1704— until we get accustomed to seeing these things,
they appear very strange to *fresh American* eyes— When I came
here two or three days since, I had just returned from a most
charming trip in the Odenwald Mountains, where the scenery is
very beautiful— also Tad & myself went to Heidelberg, to Baden for
a few hours & traveled in *the Black Forest*. At Heidelberg, we
ascended the mountain one morning, about nine o'clock, roamed
through the ruins of the magnificent old castle & took our breakfast
in the grounds, where there is a very fine restaurant— At noon, we
proceeded to Baden— and ascended another mountain height in the
evening, to visit the ruins of another grand old castle—centuries
back— & took our supper up there. Tell Mrs Grund, I do not wish
to *tantalise* her, now that she *is* in Chicago— but B— & the sur-
roundings are looking too lovely, to attempt to describe— The next
day, we went out to the "La Favorita," the abode of the "White
Lady," also to Rathstatt. You may well believe the few days, we
consumed in this journey were most pleasantly occupied. Taddie &
myself were continually wishing that yourself, Bob, & that precious
baby, were with us. Some day, & not very *far distant* either I hope,
dear Mary, you all with [will] see, just what we have so lately seen—
I so long, to have you both, *come to Europe*.

[F R A G M E N T, June 1870]

... I sent you about three weeks since, directed to your Mother— a
small box— with the light bonnet for yourself the long dress for

baby— I will tomorrow send the baby— a little light hat—just sweet enough to eat in a box not much larger than your hand. In F——— I have found a nice little set of coral— bracelets— sleeve fasteners & necklace— It is light but very pretty . . .

Be sure & get out some of these light dresses & have them made up for yourself, that is, if you do not think, they are *too plain.*

ML

[FRAGMENT]

. . . I will send *this* coral when I return from Bohemia— Which I expect to do the first of July— In the meantime— do write me often— directed as usual to Phillip, Nicoll, Schmidt Frankfurt— *Do pray*, do not remain in Chicago— *all summer.* A change, you should all have. With much love to Bob, kisses from Tad & myself to the darling baby, believe me always, lovingly yours

M L

Leamington, England
Sept 16th 1870.

My dear Mary:

Your very welcome letter of 22*d*— Aug— was received last evening. Col Weaver[22] was kind enough to send your letters to me *here*— where I am remaining with Mrs Orne a few days— I wrote Bob— from York a week since— en route for Liverpool— whither I was going to send off two boxes for you & to get some of Taddie's winter clothing. His tutor[23] & himself began their studies together on yesterday & they both appear most deeply interested— He comes to us— very highly recommended, and I shall see that not a moment— will be idly passed. The young man, has had such experience in teaching and brings such high testimonials with him— that I am sure he will faithfully perform his duty to Tad. Mrs Orne & others are greatly pleased with the tutor & his evident intention of making Tad— faithfully apply himself. I left Liverpool last Saturday afternoon— so completely sick with a cold— that I determined to come on here— to be well attended to. This is the first day, I have sat up, since then— and a physician, has been to see me each day— I cough very bad & my lungs are very sore, the Dr applied a tube on yesterday & pronounced it necessary— that as soon as possible, I should go to a dryer climate. From 8 until 1 o'clock each day Tad is seated at his table— with his tutor studying & from 5 to 7— each evening— with his tutor he is studying his lessons— On no occasion— do I intend that he shall deviate from this rule. I have just been in to see him studying— and they are earnestly engaged— for dear life. The gentleman who is teaching him, is very highly educated— very quiet & gentlemanly & patience itself. Tad— now realises the great necessity of an education, & I am sure will do well. I do hope you will, dear Mary, receive your two boxes— by the *29th* of Sept— to wear some of the pretty things to the wedding. I send you a lovely white evening dress— a rose evening silk a rose plush sack— & a charming rose bonnet— which I secured in London— from a Parisian milliner— a refuguee from Paris— Also the *newest* & most stylish walking costume— a shawl cashmere— walking suit— the *falling leaf colour*— Now— so, very fashionable. You must wear it— immediately— The baby's clothes— I know you will pronounce exquisite— If there is Custom House duty to be paid have Bob— put it— to my account. I am coughing so badly that I can scarcely write— By the 25*th* of Sept— the boxes— will be in N.Y—

It will be a great trial to me to separate myself, from dear Mrs Orne— who has proved so loving a friend to me— but my health is again beginning to fail me— as it did last winter— I can only hope— that I can secure some quite Southern nook to rest— until the disturbances in Italy, have ceased. When I see you, I can tell you a great deal about the war— which I cannot now write. Although I have thought a great deal about you, the past summer— yet living a life of such continued change, I have not had a moment to myself— On yesterday, I received a letter from Mrs Col Weaver— mentioning that Ida & herself were about crossing over to London— to join her mother— We can well imagine, that in her confinement, that she will *not* in *London* lodgings— be *quite* as comfortable as *you* were in your cozy little home— Referring to the speech Mrs Simpson made you last winter—that housekeeping & babies, were an uncomfortable state of existence for a young married lady. I think her experience was different from most Mother's— who consider that in the outset in life— a nice home— loving husband & precious child are the happiest stages of life— I fear she has grown worldly— But at the same time, I hope you will have a good rest— & enjoy yourself *free*— for *a* year or more to come— At the Langhorn, a very pleasant, gay & handsome young man, Mr Tobe[24]— who said he knew *you* in Wash[ington]— and called on you at the Hoffman House, when a bride　Do you remember him? He sailed for Quebec, last week.— The *Dr* has just left me & says he wonders to find me sitting up— As a general thing, I think they would especially like to keep one in bed. The love of money, is the root of all evil. I wish you had a girl— *never* to leave your baby on your hands for a moment— your morning of nursing, must be very tiresome. If I was in Chicago— *we* would accompanied by "Miss Lincoln," beguile *those* hours— be sometimes driving out— I would very willingly from each month of the Allston rent— give you $18— a month to hire an extra girl— so that you can have a servant— never to leave your baby— because she is so heavy & must wear you out— You should go out *every* day & do enjoy yourself you are so *very young* and should be as gay as a lark. Trouble comes soon enough, my dear child— and you must enjoy life, whenever you can— We all love you so very much— and you are blessed with a devoted husband & darling child— *so go out*— & enjoy the sunshine— Only, do not *allow the baby*, to walk too soon & *become bowlegged*— Will you remember *this*— I do so hope, that your dear Mother has recovered her health— When I can, I will write to her— Do, I pray you, write More frequently, address to me at Frankfurt a Maine, care of P. N. Schmidt— The leaf set of earings, I send you is now the fashionable shade of gold— do wear them, with your shawl suit & little straw hat in the box— Did you in July last, receive a little French straw hat for baby with feathers? Write me if you have I have a splendid watch chain to send Bob— gold links of the same colour as your leaf set—bought at Geneva It is really choice They were addressed[ed] to the care of the Collector Mr. Murp[hy?][25] I am sure—he will faithfully attend to them—I wish you would take out the double *India* shawl—with a *red* centre—which *I never* wore & make faithful use of it— from *this time on* —be *sure to do it*

Write very soon—

With much love, I remain

Most affectionately yours

　　　Mary Lincoln

London
No. 9. Woburn Place
Russell Square
W.C.
[November 1870]

My dear Mary:

Your most acceptable letter was received to day. Need I say to you, how much delight it affords me, to hear from you. That blessed baby, how dearly I would love to look upon its sweet young face, if my boy Taddie and myself *are* wanderers in a strange land, our thoughts are continually with you, & we speak of you, very frequently. I have just received another letter from Mrs. Simpson, who is now en route to Italy & when she left here, we came to *some* understanding that I might join her, *about Christmas,*— in Rome— As a matter of course even if it suited pecuniarily, which it does not, it would never do, to have Taddie or his Tutor accompany me. Taddie is closeted with his Tutor, seven & half hours each day, and from Saturday to Saturday, when I am with him for three hours to listen to his examinations of his studies, of the week. I can see a great improvement in him— But of course, if I go to Italy, the Tutor, must be relinquished & *he* placed in school or I must trust him to the stormy waves, and the Merciful Providence of of our great Father in Heaven for safety & protection— until he lands in America!

This morning, the agent of the Cunard Steamer at Liverpool enclosed me the list of steamers— that are sailing across the stormy deep, this winter— Driving down at noon to day, for letters at the bank, I proposed to Tad, with a trembling voice & aching heart, you may be sure that he would embark on *the Russia,* which sails next Saturday week for the U.S. *Dec 10th* and go home— pass his Christmas with yourself & Bob— and immediately afterwards be placed in school— Study more than he does now, he could not possibly do. If he only had the information of his Tutor, who is most persevering and indefatigable, I told him to day, I would be willing to live on a crust of bread a day. ALMOST— To night, we are engaged to meet Gov *Evans*[26] & family at the South Kensington museum (they are to see us very often) and I am going to ask Gov Evan's, candid advice on the subject— *He,* came over last week on the same vessel. To trust my beautiful, darling— GOOD boy, to the elements, at this season of the year makes my heart faint within me. Each breath, I drew, would be a prayer, for his safety, which only, those who have been as deeply bereaved as myself, could fully understand. On the other hand, the English schools— have vacation for a month *after Christmas*, which if I did not send Tad home would delay my journey to Italy, until the 1st of Feb keeping him with his Tutor, in the mean *time at hard study* direct your letters to Frankfurt a Maine I have not let the Motley's[27] know, that I am here, as I promised Every moment IS occupied.

I have a perfect love of a little white gipsy bonnet to send to the baby— I am *jealous* of the one, you have bought & hope *that* one *will* be soiled, when *this* arrives—

With great deal of love & *pardon* to Bob— Many kisses for our precious baby and much affection & tenderness for your own sweet self, I remain, ever yours

Mary Lincoln

London
Nov. 22d. [1870]

My dear Mary:

Although I wrote you a few days since, yet I will write you again a few lines this morning. Robert writes that you were quite frightened, about the baby clothes— Certainly they were made of the simplest materials & if they were a little trimmed there was certainly nothing out of the way— The *baby* is *not* supposed to be able to walk out in the street this winter & being carried in a nurse's arms, certainly a simple embroidered cloak— is not too much, for people in *our station* of life— The very *middle classes* in Europe, dress their children quite as much & as I do not consider ourselves in that catagory, I would not care what the MEAN & ENVIOUS, would say. However, I will send no more be assured. Only Robert intimates, that you have no drawing room curtains, & I do not wish Christmas, to come, *without* those windows being suitably draped. You have never mentioned to me if you had two parlors or how many windows you had. But I wish you *the day*, you receive this, to go & get *silk* biscatelle, *not worsted* curtains, to match the colour of your carpet, a piano cover— & lace curtains— cornices &&& charge to my account. Of course you will have to hurry about it— it would never do, for you to receive callers— New Year's day, with bare windows— About *the pension* paper— I am going in an hour's time to the

Consuls here— which I dislike intensely. I suppose, I shall have to present myself, before his *red-haired* dignity, Badeau.[28] I pray you, to select curtains of both kinds, worthy of your carpet— and do it, at once— At the Consul, I shall make some enquiries, about sending the diamond set— Do not let a *Chicago jeweller* have them, in their hands.

With much love, I remain, most affectionately yours,

Mary Lincoln

[FRAGMENT]

. . . If Grant had been in the least grateful for favors received from my husband, who did every thing for him, in fact *made him*, the first act he should have done, would have been to offer Robert—a *first class* foreign mission—*he* has been working too hard, for so young a man & requires a change. I wish B—— would lay aside his diffidence & make the request of Grant, *no one* ever gets an appointment, without it is asked for—I hope *Bob, will remember this.* I wrote to Bob, that some of our Phil friends, telegraphed me, immediately my bill passed the House—I very much dread, that it will not pass the senate—It will be very contemptible if it does not. By *this time*, they may have reported *adversely* upon it—If it becomes a law, I mean forthwith, to give you *two* thousand dollars—you can use it either in furnishing your house, or making a little trip to Europe. I should much prefer, to see you do the latter—Let us all hope & pray that the Senate—will act *right* in the matter—Such *long* deliberation, does not argue, well for the cause—I hope you will not remain in Chicago, the months of August & September. Why do you not go up to Mackinaw, it is such a delightful place, the air so cool & healthy— *Those* two months, *under all circumstances*, I mean you to take the Allston rents[29]—it is little to be sure—but my dear Mary, it is a widow's mite, who cannot do for you as much as the heart, so longingly desires. Remember Bob, must hand you the rent for Aug & September   It is little—but that little may *help* to give you *some* fresh air.—to get out of *horrid Chicago*—

Dear Mary, up in that large trunk, near the window—there are some *Quaker* silks   can you not have one or two of them made up for yourself, this summer? There is also a striped light Quaker silk & alpaca—which would make you so nice a travelling costume. Any thing you want up there is yours—Dear Mary, who do you think had

the impudence to write to me a few weeks since—that little mischief
making—Mrs Atwater. It appeared to be directed by Bob, but I
suppose—she requested him to do it & he could not avoid it—Of
course I would not reply & should certainly not know her, were I to
meet her— Her letter contained nothing but *boarding house* news,
in which I was not, in the *least* interested. Very much in keeping—
with Mrs Atwater's style of thinking.

[FRAGMENT]

I think it will be best—to direct them to Wash[ington]—to your
Mother—care of your father—and to his house there—It may prevent Newspaper comment—on the *recent* event[30] which is naturally
so embarrassing to a young couple. All the custom house duty, to
which they will be subjected—Robert—must settle out of my
money—I hope you will carefully remember this—I think an
arrangement will be made here—through the Consulate—between
ourselves that *it* will not be very high. It has brought back—other
and far happier days, to me—to inspect the little articles, as they
have come in—the dainty dresses—little sashs & shawls—not to
speak of precious soft little shoes—for the dear little feet—I am sure
you will be pleased. I have also—had you made—one of the most
elegant yet plain costume suits—with a black velvet hat which is
very distingué looking—with a long brown & black feather to match
the suit—I send you a scrap of the dress & trimming the dress is of
the plain brown trimmed with the brown satin plush trimming—I
have not seen so pretty a costume suit this winter—it is so plain—
yet so rich—and the hat is exquisite—the brown is any thing—the
costume will be strikingly plain & elegant—Plaids are also very
extensively worn—the larger—the better—I want you to have the
plaid I sent you from S. which you have not yet told me whether you
have received—made up after the fashion of the dress I send you—
with tunic to make it warmer & bias folds you can scarcely imagine
what large plaids are worn for dress—& very high colours—the
brown suit I send you with the lovely hat you cannot fail to be
pleased with—parasol & gloves—all to match—In a box—near the
front window up stairs—you will find a purple parasol—with a new
& very beautiful lace cover—which I never used—please accept—
the cover—over the brown the lace—it will look very well—I grieve

to learn of the moths—will you when you recover have my blk velvet dress, cloaks 2 camels hair double shawls all inspected & removed to your house—the one with the peculiar red Indian centre accept for yourself—that I never wore—

Jany 26*th* 1871
London

My dear Mary:

Your note of *Dec 31st* has been received. I am very glad, that you are pleased with your diamonds. The style of their setting, I think very pretty & effective— certainly the *pendant* form is the decided fashion, NOW— Therefore if I were in your place, I would not change it— They may need cleaning, but *that*, Bob, in *his* lawyer style, will tell you *is* a *risk*— for fear the diamonds, *might be changed*. I agree with him there.

I have my eye & *occasionally* my mind, on a beautiful *baby* chain, for the neck links of gold & turquoise, which would go beautifully with *the* turquioise locket—nous verrons, before long. I picked up a dear little gold locket a few days since to wear on the baby's gold chain and a dainty little pair of gold, acorn earrings—They are little loves— That blessed, darling baby, how I long to see it & you all— I am to day in receipt of a letter from Mrs Grund— describing the pleasant New Years day, she passed with you— Have I, not cause to be jealous? I start imm[ediately]— for Italy, to Mrs Orne, in consequence of favoritism—
I am just recovering from quite a severe billious attack. *This* climate, in the winter, is simply, miserable. Five days hence, accompanied by a very good English servant woman, I cross, the terrible channel, for the Continent. We will run down to Italy, quite as fast, as we possibly can, for I am coughing very badly. Tad enters on his school, Tuesday next, determined to resume the hard study, which he certainly went through, with his Tutor. He is an excellent boy — I enclose you a dainty little lace collar which will look very pretty with the black silk costume suit—which is just ready, to be shipped you. In the box— which is being sent, I enclose a list of the contents— I will direct it to OUR DEAR friend, Mr Murphy & perhaps— a little delicate note, would not be amiss — I *do wish* you would send me *Tom Brown's*[31]—exact address— His official Custom House

standing & &— do so, at once please. The key in this letter, is for your travelling bag—*in the box to*— *be sent.*

I am writing you, a fearfully long letter, but as I will have so little chance to write *much* when I am travelling, there will be *great* compensation to you, in the thought. But I hope you will be sure, to write often to me, for every thing connected with you & yours, is of *deep*— *deep* interest to me. How pained I am dear Mary, to hear of your beloved Mother's continued illness[32]—Tad is often very anxious too, to hear of your brother,[33] for he with his loving heart, is very much attached to him. Tad is almost wild to see Bob, yourself, & baby— he thinks the latter, must be, a rare young lady. I am also, of his opinion. I scarcely imagined when I began this letter, that my strength would hold out, for more than three pages. But the themes, which *we discuss* together, in our epistles, are decidedly *exciting & exhaustless.* Tad is enjoying his two weeks holiday, you may be sure—today

You have, my dear Mary, a warm & affectionate friend, in Mrs Grund. She is also, a most amiable & kind hearted woman. *So* different from the *usual cold* element, that predominates in Chicago

Count de Paris,[34] came in about a week since, (twelve miles, from Twickenham) to see me— Having only heard the day before, that I was in town. He *then* wished me to name a day, when I would dine with them, and on my table, this morning I find a most urgent note to come out & visit them. I will do so, on my return in the spring. Also I find, a card for a reception which Badeau gave this week & of a later date, a very kind note pressing me to come he *is* kind hearted— but very *monkeyish* & undignified in manner. I grieve, in my mind, whenever I think of Mr. Motley, being compelled to leave his place. As he says to me quietly, "it is only Grant's spite against Sumner, that has brought it about"—I think so too & *tell him* so.[35]

Will Evans[36] & himself went out to the Chrystal Palace, to see some Gulliver pantomime I hope this lace collar, will reach you safely, direct henceforth to care P. N. Schmidt banker

Frankfurt

With best love to Bob, —that darling precious baby & any quantity for yourself, believe me, always —

　　　　　　　　　Most affectionately
　　　　　　　　　　yours—
　　　　　　　　　　　M L.

London.

Jany 31*st* [1871?]

My dear Mary:

I am leaving this afternoon for Dover— thence the Continent. I am scarcely well enough to travel & will go away coughing for dear life, & a bundle of wrappings but my servant woman has proved herself a good nurse within the past week, so, if unfortunately, I should be ill on the route, I will be well taken care of. Taddie & myself, are feeling very sad over the approaching separation. Yet I have *cited an instance* for the encouragement of *us* both— *in fortitude.* On yesterday, I felt that I must make an exertion, and go to see Mrs Evans & her baby—just EIGHT days old, I found her with a very sweet little girl & she, herself, doing well. She mentioned during my call, that she hoped by the 15*th* of Feb to be able to leave her babe in London, with its monthly nurse, and travel on the Continent for some weeks with her husband. When she leaves her child— it will be a little over three 3— weeks old— she is very well— but does not nurse it herself Neither *does Mrs. Weaver* who was as plump as a *butter* ball— after the birth of her's— I think *Mrs Simpson*—has regulated the BOTTLE system, of *these two blessed* babes— Mrs Evans, is a— lovely woman, yet I cannot understand, such a *strong minded act*, as she appears to be contemplating. What I write you, concerning *these* domestic matters, please say nothing about. *Some* boxes, *are en route* to you, of which I wrote Bob. I sent you, a very stylish little Honiton lace collar in a letter, with a small key. Write me if you receive them. I hope you purchased white lace curtains, with your *coloured* parlour ones. Write me word, if you did—or not—so I can get some over here. Be sure dear Mary, to do so—also write & tell me, how many windows, you have in your parlours, & & lest you need white lace ones—*Also* write me, if you have curtains of any kind, to your chamber windows— I feel sure, you will do this, *immediately*— Direct to Frankfurt & write often— I hope to hear that your dear Mother's health, has improved. *The* Simpson's *are* great *Grant* people, so *are* the Evans's.

I will close with much love to you all—

Very affectionately yours. M. L.

Send me *Tom Browne's* address—his *official position*, in Custom House & &—

ML

Florence, Italy
Feb. 12*th* 1870[37]

My dear Mary:

This morning, I received a letter from Bob, dated as far back as Jany. 6*th* I regretted not having *one* from you. My servant woman & myself, have arrived safely, after much fatigue in this beautiful Florence. We came down the Brenner Pass, through the charming Tyrol, via Milan & Lake Como— had a day's sail on the latter, the beauties of which are simply indescribable— Passed three days at Genoa— and found Mrs Simpson & Ida,[38] *here*— wondering what had become of me. Yesterday, we went together to the Pitti Palace, where the King resides & saw the room, where the beautiful Princess Marguerite sleeps, we can only wish HER, health & happiness, *all her days*, knowing full well, by experience, that power & high position, does not *ensure a bed of roses*. Mrs S. has been here, already *four* weeks— & has passed the same *time* at Rome, having pretty much *accomplished*, Italy. I, am entirely, entre nous, surprised to see Mrs S—— with *many worldly* ideas, which *Bishop's* wives, are not supposed to cultivate, yet withal she is a loving friend— & *I like her.*

She proposes, returning with me to Rome, but I do not insist upon it, *not*, that their company, would not be very desirable, but the return would be expensive & Ida, prefers Florence. Armed, with my guide book, a desire to see all that is wonderful, and strange— and with my faithful·domestic, following in my wake, I must pursue my journey alone. At Venice, *where* Mrs Simpson has not yet been, in three weeks time, we will meet & wend our way up to dear old Frankfurt, thence to England. I received a letter this morning from dear Tad, I wrote you, that until the middle of April next, he is placed with young Evans in an Eng— school— he writes me, that *he has* set into study, but *the fare* is poor enough. Dickens told many truths, in his school narrations. Dear Mary, how is your Mother? Mrs Simpson, & myself, are exceedingly anxious to hear all about her, praying that the news may be good. The *bread* & *butter* of her son in law— is the only cause, I can assign to myself, for her *devotion* to the *present*—Republican throne in America.

I am neglecting to tell you, that we visited the Studio, on yesterday, of the man, to whom the Commission was given, for the Statue of my dearly beloved husband.[39] The bas-reliefs, of dear Bob & yourself, are completed and are, most excellent likenesses[40]—He will send them to you, I think very soon. Have you received the *four* boxes, containing NOT much, sent now, two weeks since?

Mrs Simpson, is exceedingly kind— & affectionate, but *between ourselves*— is almost *wild*, with enthusiasm & admiration, for *Grant* & his wife *She* considers them *elegant*, as *ludicrous* as *it sounds*

Write me all about your dear Mother, & about you all—Every thing, interests me— *Direct to Frankfurt*. With much love, believe me, most affectionately yours.

M L

Will you be able to decipher this scrawl, so hastily written?

M L.

[FRAGMENT]

In a little black hat box— you will find a very pretty cup & saucer— silver lined with gold—a tea pot—cream pitcher & sugar bowl & spoon pretty to use—in your room—when you are an interesting invalid—accept them from me they will need cleaning considerably Also you will find 2 different—mahogany cases of knives—both very handsome enjoy all you can in this life, you will find a box of wall papering, one set particularly . . .

[FRAGMENT]

. . . I am troubled to hear of your dear Mother's continued ill health, I *do so* wish, she was here in Europe, where change of climate, would benefit her so much. You say nothing of the offer I made you, will you not accompany her? At the same time, I wrote last week to Bob, to make some arrangement, which as a business man, he can certainly do— so that two thousand dollars, should be placed at your disposal, for furniture, to *be placed*, in your house *by Christmas*— Do let me think of you by Christmas my dear Mary, with many *niceties* around you, which I fear you have not— Do get pretty furniture for your drawing room— handsome curtains for the windows— suitable things elsewhere. The offer of this money will not prevent my giving you what I have promised you for Europe, if you wish to come over, in the spring. And I do so trust, that Bob, will come over with you, if it is, only for three months, it would do him such a world of good— and for that short time he can easily place a reliable person, in his place— He loves you *very very* dearly & misses you very greatly— I was such an excessively indulged wife— my darling husband, was so gentle and easy, that when unpleasant words are used towards me, when I am conscious I am acting, for the best, it goes very hard with my wounded spirit   Yet we know, Bob, is just as kind & noble hearted as he can be —.

Judge Bradwell:

I find another very important page of items. Notes due for $13,500 which so soon as the bills mature, must be placed in '81' bonds. My son to receive *all* the interest himself. Should my son die *before* the six years after my death, when the $13,500— *would* become his then it goes to any child *or* children he may leave, when they arrive at *21* years of age, to be equally divided [()the interest each year to be paid them— to the children[)] between them— failing of issue to go to Lincoln Home for indigent women[41]

At the expiration of six years after my death, the whole of the last mentioned sum, he can receive *in full* & must be placed at *his* disposition.

Lest you might desire some further explanation on the subject, I will come down tomorrow at 2 two P.M for a few moments.

Very respectfully yours,
Mrs A. Lincoln.

Chicago
Oct 10*th* 1872

Chicago, Illinois
July 23d— 1873.

To the County Judge, of
    Cook County
Dear Sir:

This is to certify, that I have made my will, dated the 23 of July A.D. 1873, and the same will be found after my death, in "Bryant's Fidelity and Safety depository," box No..282

Respectfully,
Mrs Abraham Lincoln

P.S. Hon David Davis and John T. Stuart are my executors. M L.
[On envelope]
To be delivered to the County Judge of Cook Co—
upon the Death of Mrs Abraham Lincoln

Private)   Jany 17*th* 1874.

Judge Bradwell

I do not wish to trouble you, *yet* I am not satisfied about the $50,[42] per month. It looks *small*, to mention the sum— and I *urgently* request you to erase it, as you can do it so neatly & return the paper by Mrs Bradwell— *Please do* NOT *fail* to comply with my request & oblige— Very truly yours—

Mrs A.Lincoln.

P.S. There is no question of it being legal, I suppose, and I feel that I cannot rest, until it is done— My time now is growing very short, *entre nous*, for leaving.

M.L.

Please burn this

Chicago Jany
18*th* 1874

Judge Bradwell

My Dear Sir:

I fear the rough lines, I wrote so hastily in Mrs. Bradwell's presence— were not entirely correct. I thought, that in the space, which you will kindly erase— it would be better to say, that any loose sum of money, that may be left after my death, not mentioned in my will, shall go *immediately* to my son. Also in the event of the death of my grandson, "Robert Lincoln,"[43] the bond which is now received number 1108341—and which was allotted the grandson— should the dear boy unfortunately not survive— the said bond, goes *at once* to my son— R. T. L. These little items, will certainly fill the vacuum, which I am sure you will erase— I have given you so much trouble, dear Judge— yet *under the* circumstances, I trust you will not consider me *whimsical* or changeable.

Hoping you will have a pleasant winter in S—— and with the sincerest regards for yourself & your dear good wife, whom I hesitate to praise because she has not paid me that promised visit, I remain,

Very truly, your friend
Mrs A Lincoln.

Private—   November 11th 1875.

Judge Bradwell

My dear friend:

A long & weary time has passed since I last saw you— Knowing well the interest you have taken in my sad fate, I feel assured that you will be pleased to hear that I am in perfect health, I am staying with my sister Mrs Edwards, who has always been tenderly attached to me— I am now writing at the suggestion of Mr. N. W. Edwards— who is desirous that you should send me— the *will* you wrote for me many months since. You will remember, that I left it, in your charge. Please send it, by return of mail. What can I say to your dear wife?— The sorrow which has been mine for the last six months, has been in a measure alleviated, by the friendship of such noble hearts as yours— I feel assured you will reply to this *note* at once— without ever mentioning that you have heard from me— The paths of life have become very rough to me— since the most loving & devoted husband & children have been called from my side. In the great hereafter, when I am reunited to my beloved ones, we will then know, why the gracious Father, has caused such deep affliction.

Be kind enough to enclose the will to Mr. N. W. Edwards—

Yours very truly
Mary Lincoln

write me— quietly—
both of you.

Springfield, Ill
Dec— 1st 1875.

Judge Bradwell:

A month since, I wrote you, requesting you to send me the *will*, which you wrote & which I entrusted to your care.[44]

Please send it to me at once & greatly oblige,

Your friend,
Mrs A. Lincoln

NOTES

1. THE TRIAL

1. Justin G. and Linda Levitt Turner, *Mary Todd Lincoln: Her Life and Letters* (New York: Knopf, 1972), 534, 536; Appendix, 171–172.

2. J. G. Randall, *Lincoln the President: Midstream* (New York: Dodd, Mead, 1953), 36.

3. Nancy F. Cott, *The Bonds of Womanhood: "Woman's Sphere" in New England, 1780–1835* (New Haven, Conn.: Yale Univ. Press, 1977), 64; Turner and Turner, *Mary Todd Lincoln*, 189. On the Victorian ideal of the family, see Walter E. Houghton, *The Victorian Frame of Mind, 1830–1870* (New Haven, Conn.: Yale Univ. Press, 1957), 343–44.

4. Benjamin P. Thomas, *Abraham Lincoln: A Biography* (New York: Knopf, 1952), 464; Turner and Turner, *Mary Todd Lincoln*, 178.

5. Elizabeth Keckley, *Behind the Scenes* (New York: G. W. Carleton, 1868), 104–5; Turner and Turner, *Mary Todd Lincoln*, 285.

6. Charles B. Strozier, *Lincoln's Quest for Union: Public and Private Meanings* (New York: Basic Books, 1982), 95–97, accurately describes the devastating impact of the presidency on the Lincolns' marriage.

7. Barbara Welter, "The Cult of True Womanhood," in *Dimity Convictions: The American Woman in the Nineteenth Century* (Athens: Ohio Univ. Press, 1976), 40; Harold Holzer, *Abraham Lincoln, Mary Todd Lincoln* (Richmond, Va.: United States Historical Society, n.d.), 5.

8. Willard King, *Lincoln's Manager: David Davis* (Cambridge: Harvard Univ. Press, 1960), 235–36. Strozier notes an earlier sign of financial trouble (*Lincoln's Quest for Union*, 87).

9. Katherine Helm, *The True Story of Mary, Wife of Lincoln* (New York:

Harper & Brothers, 1923), 267; Ishbel Ross, *The President's Wife: Mary Todd Lincoln, a Biography* (New York: G. P. Putnam's Sons, 1973), 259–65, 283–84, 292–300.

10. *Philadelphia Record*, March 29, 1931, clipping, and unidentified clipping quoting the *Waukesha Daily Freeman*, August 15, 1872, both in Louis A. Warren Lincoln Library and Museum, Fort Wayne, Ind.; Turner and Turner, *Mary Todd Lincoln*, 601.

11. *Tallahassee Weekly Floridian*, November 17, 1874; Eddie Foy and Alvin E. Harlow, "Clowning through Life," *Collier's*, December 25, 1926, 30. The nurse was the mother of entertainer Eddie Foy, and her article is riddled with factual errors but likely has some basis in truth, as other sources indicate that Mrs. Lincoln's traveling companion was a nurse (*Tallahassee Weekly Floridian*, November 24, 1874; *Savannah Morning News*, November 24, 1874; *Jacksonville Florida Union*, November 26, 1874). Newspaper references courtesy of August E. Johansen and Gary R. Planck.

12. John Coyne to Robert Todd Lincoln, March 12, 1875 (telegram); Mary Todd Lincoln to Edward Swift Isham, March 12, 1875 (two telegrams of same date), Insanity File, Louis A. Warren Lincoln Library and Museum, Fort Wayne, Ind. All previous studies have stated that Mrs. Lincoln addressed her telegram to Ralph Isham rather than Edward Isham. The factual error is insignificant except as a symptom of the primitive state of research on Mrs. Lincoln's case, for the information about the addressee was available to researchers before the discovery of the Insanity File.

13. J. J. S. Wilson to [John Coyne] n.d. (pencil draft of telegram); John Coyne to J. J. S. Wilson (telegram), March 12, 1875, Insanity File.

14. Mary Todd Lincoln to Robert Todd Lincoln (telegram), March 13, 1875; John Coyne to J. J. S. Wilson, March 13, 1875 (two telegrams of same date), Insanity File.

15. Carl Sandburg and Paul M. Angle, *Mary Lincoln: Wife and Widow* (New York: Harcourt, Brace, 1932), 309.

16. Miscellaneous account book pages, 9, Insanity File.

17. Leonard Swett to David Davis, May 24, 1875, David Davis Family Papers, Illinois State Historical Library, Springfield.

18. Turner and Turner, *Mary Todd Lincoln*, 590; *Biographical Sketches of the Leading Men of Chicago* (Chicago: Wilson & St. Clair, 1868), 229–34.

19. Sandburg and Angle, *Mary Lincoln: Wife and Widow*, 306–7.

20. Charles D. Mosher, *Centennial Historical Albums of Biographies . . . ; Biographical Sketches of the Leading Men of Chicago*, 81–89.

21. Albert Deutsch, *The Mentally Ill in America: A History of Their Cure and Treatment from Colonial Times*, 2d ed., rev. (New York: Columbia Univ. Press, 1949), 152 n.

22. Andrew McFarland, "Insanity as a Defense: The Late Leonard Swett One of Its Most Successful Advocates," *Chicago Tribune*, June 20, 1889, clipping in scrapbook, Leonard Swett Papers, Illinois State Historical Library, Springfield. McFarland, who frequently testified in court cases in-

volving insanity, had doubtless encountered Swett in the courtroom and therefore admired his ability in such cases. However, a check of all the cases involving insanity reported by the Illinois Supreme Court through 1876 failed to uncover a single case in which Swett was counsel. Thus it seems an exaggeration to imply that he left a lasting mark on the law of the state.

23. Sherman Day Wakefield, *How Lincoln Became President: The Part Played by Bloomington, Illinois* . . . (New York: Wilson-Erickson, 1936), 75–76; McFarland, "Insanity as a Defense"; "In Memoriam: Leonard Swett's Oration on the Life of . . . Judge Dickey," clipping from *Chicago Times*, May 10, 1887, Swett Papers. When Lincoln later learned from an old friend of Wyant's that the defendant had often been in trouble before the murder, he was surprised and chastened. Lincoln had thought Wyant was "possuming" insanity, but now he admitted that he may have been wrong to press his prosecution relentlessly. This anecdote contains an incorrect date but may well be true in substance (See Paul M. Angle, ed., *Herndon's Life of Lincoln* [Cleveland: World Publishing, 1965], 278).

24. McFarland, "Insanity as a Defense"; *Transactions of the McLean County Historical Society, Bloomington, Illinois* (Bloomington: Pantagraph Printing & Stationery, 1903), 2: 343–44.

25. Leonard Swett to David Davis, May 24, 1875, David Davis Family Papers.

26. Sandburg and Angle, *Mary Lincoln: Wife and Widow*, 306–7.

27. Leonard Swett to David Davis, May 24, 1875, David Davis Family Papers.

28. John Todd Stuart to Robert Todd Lincoln, Insanity File.

29. David Davis to Leonard Swett, May 19, 1875, Insanity File.

30. Leonard Swett to David Davis, May 24, 1875, David Davis Family Papers.

31. On Swett's skill, especially in cases involving insanity, see Leonard Swett to Rose Swett, April 22, 1854, and obituaries in Leonard Swett Papers.

32. Rhodes and Jauchius, *The Trial of Mary Todd Lincoln* (Indianapolis: Bobbs-Merrill, 1959), 68; John Clayton, *The Illinois Fact Book and Historical Almanac, 1673–1968* (Carbondale: Southern Illinois Univ. Press, 1970), 112, 497; Henry Horner to Otto L. Schmidt, October 16, 1925 (photocopy), Illinois State Historical Library, Springfield.

33. Application to Try the Question of Insanity, County Court of Cook County, May 19, 1875 (photostat), Illinois State Historical Library, Springfield.

34. *Chicago Times*, May 20, 1875.

35. Leonard Swett to David Davis, May 24, 1875, David Davis Family Papers.

36. Rhodes and Jauchius, *Trial of Mary Todd Lincoln*; Homer Croy, *The Trial of Mrs. Abraham Lincoln* (New York: Duell, Sloan & Pearce, 1962), 51–114.

37. Deutsch, *Mentally Ill in America*, 419–23; Isaac Ray, "Project of a

Law for Determining the Legal Relations of the Insane," *American Journal of Insanity* 7 (1851): 217, 223, 226.

38. Maxwell Bloomfield, *American Lawyers in a Changing Society, 1776–1876* (Cambridge: Harvard Univ. Press, 1976), 91–135; Lawrence M. Friedman, *A History of American Law* (New York: Simon & Schuster, 1973), 187–91; Deutsch, *The Mentally Ill in America*, 420–21; *The Revised Laws of Illinois* (Vandalia: Greiner & Sherman, 1833), 332–33.

39. Carl E. Black, "Origin of Our State Charitable Institutions," *Journal of the Illinois State Historical Society* 18 (April 1925): 183–91; Don Harrison Doyle, *The Social Order of a Frontier Community: Jacksonville, Illinois, 1825–70* (Champaign: Univ. of Illinois Press, 1978), 70–71, 73; *General Laws of the State of Illinois, Passed by the Seventeenth General Assembly . . .* (Springfield: Lanphier & Walker, 1851), 98. The statute is inaccurately reproduced in Deutsch, *The Mentally Ill in America*, 424—proof that the statutes are rarely examined, even by students of the commitment laws. Deutsch probably reproduced the statute from one of Elizabeth Packard's books.

40. Myra Samuels Himmelhoch with Arthur H. Shaffer, "Elizabeth Packard: Nineteenth-Century Crusader for the Rights of Mental Patients," *Journal of American Studies* 8 (December 1979): 343–75; Mrs. E. P. W. Packard, *The Prisoner's Hidden Life, or Insane Asylums Unveiled . . .* (Chicago: privately published, 1868), 14–15, 34–44, 83–84. Himmelhoch and Shaffer, like Mrs. Packard's critics, overrated her effect on Illinois law because they failed to examine the history of commitment laws in Illinois and neighboring states. The Packards became Presbyterians in Illinois by virtue of an agreement between Presbyterians and Congregationalists to divide territory in order to supply churches to the West.

41. Isaac Ray, "American Legislation on Insanity," *American Journal of Insanity* 21 (July 1864): 49–50, 53.

42. Hugh Ross, "Analysis of Legal and Medical Considerations in Commitment of the Mentally Ill," *Yale Law Journal* 61 (August 1947): 1192–93.

43. Foster Pratt, "Insane Patients and Their Legal Relations," *American Journal of Insanity*, 35 (July 1878): 185; Isaac Ray, "A Modern Lettre de Cachet Reviewed," *Atlantic Monthly* 22 (August 1868): 230.

44. Emil Joseph Verlie, *Illinois Constitutions*, Collections of the Illinois State Historical Library, vol. 13, Constitutional Series, vol. 1 (Springfield: Illinois State Historical Library, 1919), 105.

45. Eddy v. The People, 15 Ill. Reports 386–87 (1854); Isaac Ray, "American Legislation on Insanity," *American Journal of Insanity* 21 (July 1864): 54–55; Writ of Inquisition, May 19, 1875, Cook County Court documents (photostat), Illinois State Historical Library, Springfield. Referring to *Eddy v. The People*, the 1874 statute required notice of appointment of a conservator and spelled out what constituted proper notice. With those stipulations, Robert complied in full (W. H. Underwood, *Statutes of Illinois Construed* [St. Louis: W. J. Gilbert, 1878], 847).

46. Benjamin P. Thomas, *Portrait for Posterity: Lincoln and His Biog-*

raphers (New Brunswick, N.J.: Rutgers Univ. Press, 1947), 19, 21; "Proceedings," *American Journal of Insanity* 33 (October 1876): 254.

2. COMMITMENT

1. Peter McCandless, "Liberty and Lunacy: The Victorians and Wrongful Confinement," in Andrew Scull, ed., *Madhouses, Mad-Doctors, and Madmen: The Social History of Psychiatry in the Victorian Era* (Philadelphia: Univ. of Pennsylvania Press, 1981), 340; Deutsch, *The Mentally Ill in America*, page 152 n. Men who dealt with insanity as a practical problem in the Victorian era knew better, of course. Judges frequently commented on the difficulties inherent in cases involving insanity. Pinkney H. Walker, of the Illinois Supreme Court, for example, noted in 1862: "It may be truly said, that there are few questions which present greater difficulties in their solution, than this of insanity. It assumes such a variety of forms, from that of the raving madman, to the monomaniac; from total dementia, to that of scarcely perceptible insanity, that it has almost been denied, that any person is perfectly sane, on every subject" (Lilly v. Waggoner, 27 Ill. Reports [1862], 395). Justice Sidney Breese likewise noted a year later that writers on the subject of insanity "furnish, as yet, no true and safe guide for courts and juries" (Hopps v. The People, 31 Ill. Reports [1863], 390).

2. David J. Rothman, *Conscience and Convenience: The Asylum and Its Alternatives in Progressive America* (Boston: Little, Brown, 1980), 326. See also Rothman's *The Discovery of the Asylum: Social Order and Disorder in the New Republic* (Boston: Little, Brown, 1971), 143.

3. Gerald N. Grob, *Mental Institutions in America: Social Policy to 1875* (New York: Free Press, 1973), 202, 167–68, 240; J. Sanbourne Bockoven, *Moral Treatment in American Psychiatry* (New York: Springer Publishing, 1963), 12.

4. Grob, *Mental Institutions*, 98.

5. Bockoven, *Moral Treatment*, 47–48.

6. Deutsch, *The Mentally Ill in America*, 55–57.

7. Norman Dain, *Concepts of Insanity in the United States, 1789–1865* (New Brunswick, N.J.; Rutgers Univ. Press, 1964), 58; Pliny Earle, "The Curability of Insanity," *American Journal of Insanity* 32 (April 1877): 485–533; Bockoven, *Moral Treatment*, 65–66.

8. Deutsch, *The Mentally Ill in America*, 423–24.

9. David Davis to Leonard Swett, May 19, 1875; Ralph N. Isham to Ayer & Kales, May 18, 1875; and Nathan Smith Davis to Ayer & Kales, May 18, 1875, Insanity File.

10. See, for example, Barbara Welter, "Female Complaints: Medical Views of American Women (1790–1865)," in *Dimity Convictions*, 57–70; Carroll Smith-Rosenberg and Charles Rosenberg, "The Female Animal: Medical and Biological Views of Woman and Her Role in Nineteenth-

Century America," *Journal of American History* 60 (September 1973): 332–56; Barbara Ehrenreich and Deirdre English, *Complaints and Disorders: The Sexual Politics of Sickness* ([New York]: Feminist Press, 1973); Ann Douglas Wood, " 'The Fashionable Diseases': Women's Complaints and Their Treatment in Nineteenth-Century America," *Journal of Interdisciplinary History* 4 (Summer 1973): 25–52; and John S. Haller, *The Physician and Sexuality in Victorian America* (Champaign: Univ. of Illinois Press, 1974).

11. Elizabeth Todd Edwards to Robert Todd Lincoln, November 5, 1875, Insanity File.

12. Chloral was a major subject of interest in the Association of Medical Superintendents of American Institutions for the Insane in this period. See, for example: "Proceedings of the Association," *American Journal of Insanity* 27 (October 1870): 210; J. B. Andrews, "The Physiological Action and Therapeutic Use of Chloral," *American Journal of Insanity* 28 (July 1871): 35–36; and Carlos F. MacDonald, "Hydrate of Chloral," *American Journal of Insanity* 34 (January 1878): 360–67.

13. *Chicago Times*, May 21, 1875; Leonard Swett to David Davis, May 24, 1875, David Davis Family Papers. Mrs. Lincoln's treatment for neuralgia was not unusual in the nineteenth century. See Haller, *Physician and Sexuality in Victorian America*, 276.

14. Robert Todd Lincoln to Leonard Swett, May 25, 1884, Robert Todd Lincoln Letterbooks, Illinois State Historical Library, Springfield.

15. *Chicago Times*, May 21, 1875.

16. W. H. Underwood, *Statutes of Illinois Construed*, 844; "Proceedings of the Association," *American Journal of Insanity* 21 (July 1864): 132 ff; Robert Todd Lincoln to Elizabeth Todd Edwards, August 7, 1875, Robert Todd Lincoln Letterbooks.

17. John Todd Stuart to Robert Todd Lincoln, May 10, 1875 and May 21, 1875, Insanity File.

18. *Chicago Times*, May 21, 1875.

19. Rodney A. Ross, "Mary Todd Lincoln, Patient at Bellevue Place, Batavia," *Journal of the Illinois State Historical Society* 63 (Spring 1970): 5–10.

20. Robert Todd Lincoln to Henry T. Blow, August 4, 1876, Robert Todd Lincoln Letterbooks.

21. Bockhoven, *Moral Treatment*, 69–70, 74; Grob, *Mental Institutions in America*, 202; Robert Todd Lincoln to Mrs. J. H. Orne, June 1, 1875 (typed copy), Insanity File.

22. Patient progress reports for Bellevue Place, photographic slide copies, Louis A. Warren Lincoln Library and Museum, Fort Wayne, Ind.

3. RELEASE

1. Ross, "Mary Todd Lincoln, Patient at Bellevue Place," 26, 27, 28, 29.

2. W. A. Evans, *Mrs. Abraham Lincoln: A Study of Her Personality and Her Influence on Lincoln* (New York: Knopf, 1932), 43–45; Emanuel Hertz, *The Hidden Lincoln: From the Letters and Papers of William H. Herndon* (New York: Viking, 1938), 373; Mark E. Neely, Jr., *The Abraham Lincoln Encyclopedia* (New York: McGraw-Hill, 1982), 95–96; Turner and Turner, *Mary Todd Lincoln*, 705–6.

3. Turner and Turner, *Mary Todd Lincoln*, 105.

4. Ibid., 122.

5. Roy P. Basler et al., eds., *The Collected Works of Abraham Lincoln*, 9 vols. (New Brunswick, N.J.: Rutgers Univ. Press, 1953–55), 3: 10, 55, 61, 133, 140, 174, 176, 241; John F. Farnsworth to Abraham Lincoln, September 20, 1858, and May 22, 1860, Abraham Lincoln Papers, Library of Congress (microfilm); Newton Bateman and Paul Selby, eds., *Historical Encyclopedia of Illinois* (Chicago: Mumsell Publishing, 1900), 162; Roy P. Basler, ed., *The Collected Works of Abraham Lincoln: Supplement, 1832–1865* (Westport, Conn.: Greenwood, 1974), 205; *Ritchie's Historical Picture, Death of President Lincoln . . .* (New York: A. H. Ritchie, n.d.), 10.

6. Ross, "Mary Todd Lincoln, Patient at Bellevue Place," 30.

7. Bateman and Selby, *Historical Encyclopedia of Illinois*, 58–59; Appendix, 182. There is no evidence that Mrs. Lincoln shared the feminist views of the Bradwells, but a letter opposing female suffrage allegedly written by Mrs. Lincoln, which appears in Sandburg and Angle, *Mary Lincoln: Wife and Widow*, 303, is almost certainly a forgery. It is not reprinted in Turner and Turner, *Mary Todd Lincoln: Her Life and Letters*, but the Turners never explain their decisions on documents. The letter in question, originally a part of Oliver R. Barrett's collection, cannot now be located.

8. Ross, "Mary Todd Lincoln, Patient at Bellevue Place," 31, 32.

9. Myra Bradwell to A[bram] Wakeman, August 12, 1875, Louis A. Warren Lincoln Library and Museum, Fort Wayne, Ind.

10. Ross, "Mary Todd Lincoln, Patient at Bellevue Place," 32; *Biographical Sketches of the Leading Men of Chicago*, 577–81.

11. Robert Todd Lincoln to Elizabeth Todd Edwards, August 7, 1875, Robert Todd Lincoln Letterbooks.

12. Robert Todd Lincoln to Elizabeth Todd Edwards, August 10, 1875, Robert Todd Lincoln Letterbooks.

13. Elizabeth Todd Edwards to Robert Todd Lincoln, August 11, [1875], Insanity File.

14. Elizabeth Todd Edwards to Robert Todd Lincoln, August 12, [1875], Insanity File.

15. Robert Todd Lincoln to Myra Bradwell, August 13, 1875, Insanity File.

16. Robert Todd Lincoln to Myra Bradwell, August 14, 1875; Robert Todd Lincoln to Mary Todd Lincoln, August 15, 1875, Insanity File.

17. *Chicago Times*, August 24, 1875; *Biographical Sketches of the Leading Men of Chicago*, 579–80.

18. Turner and Turner, *Mary Todd Lincoln*, 344, 376, 377; George B.

Lincoln to Gideon Welles, April 25, 1874, Louis A. Warren Lincoln Library and Museum, Fort Wayne, Ind.

19. R[ichard] J. Patterson to J[ames] B. Bradwell, August 18, 1875, Insanity File.

20. *Chicago Tribune*, August 31, 1875.

21. Elizabeth Todd Edwards to Robert Todd Lincoln, August 13, 1875, Insanity File.

22. Elizabeth Todd Edwards to Robert Todd Lincoln, August 17, 1875, Insanity File.

23. *Chicago Post and Mail*, August 23, 1875 (clipping), Insanity File.

24. Myra Samuels Himmelhoch with Arthur H. Shaffer, "Elizabeth Packard: Nineteenth-Century Crusader for the Rights of Mental Patients, *Journal of American Studies* 13 (December 1979): 362, 367, 371–72.

25. Robert Todd Lincoln to Henry T. Blow, Aug. 4, 1875 (copy), Robert Todd Lincoln Letterbooks; *Chicago Tribune*, August 29, 1875.

26. Isaac Ray, *A Treatise on the Medical Jurisprudence of Insanity*, ed. Winfred Overholser (Cambridge: Harvard Univ. Press, 1962).

27. Isaac Ray, "A Modern Lettre de Cachet Reviewed," 231–32.

28. R[ichard] J. Patterson to Rob[er]t T[odd] Lincoln, September 2, 1875, Insanity File.

29. Andrew W. McFarland to Robert Todd Lincoln, October 1, 1875, Insanity File.

30. Andrew W. McFarland to Robert Todd Lincoln, September 8, 1875, Insanity File. The consultation was costly. Robert paid Dr. McFarland $100 from his mother's estate for the appointment and traveling expenses. Account of Receipts and Disbursements, as . . . Conservator, June 15, 1876, Insanity File.

31. A. G. McDill to Rob[er]t T[odd] Lincoln, September 6, 1875, Insanity File.

4. THE EXPERIMENT

1. Robert Todd Lincoln to Richard J. Patterson, September 9, 1875, Robert Todd Lincoln Letterbooks.

2. Andrew McFarland to Robert Todd Lincoln, September 10, 1875, Insanity File.

3. Elizabeth Todd Edwards to Robert Todd Lincoln, September 15, [1875], Insanity File.

4. Elizabeth Todd Edwards to Robert Todd Lincoln, September 15, [1875], Insanity File.

5. Elizabeth Todd Edwards to Robert Todd Lincoln, September 15, [1875], Insanity File.

6. Elizabeth Todd Edwards to Robert Todd Lincoln, September 22, [1875], Insanity File.

7. Elizabeth Todd Edwards to Robert Todd Lincoln, November 5, 1875, Insanity File.

8. Elizabeth Todd Edwards to Robert Todd Lincoln, November 12, 1875, Insanity File.

9. Robert Todd Lincoln to Ninian W. Edwards, November 15, 1875 (copy), Insanity File.

10. Elizabeth Todd Edwards to Robert Todd Lincoln, November 12, 1875, Insanity File.

11. Ninian W. Edwards to Robert Todd Lincoln, November 12, 1875 and November 18, 1875, Insanity File. He had written much the same thing to Robert the day before (Ninian W. Edwards to Robert Todd Lincoln, November 17, 1875, Insanity File).

12. Rhodes and Jauchius, *Trial of Mary Todd Lincoln*, 21–16; John S. Goff, *Robert Todd Lincoln: A Man in His Own Right* (Norman: Univ. of Oklahoma Press, 1969), 108–18.

13. Robert Todd Lincoln to John Todd Stuart, Nov. 15, 1875 (copy), Insanity File; F. Lauriston Bullard, "Mrs. Lincoln's Pension," *Lincoln Herald*, 49 (June 1947): 26–27. Congress voted Mrs. Lincoln a $3,000 annual pension in 1870. Republican senators split 28–11 in favor of the bill (20 absent). Nine Democrats voted against the bill, and 4 were absent. The House passed the bill by a vote of 85–65 (with 77 absent).

14. Robert Todd Lincoln to David Davis, November 16, 1875 (copy), Insanity File.

15. Jay Monaghan, "Was Abraham Lincoln Really a Spiritualist?" *Journal of the Illinois State Historical Society* 34 (June 1941): 209–32.

16. Ruth Painter Randall, *Mary Todd Lincoln*, 294; Turner and Turner, *Mary Todd Lincoln: Her Life and Letters*, 525; Strozier, *Lincoln's Quest for Union*, 99.

17. Monaghan, "Was Abraham Lincoln Really a Spiritualist?" 226, 216.

18. Robert Todd Lincoln to David Davis, November 16, 1875 (copy), Insanity File.

19. David Davis to Robert Todd Lincoln, November 20, 1875, Insanity File.

20. David Davis to Robert Todd Lincoln, November 30, [1875], Insanity File.

21. Ninian W. Edwards to Robert Todd Lincoln, December 1, 1875, Insanity File.

22. Elizabeth Todd Edwards to Robert Todd Lincoln, December 1, 1875, Insanity File.

23. Ninian W. Edwards to Robert Todd Lincoln, December 14, 1875, Insanity File.

24. Ninian W. Edwards to Robert Todd Lincoln, December 18, 1875, Insanity File.

25. Robert Todd Lincoln to Ninian W. Edwards, December 21, 1875, Insanity File.

26. Robert Todd Lincoln to Ninian W. Edwards, December 21, 1875, Insanity File; Turner and Turner, *Mary Todd Lincoln: Her Life and Letters*, 445.

27. George Thomas Palmer, *A Conscientious Turncoat: The Story of John M. Palmer, 1817–1900* (New Haven: Yale Univ. Press, 1941), 244–45; Neely, *Abraham Lincoln Encyclopedia*, 231–32.

28. John M. Palmer to Robert Todd Lincoln, December 21, 1875, Insanity File.

29. Ninian W. Edwards to Robert Todd Lincoln, December 22, 1875, Insanity File.

30. Ninian W. Edwards to Robert Todd Lincoln, January 14, 1876, Insanity File.

5. A NEW TRIAL

1. Robert Todd Lincoln to John M. Palmer, December 23, 1875, Insanity File.

2. Ayers v. Mussetter, 46 Ill. Reports 475 (1868).

3. Daniel Scott Smith, "Family Limitation, Sexual Control, and Domestic Feminism in Victorian America," in Nancy F. Cott and Elizabeth H. Pleck, eds., *A Heritage of Her Own: Toward a New Social History of American Women* (New York: Simon & Schuster, 1979), 223–24; Kathryn Kish Sklar, "Victorian Women and Domestic Life: Mary Todd Lincoln, Elizabeth Cady Stanton, and Harriet Beecher Stowe," in Cullom Davis et al., eds., *The Public and the Private Lincoln: Contemporary Perspectives* (Carbondale: Southern Illinois Univ. Press, 1979), 30–31.

4. Elizabeth Todd Edwards to Robert Todd Lincoln, January 15, 1876, Insanity File.

5. Ninian W. Edwards to Robert Todd Lincoln, January 14, 1876, Insanity File.

6. Elizabeth Todd Edwards to Robert Todd Lincoln, January 15, 1876, Insanity File.

7. Ninian W. Edwards to Robert Todd Lincoln, January 15, 1876, Insanity File.

8. Robert Todd Lincoln to Ninian W. Edwards, January 17, 1876; Robert Todd Lincoln to Elizabeth Todd Edwards, January 17, 1876; Robert Todd Lincoln to Edward Swift Isham, January 17, 1876, Insanity File.

9. Elizabeth Todd Edwards to Robert Todd Lincoln, February 9, 1876, Insanity File; Robert Todd Lincoln to Elizabeth Todd Edwards, February 12, 1876 (copy), Letterbooks.

10. Robert Todd Lincoln to Elizabeth Todd Edwards, February 16, 1876, Letterbooks.

11. Ninian W. Edwards to Robert Todd Lincoln, April 6, 1876, Insanity File.

12. Ninian W. Edwards to Robert Todd Lincoln, April 18, 1876, Insanity File.

13. John M. Palmer to Robert Todd Lincoln, April 19, 1876, Insanity File; Robert Todd Lincoln to John M. Palmer, April 20, 1876 (copy), Letterbooks.

14. Ninian W. Edwards to Robert Todd Lincoln, April 21, 1876, Insanity File.

15. Robert Todd Lincoln to Ninian W. Edwards, April 24, 1876 (copy), Letterbooks.

16. John M. Palmer to Leonard Swett, April 24, 1876, Insanity File.

17. Ninian W. Edwards to David Davis, May 23, 1876, Insanity File.

18. Ninian W. Edwards to David Davis, June 8, 1876, Insanity File.

19. *Chicago Times*, June 16, 1876.

20. Mary Lincoln Verdict, June 15, 1876, Cook County Court documents (photostat), Illinois State Historical Library, Springfield; *Chicago Times*, June 16, 1876.

21. Ninian W. Edwards to Robert Todd Lincoln, June 17, 1876 (three letters of same date), Insanity File.

22. Smith v. The People, 65 Ill. Reports 378 (1872).

23. Robert Todd Lincoln, Waiver of Notice, June 15, 1876; Ninian W. Edwards, "In the matter of . . . ," June 15, 1876; Mary Lincoln Verdict, June 15, 1876, Cook County Court documents (photocopies), Illinois State Historical Library, Springfield.

24. Smith v. The People. 65 Ill. Reports 378 (1872); Menkins v. Lightner, 18 Ill. Reports 282 (1857).

25. W. H. Underwood, *Statutes of Illinois Construed*, 851.

26. Ninian W. Edwards to Robert Todd Lincoln, June 17, 1876, Insanity File; Turner and Turner, *Mary Todd Lincoln*, 615–16.

27. Leonard Swett to Ninian W. Edwards, June 20, 1876 (copy), Insanity File.

28. Ninian W. Edwards to Leonard Swett, June 22, 1876, Insanity File.

6. CONCLUSION

1. Elizabeth Todd Edwards to Robert Todd Lincoln, October 26, 1876 Insanity File.

2. Elizabeth Todd Edwards to Robert Todd Lincoln, October 29, 1876 Insanity File.

2. Robert Todd Lincoln to Henry Darling, November 15, 1877, Barton Collection, University of Chicago; Elizabeth Todd Edwards to Mary Todd Lincoln, November 5, 1876 and March 31, 1876.

4. Turner and Turner, *Mary Todd Lincoln: Her Life and Letters*, 690; Robert Todd Lincoln to Elizabeth Todd Edwards, April 18, 1879, Louis A. Warren Lincoln Library and Museum, Fort Wayne, Ind.

5. Turner and Turner, *Mary Todd Lincoln: Her Life and Letters*, 704–6.

6. Ross, *The President's Wife*, 330; Randall, *Mary Lincoln: Biography of a Marriage*, 440–1.

7. Paul M. Angle to William E. Barton (extracting from a letter of Mary L. D. Putnam to St. Clair and Clement Putnam, December 8, 1882), January 10, 1927, Barton Collection.

8. William E. Barton to Henry Horner, February 15, 1926 (carbon copy) and Henry Horner to William E. Barton, February 12, 1926, Barton Collection, Univ. of Chicago. Horner was judge of the probate court. The county court had jurisdiction in all matters requiring conservators for estates, and, as Robert Todd Lincoln became his mother's conservator after the court declared her insane, the files on the case were originally in the county court's records. In 1878 the probate court was created with jurisdiction in all conservatorship matters, and the records transferred to the probate court. Thus Barton found the papers in Horner's court, and the transfer may have been the reason for the clerk's difficulties in locating them at first. Henry Horner to Otto L. Schmidt, October 16, 1925 (photocopy), Illinois State Historical Library, Springfield.

9. Henry Horner to Paul M. Angle, October 20, 1925; Paul M. Angle to Henry Horner, October 27, 1925 (photocopies), Illinois State Historical Library, Springfield.

10. William E. Barton, *The Life of Abraham Lincoln*, 2 vols. (Indianapolis: Bobbs-Merrill, 1925), 3: 419. Barton suggested another element of mystery by saying, "No docket number appears to have been given in the case." In fact, most of the documents bear the number "1/920" (Documents, Mary Todd Lincoln Case, Cook County Court [photostats], Illinois State Historical Library, Springfield). Barton also mentioned "a transcript of the evidence." No such thing ever existed, as there were no transcripts of trials below the appellate level in that era (William E. Barton, *The Women Lincoln Loved* [Indianapolis: Bobbs-Merrill, 1927], 362). Horner termed Barton's treatment of the matter in the first book "gentle and considerate" (Henry Horner to Otto L. Schmidt, October 16, 1926 [photocopy], Illinois State Historical Library, Springfield).

11. See Katherine Helm, *The True Life of Mary, Wife of Lincoln* (New York: Harper, 1928), 295–98; William E. Barton to Katherine Helm, January 22, 1927 (carbon), and Helm to Barton, January 27, 1927, Barton Collection.

12. Sandburg and Angle, *Mary Lincoln: Wife and Widow*, 310–18.

13. Barton, *The Women Lincoln Loved*, 364; Evans, *Mrs. Abraham Lincoln*, 8, 27, 25.

14. Ruth Painter Randall, *Mary Lincoln: Biography of a Marriage* (Boston: Little, Brown, 1953), 434–35.

15. Turner and Turner, *Mary Todd Lincoln*, 436, 435; Randall, *Mary Lincoln: Biography of a Marriage*, 412. See also Keckley, *Behind the Scenes*, 296. Mrs. Randall used the Keckley book and thus knew Mrs. Lincoln gave the letters to the *World*.

16. Rhodes and Jauchius, *The Trial of Mary Todd Lincoln*, 5, 19.

17. Croy, *The Trial of Mrs. Abraham Lincoln*, v.

18. Ross, *The President's Wife*, 310, 319.

19. Turner and Turner, *Mary Todd Lincoln*, 620.

20. See David C. Mearns, *The Lincoln Papers*, 2 vols. (Garden City, N.Y.: Doubleday, 1948), 1: 121–29.

21. James T. Hickey, "Robert Todd Lincoln and the 'Purely Private' Letters of the Lincoln Family," *Journal of the Illinois State Historical Society* 74 (Spring 1981): 59. Frederick N. Towers, a Lincoln family attorney, wrote Jessie Lincoln Randolph in the Library of Congress' behalf. Mrs. Randolph would die the next year. Mary Lincoln Isham, Robert's first daughter, died in 1938. His son, Abraham "Jack" Lincoln, died in 1890.

22. Ed Russo, "What Was It Like Being Abraham Lincoln's Son?" *Illinois Times*, February 6–12, 1981, 4.

23. Hickey, "Robert Todd Lincoln and the 'Purely Private' Letters," 73–78; John S. Goff, *Robert Todd Lincoln: A Man in His Own Right* (Norman: Univ. of Oklahoma Pres, 1969), 235.

24. Russo, "What Was It Like Being Abraham Lincoln's Son?" 4. Lacking carbon paper, businessmen in Robert Lincoln's day sometimes kept copies of their correspondence made by running through a press a dampened sheet of thin paper placed over the letter. The damp paper picked up some of the original ink and was thin enough to be read from the other side of the sheet.

25. Turner and Turner, *Mary Todd Lincoln*, 620.

26. John Todd Stuart to Robert Todd Lincoln, May 10, 1875, Insanity File.

27. Isaac Ray, *A Treatise on the Medical Jurisprudence of Insanity*, vii; Justice Sidney Breese cited Ray's book in Hopps v. The People, 31 Ill. Reports 391 (1863).

28. Ray, *Treatise on the Medical Jurisprudence of Insanity*, vii, 5, 388, 339, 341.

29. Underwood, *Statutes of Illinois Construed*, 847, 843.

30. The 1823 law may have been aimed at taking such cases out of chancery courts to save time and expense.

31. Certified copy of proceedings . . . [Mary Lincoln], May 19, 1875, Insanity File.

32. Application to Try the Question of Insanity, County Court of Cook County, May 19, 1875 (photostat), Illinois State Historical Library, Springfield.

33. In the Matter of the Estate of Mary Lincoln, May 19, 1875, Cook County Court documents (photostat), Illinois State Historical Library, Springfield; certified copy of proceedings and order appointing a Conservator . . . [Mary Lincoln], June 14, 1875, Insanity File.

34. Ray, *Treatise on the Medical Jurisprudence of Insanity*, 338.

35. On the effects of individualism on American law see Stanley Elkins, *Slavery: A Study in American Institutional and Intellectual Life* (Chicago: Univ. of Chicago Press, 1959), 27–62.

36. Norman Dain, *Concepts of Insanity*, 6, 7, 45. Expert medical witnesses in trials probably described mental diseases with technical terms. When Andrew McFarland testified in *Hamaker v. Hamaker* in 1856, for example, he said that the accused showed "the usual symptoms of dementia" (18 Ill. Reports 139 [1856]). Only newspaper reports exist to reveal the evidence at Mary Todd Lincoln's trial, however, and they contain no technical medical terminology. In 1921 William E. Barton asked Lyman J. Gage, a member of the jury, about his memories of the trial. Gage recalled that "It did not appear the accused was violently insane, but suffered from phobias or occasional insane delusions." Dr. Danforth told Gage privately after the trial "that there was no doubt whatever of the fact of her mental aberration. He told me in substance that it was a case of dementia, or degeneration of brain tissue, that she would steadily degenerate and that within a year or a year and a half, or two years, she would die." Gage admitted to having a poor memory, and this evidence, gathered almost fifty years later from a very old man, seems suspect (Lyman J. Gage to William E. Barton, January 20, 1921, Barton Collection).

37. Turner and Turner, *Mary Todd Lincoln*, 616, 618.

38. Goff, *Robert Todd Lincoln*, 235.

APPENDIX

1. Mary Eunice Harlan married Robert Todd Lincoln on September 24, 1868.

2. Tad Lincoln was a student in Dr. D. Hohagen's Institute near Frankfurt, Germany, from October 1868 to April 1870.

3. James Smith, formerly pastor of the First Presbyterian Church in Springfield, Illinois, which the Lincolns attended in the 1850s, was later appointed to the United States Consular Service in Scotland by President Lincoln.

4. Mary Harlan Lincoln's letters are not present in the Insanity File.

5. In 1866 Mrs. Lincoln used $17,000 of the unpaid portion of President Lincoln's salary for 1865 (granted her by Congress) to buy a house at 375 West Washington Street in Chicago. She proved unable or unwilling to keep it up, moved out in 1867, and thereafter rented it.

6. Doubtless, Elizabeth Todd Edwards.

7. Unidentified.

8. Bettie Stuart (Mrs. Christopher Brown) was the daughter of John Todd Stuart. She died on March 2, 1869.

9. Lizzie Brown was Mrs. Lincoln's widowed cousin Elizabeth Todd Grimsley, who had remarried in 1867 the Reverend John H. Brown.

10. This was probably the horn chair presented to President Lincoln by California hunter and trapper Seth Kinman, who made a practice of presenting American presidents with these symbols of the great West.

11. Mrs. Lincoln vacationed in Scotland in July and August 1869, visiting Dr. James Smith—hence the placement of this fragment.

12. Mrs. James H. (Sally) Orne was Mrs. Lincoln's closest friend.

13. Unidentified.

14. Mrs. Samuel T. (Elizabeth Emerson) Atwater was the wife of a successful Chicago insurance agent and a prominent woman in civic circles. Mrs. Lincoln had been quite friendly with her in 1867.

15. Sally Orne's brother, Charles O'Neill, was a Republican member of the House of Representatives from Philadelphia.

16. Mary (Mamie) Lincoln was born to Robert and Mary on October 15, 1869.

17. The houses were the Chicago house at 375 West Washington Street and the Lincolns' old Springfield home, at Eighth and Jackson Streets.

18. Unidentified.

19. This fragment was written between the birth of Mrs. Lincoln's granddaughter Mary in October 1869 and the granting of Mrs. Lincoln's pension by Congress in July 1870.

20. Reuben E. Fenton served as governor of New York from 1865 to 1866 and began his first term in the United States Senate in 1869.

21. Matthew Simpson, the Methodist bishop in Washington, D.C., had delivered the eulogy for Abraham Lincoln's funeral service in Springfield.

22. Col. Riley Weaver, a Civil War veteran, was married to Ann Simpson, the daughter of Bishop Matthew Simpson. At the bishop's urging, President Grant had appointed him consul at Brindisi.

23. Tad Lincoln's talented tutor in England has never been identified.

24. Unidentified.

25. William Walton Murphy was the consul at Frankfurt from 1861 to 1864.

26. John Evans, the former governor of Colorado Territory, 1863–65, had been a Lincoln appointee. A prominent Methodist layman, Evans had gained his appointment through the urging of Bishop Matthew Simpson.

27. Historian John Lothrop Motley was appointed minister to Austria by President Lincoln and served from 1861 to 1867. President Grant appointed him minister to England in 1869.

28. General Adam Badeau served as military secretary to General Grant from 1864 to 1866. President Grant later appointed him consul general at London.

29. Unidentified.

30. The event, no doubt, was the final passage on July 14, 1870, of the bill granting Mrs. Lincoln a $3,000 lifetime annual pension.

31. Unidentified.

32. Ann Peck Harlan died on September 4, 1884.

33. William A. Harlan, James Harlan's only son, was eighteen in 1871.

34. Louis Philippe Albert d'Orleans, Count of Paris, son of the deposed king of France Louis Philippe, had visited the United States during the Civil War and served on Gen. George B. McClellan's staff.

35. John Lothrop Motley was removed from his post as minister to Great Britain by President Grant on November 10, 1870, probably because Grant was angry with Motley's political champion and protector, Senator Charles Sumner of Massachusetts, who had opposed Grant's policy toward Santo Domingo.

36. Will Evans was the son of John Evans.

37. Misdated by Mrs. Lincoln. It should be 1871.

38. Ellen Verner Simpson was Matthew Simpson's wife. Ida Simpson, one of their daughters, was 15 in 1870.

39. Randolph Rogers was in Italy modeling a statue of Abraham Lincoln for the city of Philadelphia.

40. The plaques of Robert and Mary Harlan Lincoln, by Randolph Rogers, are now on display in the Illinois State Historical Library, Springfield.

41. No such home is known to have existed.

42. In the actual letter the "50" was underlined twice.

43. Mrs. Lincoln's only grandson was named Abraham "Jack" Lincoln. He was born on August 14, 1873.

44. Mary Todd Lincoln died intestate, as her husband had. She left an estate valued at $84,035. It included $72,000 in government bonds. The final probate, dated November 6, 1884, included $6,480 in interest payments accumulated after her death. See photocopies of probate documents in the Estate of Mary Lincoln, Deceased, Robert T. Lincoln, Administrator, Illinois State Historical Library, Springfield.

INDEX

Mark E. Neely, Jr., is a professor of history at St. Louis University. He earned B.A. and Ph.D. degrees from Yale University. He is the author of the Pulitzer Prize winning *The Fate of Liberty: Abraham Lincoln and Civil Liberties* and *The Abraham Lincoln Encyclopedia*. He is the coauthor, with Harold Holzer and Gabor S. Boritt, of *The Lincoln Image: Abraham Lincoln and the Popular Print*.

R. Gerald McMurtry spent more than fifty years in the Lincoln field. He headed the Department of Lincolniana at Lincoln Memorial University and was editor of the *Lincoln Herald* from 1937 to 1956. He then became the Director of the Lincoln National Life Foundation, now the Louis A. Warren Lincoln Library and Museum. He is the author or coauthor of numerous monographs on Abraham Lincoln.